Adventures in Social Research

Data Analysis Using *SPSS*™

for Windows 95®

TITLES OF RELATED INTEREST FROM PINE FORGE PRESS

Adventures in Social Research: Data Analysis Using SPSS® by Earl Babbie and Fred Halley

Adventures in Social Research: Data Analysis Using SPSS® for Windows™ by Earl Babbie and Fred Halley

Adventures in Criminal Justice Research: Data Analysis Using SPSS® for Windows™ by George W. Dowdall, Earl Babbie, and Fred Halley

Exploring Social Issues Using SPSS® for Windows™ by Joseph R. Healey, Earl Babbie, and Fred Halley

Building Community: Social Science in Action edited by Philip Nyden, Anne Figert, Mark Shibley, and Darryl Burrows

---

The Pine Forge Press Series in Research Methods and Statistics
Edited by Kathleen S. Crittenden

> *Regression: A Primer* by Paul Allison

> *A Guide to Field Research* by Carol A. Bailey

> *Designing Surveys: A Guide to Decisions and Procedures* by Ronald Czaja and Johnny Blair

> **Social Statistics for a Diverse Society** by Chava Frankfort-Nachmias

> *Experimental Design and the Analysis of Variance* by Robert Leik

> *How Sampling Works* by Richard Maisel and Caroline Hodges Persell

> *Program Evaluation* by George McCall

> **Investigating the Social World: The Process and Practice of Research** by Russell K. Schutt

Adventures in Social Research

Data Analysis Using *SPSS*™
for Windows 95®

Earl Babbie

Chapman University

Fred Halley

SUNY-Brockport

PINE FORGE PRESS

Thousand Oaks • London • New Delhi

For information, address:

Pine Forge Press
A Sage Publications Company
2455 Teller Road
Thousand Oaks, California 91320
E-mail: sales@pfp.sagepub.com

SAGE Publications Ltd.
6 Bonhill Street
London EC2A 4PU
United Kingdom

SAGE Publications India Pvt. Ltd.
M-32 Market
Greater Kailash I
New Delhi 110 048 India

Production Coordinator: Windy Just
Production Editor: Sanford Robinson
Production Assistant: Denise Santoyo
Typesetter: Janelle LeMaster
Cover: Ravi Balasuriya
Print Buyer: Anna Chin

Printed in the United States of America

98 99 00   2 3 4 5 6 7 8 9 10

ISBN 0-7619-8524-7

SPSS® is a registered trademark of SPSS, Inc., Chicago, Illinois.

This book is printed on acid-free paper that meets Environmental Protection Agency standards for recycled paper.

To our students:
past, present, and future.
We challenge each other and profit from it.

About the Authors

Earl Babbie was born in Detroit, Michigan, in 1938, although he chose to return to Vermont three months later, growing up there and in New Hampshire. In 1956, he set off for Harvard Yard, where he spent the next four years learning more than he initially planned. After three years with the U.S. Marine Corps, mostly in Asia, he began graduate studies at the University of California, Berkeley. He received his Ph.D. from Berkeley in 1969. He taught sociology at the University of Hawaii from 1968 through 1979, took time off from teaching and research to write full-time for eight years, and then joined the faculty at Chapman University in southern California in 1987. Although an author of research articles and monographs, he is best known for the many texts he has written, which have been widely adopted in colleges throughout the United States and the world. He also has been active in the American Sociological Association for 25 years and currently serves on the ASA's executive committee. He has been married to his wife, Sheila, for more than 30 years, and they have a son, Aaron, who would make any parent proud.

Fred Halley, Associate Professor of Sociology, the State University of New York College at Brockport, has been developing computer-based tools for teaching sociology since 1970. His major projects have included the design of a computer-managed social statistics course and an introduction to sociology course with computer labs. Halley has served as a collegewide social science computing consultant, directed Brockport's Institute for Social Research, and now directs the college's Data Analysis Laboratory. He is the author of GENSTAT, an IBM PC-based program that generates individualized data sets for statistics students and correct answers for their instructors. He recently codirected a three-year evaluation project concerning a Head Start Family Service Center in Rochester, New York and an evaluation of a community action program in two rural upstate New York counties.

About the Publisher

Pine Forge Press is a new educational publisher dedicated to publishing innovative books and software throughout the social sciences. On this and any other of our publications, we welcome your comments and suggestions.

Please call or write us at:

Pine Forge Press
2455 Teller Road
Thousand Oaks, CA 91320
805-499-4224
E-mail: sales@pfp.sagepub.com

Visit our new World Wide Web site, your direct link to a multitude of online resources:

http://www.sagepub.com/pineforge

Contents

Preface for Instructors

This book is offered to you with a number of aims in mind. To begin, we want to introduce students to the logic of social science research, particularly survey research. Furthermore, we present the essentials of using SPSS as a vehicle for putting that logic into practice. As we pursue these twin goals, however, there are a number of agendas in the background of this book. For example, students who complete the book will have learned a very useful, employable skill. Increasingly, job applicants are asked about their facility with various computer programs: word processing, spreadsheets, and data analysis. As of this writing, SPSS is still clearly the most popular professional program available for social science data analysis, hence our choice of it as a vehicle for teaching social research.

A Focus on Developing Professional and Intellectual Skills

What sets this book apart from others that teach SPSS or similar programs is that we cast that particular skill within the context of social research as a logical enterprise. Thus, in addition to learning the use of SPSS, students are learning the intellectual "skills" of conceptualization, measurement, and association. Whereas those who know only SPSS can assist in data analysis, our intention is that our students will also be able to think for themselves, mapping out analytic paths into the understanding of social data. As they polish these intellectual skills, they should be able to progress to higher levels of research and to the administration of research enterprises.

More generally, we aim to train students who will use computers rather than be used by them. It is our experience that when students first confront computers in school, they tend to fall into two groups: those who recognize computers as powerful instruments for pursuing their goals in life, or at least as the grandest of toys; and those who are intimidated by computers and seek the earliest possible refuge from them. Our intention is to reveal the former possibility to students and to coax them into that relationship with computers.

Educators are being challenged increasingly to demonstrate the practical value of instruction, in the social sciences no less than in other fields. Too often, the overreaction to this demand results in superficial vocational courses that offer no intellectual meaning or courses hastily contrived as a home for current buzzwords, whose popularity is often short-lived. We are excited to be able to offer an educational experience that is genuinely practical for students and that also represents an intellectual adventure.

Those who have taught methods or statistics courses typically find themselves with a daunting task—to ignite their often involuntary students with the fire of enthusiasm they themselves feel for the detective work of social research at its best. In this book, we seek to engage students' curiosity by setting them about the task of understanding issues that are already points of interest for them: topics such as abortion, religion, politics, and poverty. For many of our readers, we imagine that mathematical analysis still smacks of trains leaving Point A and Point B at different speeds, and so on. Now, they are going to learn that some facility with the logic and mathematics of social research can let them focus the light of understanding on some of the dark turbulence of opinion and hysteria. We do not tell students about opinions on abortion as much as we show them how to find out for themselves. We think that will get students to Point C ahead of either of the trains.

A Focus on Active Learning

As we are teaching students to learn for themselves, this book offers a good example of what educators have taken to calling "active learning." We have set up all of our exercises so that students should be executing the same SPSS operations we are discussing at any given point. Although we may give them the "answers" to assure them that they are on the right track, we leave them on their own often enough to require that they do the work rather than simply read about it. Finally, the culture of personal computers has been one of "collaborative learning" from its very beginning. More than people in any other field of activity, perhaps, computer users have always delighted in sharing what they know with others. There is probably no better context within which to ask for help: Those who know the answer are quick to respond, and those who do not often turn their attention to finding an answer, delighting in the challenge.

We imagine that students will often want to work together as they progress through this book. That has been our experience in student testing it and in earlier courses we have taught involving computers. We suggest that you encourage cooperation among students; we are certain they will learn more that way and will enjoy the course more. In fact, those who are initially intimidated by computers should especially be encouraged to find buddies with whom to work.

We have designed this book to support students' first "doing" course in social research. If they have had earlier introductory methods or statistics courses, they will probably come to this book at full speed, but those who have never taken a methods or statistics course can easily make it through this book. At the same time, it is not too elementary for graduate students who are having their first hands-on experience in social research.

The Book and the Disk: What Is Included?

The book your students buy contains everything they need, except for SPSS itself. We have included a data set comprising 42 variables from the 1996 General Social Survey, which can be analyzed by most versions of SPSS, including StudentWare. As you will see, the variables cover a fairly broad terrain, although we have provided for analysis in some depth in a few instances. In addition to working their way through the exercises presented in the book, students will be able to find original lines of inquiry that grow out of their own interests and insights.

This book will illustrate the use of SPSS, using Version 7.0 or 7.5 for Windows 95. Readers using Version 6.0 for Windows 3.1 or Version 6.3.1 for Windows 95 will find that most procedures are the same in the two versions, although the outputs are somewhat different. We will refer to the program simply as "SPSS for Windows." Where a different procedure is required in Version 6.0, we will indicate that with the notation: ☐

Using the General Social Survey on your disk data is easy. After starting SPSS for Windows, click the following sequence

File → Open [☐ File → Open → Data]

to display the Open File window. Click on the "Look in" field and select the drive that contains your disk. Next, move the mouse to the "Files of type" dialog box and click on the suffix for SPSS for Windows data files, "SPSS(*.sav)." Now you should see the name of the General Social Survey system file, GSS.SAV, in the list of files. Select GSS.SAV by placing the mouse on it and clicking. Click the Open button near the lower right corner of the Open File window. In a few seconds, SPSS will display the GSS data in its data window. Specific instructions on using SPSS with these data are provided in later chapters.

SPSS for Windows comes with extensive help screens. They are almost like having a coach built in to your computer! Begin with the menu farthest to the right. You can click Help or hit ALT-H to see the options available to you. "Topics" will usually be your most useful choice. This will give you three options. "Contents" and "Index" present you with two ways of zeroing in on the topic of interest to you. "Find" will search for the specific terms you indicate. You should experiment with these several options to discover what works best for you.

Software Support and Service

If you or your students should run into any problems using this package, there are several sources of support that should serve your needs. Frequently, college and university computing centers have student assistants who are very helpful to new computer users. In fact, most academic computing centers employ a user services coordinator who can help faculty plan student use of the school's computers and provide aid when problems arise.

There are at least two sources of SPSS assistance available via the Internet. The first is a home page (http://www.spss.com/) maintained by SPSS, Inc. In addition to providing answers to frequently asked questions, it provides variety tips and white papers on important issues in data analysis. Specific questions may be submitted to consultants via e-mail from the homepage. SPSS requests that a legitimate license or serial number be submitted with questions for questions to receive a response.

A second source of help on the Internet is a listserve for SPSS users maintained at the University of Georgia (SPSSX-L@UGA.CC.UGA. EDU). It provides a forum where SPSS users can ask questions of other SPSS users. SPSS programmers and statisticians informally monitor the listserve and frequently offer their expertise in answering users' problems. The listserve is primarily intended to meet the needs of academics and professionals using SPSS as part of their work. This virtual community is very good at identifying questions that come from students rather than professionals. Students posting questions are warned that if detected, they may be severely flamed (admonished) for attempting to take a short cut in completing their assignments!

If you cannot find local help to solve a problem, you can call Fred Halley at Socware, Inc., in Brockport, New York, at (716) 352-1986. If you get the answering machine, please leave a time and phone number where you can be reached. As a last resort, you can call SPSS, Inc., in Chicago for technical support at (312) 329-2400. Be forewarned that SPSS cannot give assistance with pedagogical or substantive problems and that you may have a long wait in a telephone queue for your turn to talk to a technical support person. It has been our experience that our best help comes from local resources.

Acknowledgments

In conclusion, we would like to acknowledge a number of people who have been instrumental in making this book a reality. First and foremost, Steve Rutter and Sherith Pankratz of Pine Forge Press have been full partners from start to finish. They are able to bring full measures of enthusiasm, commitment, and ingenuity to every book on which they work, and it is a joy for us to play together in that environment, even if we expressed our joy by whining and complaining at times.

We would also like to thank the many reviewers who helped us along the way: Marybeth Ayella, Saint Joseph's University; James David Ballard, University of Nevada, Las Vegas; Neal DeChillo, Salem State College; David Decker, California State University at San Bernardino; Sister Ellen Desmond, The College of Saint Elizabeth; Karen Donahue, Hanover College; Don Freeman, University of Evansville; Robert H. Freymeyer, Presbyterian College; John Gartrell, University of Alberta; Barbara Hart, University of Texas at Tyler; Richard Kendrick, SUNY-Cortland; Hoda Mahmoudi, California Lutheran University; Kathy McKinley, Cabrini College; Joan Morris, University of Central Florida; Vicki L. Sommer, Augustana College; Judith Stull, Temple University; and Terri Watson, University of Southern Indiana.

We reserve our final acknowledgment for our students, to whom this book is dedicated. We recognize that we have often asked them to think and do things they sometimes felt were beyond their abilities. We have admired their courage for trying anyway, and we have shared their growth.

Part I Preparing for Social Research

In the opening chapters, we address this book's two main purposes: to introduce you to the logic of social science research, and to give you some practical experience through the use of the SPSS computer program.

Chapter 1 discusses these purposes in more depth and will give you some of the historical background that lies behind computerized social research.

In Chapter 2, you will discover that social research (like other forms of scientific inquiry) is based on two pillars: logic and observation. You will see how theory (the logic component) informs our investigations, making sense out of our observations, and sometimes offers predictions about what we will find. The other aspect of research, on which we will focus in this book, is the collection and analysis of data, such as those collected in a survey.

Chapter 3 delves more deeply into one central component of scientific inquiry: measurement. We look at some of the criteria for measurement quality and start examining the kinds of measurements represented by the data at hand. Chapter 4 describes those data, which come from the 1996 General Social Survey, conducted among a national sample of American adults.

The computer program we will be using, SPSS, is introduced in Chapter 5, where you will learn that there are several different versions of SPSS. Chapter 5 provides you with some initial familiarization with the version you will be using, and you will see how it differs from the others available.

By the time you have gone through the chapters in Part I, you should be amply prepared to undertake your adventure in social research.

Chapter 1 Introduction

Social research is the detective work of big questions. Whereas a conventional detective tries to find out who committed a specific crime, the social researcher looks for the causes of crime in general. The logic of social scientific investigation extends beyond crime to include all aspects of social life: careers, marriage and family, voting, health, prejudice, poverty—in fact, anything that is likely to concern you as an individual is the subject of social science research.

1.1 Overview

The purpose of this book is to lead you through a series of investigative adventures in social research. We can't predict exactly where these adventures will lead, because you are going to be the detective. Our purpose is to show you some simple tools (and some that are truly amazing) that you can use in social investigations. We'll also provide you with a body of data, collected in a national survey, that is so rich you will have the opportunity to undertake investigations that no one else has ever pursued.

If you have access to an IBM-type microcomputer and SPSS for Windows (Versions 6 or 7), this book and the computer disk included with it contain everything you need for a wide range of social investigations.

This tool is designed specifically for exploring data. If you are already comfortable with computers, you can jump right in, and very quickly you will find yourself in the midst of a fascinating computer game. Instead of fighting off alien attacks or escaping from dank dungeons, you'll be pitting your abilities and imagination against real life—but you'll be looking at a side of life that you may not now be aware of.

This tool is also well designed for the creation of college term papers. Throughout, we suggest ways to present the data you discover in the context of a typical term paper in the social sciences. Whereas most students are limited in their term papers to reporting what other investigators have learned about society, you will be able to offer your own insights and discoveries.

Finally, the data set included here is being analyzed by professional social scientists today. Moreover, the analytical tools that we've provided for you are as powerful as those used by many professional researchers.

Frankly, there's no reason you can't use these materials for original research worthy of publication in a research journal. All it takes is curiosity, imagination, practice, and a healthy obsession with knowing the answers to things. In our experience, what sets professional researchers apart from others is that they have much greater curiosity about the world around them, are able to bring powerful imagination to bear on understanding it, are willing to put in the time required of effective investigation, and are passionately driven to understand.

1.2   Why Use a Computer?

Sociologists' use of data-processing machinery has evolved to its present state over a period of 50 years. As sociology moved from a social philosophy to a social science in the late 1800s, there emerged a greater need to record, organize, and analyze observations of social phenomena. Data analysis needs quickly became so great that it was too time consuming, if not impossible, to keep track of data in ledgers or on index cards.

In 1885, Herman Hollerith, an employee of the U.S. Census Bureau, developed the punch card, a prototype of the now obsolete "IBM card," to help meet the data analysis needs of the Census Bureau at a time when the U.S. population was growing and changing rapidly. By the 1930s, sociologists had adapted the new technology for more sophisticated research purposes. (In 1896, by the way, Herman Hollerith established the Tabulating Machine Company, later renamed International Business Machines: IBM.)

In the early 1960s, the electromechanical data tabulation machinery was replaced by electronic computers. Although by today's standards the early computers had small capacity and were expensive and very prone to breakdowns, they greatly enhanced sociologists' ability to organize and analyze data. Tasks that took days or weeks using data tabulation equipment took only a few hours on computers.

In addition to the development of electronic computers, or hardware, sociologists' use of computing was also advanced by the development of computer programs, or software. In 1962, the computer programming language FORTRAN (an acronym for *formula translation*) was developed. FORTRAN made it possible for sociologists to write programs for data analysis that could be used on different kinds of computers. Prior to FORTRAN, programming could be accomplished only by manually rewiring accounting machinery or by using machine languages limited to specific computers.

In the 1960s, sociologists used programs written by themselves and by colleagues, graduate students, and programmers in university computing centers. Most information about programs was gained informally through professional grapevines. This greatly expanded the research capabilities of social scientists, but there was no standardization of programs or of the format of data to be analyzed by them.

Searching for and using a statistical program could be a harrowing and time-consuming experience. Most of the programs were transported on punch cards, and if one card got out of order, the program might not run; worse yet, it might run and produce inaccurate results.

By 1970, the data analysis problems of sociologists and other social and behavioral scientists were well recognized. To answer these needs, sociologist-programmers (most notably at the University of Chicago and the University of Michigan) developed the concept of a "program package." In addition to statistical calculations, these program packages allowed researchers to modify or recode data, to create indexes and scales, and to employ many other techniques you will learn in this workbook.

Today, the two statistical packages most widely used by social scientists are SPSS (the Statistical Package for the Social Sciences) and SAS (the Statistical Analysis System). Until the mid-1980s, these large, generalized statistical packages were available only for large mainframe computers.

The advent of personal computers created a revolution in how social science data analysis was done. By the mid-1980s, personal computers became powerful enough to run statistical packages and cheap enough for individuals to purchase. This made it feasible for statistical package producers to rewrite their packages for personal computers. Although personal computers do not have the storage capacity to work with extremely large amounts of data, they are very appropriate for moderate data analysis needs.

We have selected SPSS for your use in these exercises for three reasons. First, early versions of SPSS date back to 1968. The package is well-known, and there is hardly a social scientist who has earned a graduate degree in the past 20 years who has not had some contact with SPSS. Second, SPSS takes you through all the basic issues of using a statistical package. This knowledge will give you a head start if you learn some other package later. Finally, SPSS comes in several versions. The mainframe version is called SPSSX. It is available for all of the major mainframe computers, such as IBM, Honeywell, and Unisys. There is also a version for personal computers called SPSS/PC+. It is limited to handling 500 variables at a time; the number of cases is limited to the disk space on your personal computer. Although SPSS/PC+ also has fewer statistical procedures than SPSSX, it has everything most social researchers would want. The third version is SPSS Studentware, a scaled-down version of SPSS/PC+ that will run on a minimal IBM-compatible personal computer. It can handle up to 50 variables. SPSS Studentware has fewer statistical procedures than SPSS/PC+, but it has most of the procedures that would ever be needed by an undergraduate sociology major or a master's-level graduate student. One of our earlier books, *Adventures in Social Research* (1993), was written specifically for students using SPSS Studentware. The most recent versions of SPSS are designed for use with Windows, and the present book is designed specifically for that. Specifically, it illustrates the use of SPSS Version 7.5 for Windows 95, although it can also be used with Version 6.0 for Windows 3.1.

SPSS is a professional tool used across the social and behavioral sciences. Mainframe versions are not sold but are leased to organizations on a yearly basis. The costs range from $1,000 to tens of thousands of dollars, depending on the type and size of the organization. The Base System of SPSS Version 7.5 can be purchased by faculty and undergraduate students for about $495. Optional features that include graphics, data entry, advanced statistics, and specialized statistics can be added to the Base System for Windows. SPSS offers a "grad pack" to graduate students that includes the Base System plus two modules for about $200. The student version of SPSS for Windows costs about $57, but it can be purchased only through college and university bookstores. SPSS offers substantial discounts for courses using its products. For up-to-date information, call SPSS's sales and marketing office at 1-800-543-2185. The SPSS programmers have made an effort to keep the structure and syntax of all of the SPSS versions very similar. If you learn any version, you should have little difficulty using the other versions.

The exercises presented in this book have been designed specifically for both the professional and student versions of SPSS for Windows. We think you are going to enjoy the book. If you have half as much fun working with the exercises as we had creating them, you're in for a treat. Probably the determining factor is your level of enjoyment in solving an engaging puzzle. If you like figuring out how the pieces fit, you're ready to set out on your search for society.

1.3 Summary

This book has two educational aims. First, we want to share with you the excitement of social scientific research. You are going to learn that a table of numerical data—pretty boring on the face of it—can hold within it the answers to many questions about why people think and act as they do. Finding those answers requires that you learn some skills of logical inquiry.

Second, we will show you how to use a computer program that is very popular among social scientists. SPSS is the tool you will use to unlock the mysteries of society, just as a biologist might use a microscope or an astronomer a telescope.

You may have seen those prepared foods with the instruction: "Just add water and heat." Well, the package in your hands is something like that, but the instructions read, "Just add you, and let's get cooking."

Chapter 2   Theory and Research

This book is addressed primarily to the techniques of social science data analysis. Thus, we're going to be spending most of our time analyzing data and reaching conclusions about the people who answered questions in the General Social Survey, which is described in more detail in Chapter 3. Data analysis, however, doesn't occur in a vacuum. Scientific inquiry is a matter of both observing and reasoning. Before getting into the techniques of data analysis, then, let's take a minute to consider the role of theory in conjunction with research.

Given the variety of topics examined in social science research, there is no single, established set of procedures that is always followed in social scientific inquiry. Nevertheless, data analysis almost always has a bigger purpose than the simple manipulation of numbers. Our larger aim is to learn something of general value about human social behavior. This commitment lies in the realm of theory.

Social scientific inquiry involves a bringing together of **concepts** and data: ideas and observations about human social life. Ultimately, we seek to establish a correspondence between what we observe and our conceptual understanding of the way things are. Some of the social scientific concepts with which you are familiar might include social class, deviance, political orientations, prejudice, alienation, and so forth.

Many concepts, such as those just mentioned, distinguish variations among people. Gender, for example, distinguishes "men" and "women." Social class might distinguish "upper class," "middle class," and "working class." When social scientists actually measure concepts that capture variations among people, we shift terminology from concepts to **variables**. As an idea, then, gender is a concept; when actually measured, in a questionnaire, for example, it becomes a variable for analysis.

Explanatory social inquiry is a matter of discovering which attributes of different variables are causally associated with one another. Are men or women the more religious? Which ethnic groups are the most liberal and which the most conservative? These are the kinds of questions that social scientists address.

2.1 Religiosity

A **theory** is a statement or set of statements pertaining to the relationships among variables. As one example from the sociology of religion, Glock, Ringer, and Babbie (1967) offer what they call the "deprivation theory of church involvement." Having asked why some church members participated more in their churches than others, the researchers' analyses led them to conclude that those who were deprived of gratification in the secular society would be more likely to be active in church life than were those who enjoyed the rewards of secular society.

In accordance with the deprivation theory, therefore, it was to be expected that poor people would be more active in the church than rich people, given that the former would be denied many secular gratifications enjoyed by the latter. Or, in a male-dominated society, it was suggested that women—being denied gratifications enjoyed by men—would be more likely to participate actively in the church. Similarly, in a youth-oriented society, the theory would suggest that older people would be more active in church than the young.

A theory, therefore, is a set of logical explanations about patterns of human social life: patterns among the variables that describe people. In this example, the variables are church involvement, wealth, gender, and age. The theory explains why these variables are related to one another in a particular way.

Looked at only a little differently, the theory offers expectations about the ways variables would be found to relate to one another in life. In scientific language, these are called **hypotheses**. One hypothesis to be derived from the deprivation theory is that women will be more involved in church than will men.

It is important to recognize that relationships such as the one predicted in this hypothesis are **probabilistic**. The hypothesis says that women, as a group, will have a higher average level of church involvement than men will—as a group. This does not mean that all women are more involved than any men. It does mean, for example, that if we asked men and women whether they attend church every week, a higher percentage of women than of men would say yes, even though some men would say yes and some women would say no. That is the nature of probabilistic relationships.

Sometimes, theories and the hypotheses derived from them are the result of largely intellectual procedures: thinking about and reasoning what should be the relationships among some set of variables. Other times, researchers build theories later to explain the relationships they've already observed in their analysis of data. In the case of church involvement, discussed above, the data analysis occurred first, and the researchers then faced the task of making sense out of the several relationships they had uncovered.

Stepping back a pace for a larger perspective on the process of social scientific inquiry, we find an alternation between the two approaches just described. Understandings and expectations are reached; they are tested through the collection and analysis of data; the findings arrived at in the data analysis are then subjected to further evaluation and understanding, producing a modified theory. Often, the phase that involves moving from theoretical understandings and the derivation of specific hypotheses to the collection and analysis of data is called **deduction**, and the process that proceeds from data back to theory is called **induction**. More simply, deduction can be seen as reasoning from general understandings to specific expectations, whereas induction can be seen as reasoning from specific observations to general explanations. Both deduction and induction are essential parts of any scientific inquiry.

Now, let's examine some of the theoretical work that informs other subjects we are going to analyze together in this book.

2.2 Political Orientations

One of the more familiar variables in social science is political orientation, which typically ranges from liberal to conservative. It lies at the heart of much voting behavior, and it relates to a number of nonpolitical variables as well, which you are going to discover for yourself shortly.

There are several **dimensions** of political orientations, and it will be useful to distinguish them here. Three commonly examined dimensions are social attitudes, economic attitudes, and foreign policy attitudes. Let's examine each dimension briefly.

Some specific social attitudes and related behaviors might include abortion, premarital sex, and capital punishment. Let's see where liberals and conservatives would generally stand on these issues:

Issue	Liberals	Conservatives
abortion	permissive	restrictive
premarital sex	permissive	restrictive
capital punishment	opposed	in favor

In terms of economic issues, liberals are more supportive than are conservatives of government programs such as unemployment insurance, welfare, and Medicare, and of government economic regulation, such as progressive taxation (the rich taxed at higher rates), minimum wage laws, and regulation of industry. By the same token, liberals are likely to be more supportive of labor unions than are conservatives.

2.3 Attitudes toward Abortion

Abortion is a social issue that has figured importantly in religious and political debates for years. The General Social Survey contains several variables dealing with attitudes toward abortion. Each asks whether a woman should be allowed to get an abortion for a variety of reasons. The following list shows these reasons, along with the abbreviated variable names you'll be using for them in your analyses later on.

ABDEFECT	because there is a strong chance of a serious defect
ABNOMORE	because a family wants no more children
ABHLTH	because the woman's health would be seriously endangered
ABPOOR	because a family is too poor to afford more children
ABRAPE	because the pregnancy resulted from rape
ABSINGLE	because the woman is unmarried
ABANY	because the woman wants it, for any reason

Before we begin examining answers to the abortion attitude questions (in Chapter 8), it is worth taking a moment to reflect on their logical implications. Which of these items do you suppose would receive the least support? That is, which will have the smallest percentage of respondents agreeing with it? Think about that before continuing.

Logically, we should expect the smallest percentage to support ABANY, because it "contains" all the others. For example, those who would support abortion in the case of rape might not support it for other reasons, such as the family's poverty. Those who support ABANY, however, would have to agree with both of those more specific items.

Three of the items tap into reasons that would seem to excuse the pregnant woman from responsibility:

ABDEFECT	because there is a strong chance of a serious defect
ABHLTH	because the woman's health would be seriously endangered
ABRAPE	because the pregnancy resulted from rape

We might expect the highest percentages to agree with these items. Let's see if our expectations are correct.

When we analyze this topic with data, we'll begin by finding useful ways of measuring overall attitudes toward abortion. Once we've done that, we'll be in a position to find out why some people are generally supportive and others generally opposed.

2.4 Summary

By now, you should have gained an initial appreciation of the relationship between theory and research in the social sciences. This examination will continue throughout the book. While our most direct attention will focus on the skills of analyzing data, we will always want to make logical sense out of what we learn from our manipulations of the numbers.

Measurement is a fundamental topic that bridges theory and research. We turn our attention to that topic next.

Chapter 3   The Logic of Measurement

Measurement is one of the most fundamental elements of science. In the case of social research, the task typically is one of characterizing individuals in terms of the issues under study. Thus, a voting study will characterize respondents in terms of which candidate they plan to vote for. A study of abortion attitudes will describe people in terms of their attitudes on that topic.

3.1 Validity Problems

Validity is a term used casually in everyday language, but it has a more precise meaning in social research. It describes an indicator of a concept. Most simply, the indicator is said to be valid if it really measures what it is intended to measure, and invalid if it doesn't.

As a simple example, let's consider political orientations, ranging from very liberal to very conservative. For an example of a clearly valid measure of this concept, here's the way the General Social Survey asked about it:

> We hear a lot of talk these days about liberals and conservatives. I'm going to show you a seven-point scale on which political views that people might hold are arranged from extremely liberal to extremely conservative. Where would you place yourself on this scale?
>
> 1. Extremely liberal
> 2. Liberal
> 3. Slightly liberal
> 4. Moderate, middle of the road
> 5. Slightly conservative
> 6. Conservative
> 7. Extremely conservative

At the opposite extreme, a simple question about respondent gender obviously would not be a valid measure of political orientations. It has nothing to do with politics. But now let's consider another questionnaire item that lies somewhere in between these two extremes of validity with regard to measuring political orientations.

Which of these two political parties do you most identify with?

☐   Democratic Party

☐   Republican Party

☐   Neither

This second item is another reasonable measure of political orientation. Moreover, it is related to the first, because Democrats are, on the whole, more liberal than Republicans. On the other hand, there are conservative Democrats and liberal Republicans. If our purpose is to tap into the liberal-conservative dimension, the initial item that asks directly about political orientations is obviously a more valid indicator of the concept than is the item about political party.

This particular example offers us a clear choice as to the most valid indicator of the concept at hand, but matters are not always that clear. If we were measuring levels of prejudice, for example, we could not simply ask "How prejudiced are you?" because no one is likely to admit to being prejudiced. As we search for workable indicators of a concept such as prejudice, the matter of validity becomes something to which we must pay more attention.

Validity is also a problem whenever you are reanalyzing someone else's data—as you are doing in this book. Even if you can think of a survey question that would have captured your concept perfectly, the original researchers might not have asked it. Hence, you often need to use ingenuity in constructing measures that nevertheless tap the quality in which you are interested. In the case of political orientations, for example, you might combine the responses to several questions: asking for attitudes about civil liberties, past voting behavior, political party identification, and so forth. We'll return to the use of multiple indicators shortly.

In large part, the question of validity is settled on prima facie grounds: We judge an indicator to be relatively valid or invalid "on the face of it." It was on this basis that you had no trouble seeing that asking directly about political orientations was a valid indicator of that concept, whereas asking a person's gender was definitely not a valid measure of political orientations. Later in the book, we'll explore some simple methodological techniques that are also used to test the validity of measures.

3.2   Reliability Problems

Reliability is a different but equally important quality of measurements. In the context of survey research, reliability refers to the question of whether we can trust the answers that people give us—even when their misstatements are honest ones.

Years ago, one of us was asked to assist on a survey of teenage drivers in California. Over researcher objections, the client insisted on asking the question, "How many miles have you driven?" and providing a space for the teenager to write in his or her response. Perhaps you can recognize the problem in this question by attempting to answer it yourself. Unless you have never driven an automobile, we doubt that you can report how many miles you have driven with any accuracy. In the survey mentioned, some teenagers reported driving hundreds of thousands of miles.

A better technique in that situation, by the way, would be to provide respondents with a set of categories reflecting realistically the number of miles respondents are likely to have driven: fewer than 1,000 miles, 1,000 to 5,000 miles, 5,000 to 10,000 miles, and so on. Such a set of categories gives respondents a framework within which to place their own situations. Even though they still may not know exactly how much they had driven, there would be a fair likelihood that the categories they chose would actually contain their correct answers. The success of this technique, of course, would depend on our having a good idea in advance of what constitutes reasonable categories, determined by previous research, perhaps. As an alternative, we might ask respondents to volunteer the number of miles they have driven, but limit the time period to something they are likely to remember. Thus, we might ask how many miles they drove during the preceding week or month, for example.

Conceptually, the test of reliability is whether respondents would give the same answers repeatedly if the measurement could be made in such a way that (a) their situations had not changed (hadn't driven any more miles), and (b) they couldn't remember the answer they gave before.

Perhaps the difference between validity and reliability can be seen most clearly in reference to a simple bathroom scale. If you step on a scale repeatedly (scales don't remember) and it gives you a different weight each time, then the scale has a reliability problem. On the other hand, if the scale tells you that you weigh 125 pounds every time you step on it, it's pretty reliable, but if you actually weigh 225, the scale has a problem in the validity department: It doesn't indicate your weight accurately.

Both validity and reliability are important in the analysis of data. If you are interested in learning why some people have deeply held religious beliefs and others do not, then asking people how often they attend church would be problematic. This question doesn't really provide a valid measure of the concept that interests you, and anything you learn will explain the causes of church attendance, not religious belief. And suppose you asked people how many times they had attended church in the past year—any answers you received would probably not be reliable, so anything you might think you learned about the causes of church attendance might be only a function of the errors people made in answering the question. (It would be better to give them categories from which to choose.) You would have no assurance that another study would yield the same result.

3.3 Multiple Indicators

Often, the solution to the problems discussed above lies in the creation of composite measures using multiple indicators. As a simple example, to measure the degree to which a sample of Christian church members held the beliefs associated with Christianity, you might ask them questions about several issues, each dealing with a particular belief, such as the following:

- belief in God
- belief that Jesus was divine
- belief in the existence of the devil
- belief in an afterlife: heaven and hell
- belief in the literal truth of the Bible

The several answers given to these questions could be used to create an overall measure of religious belief among the respondents. In the simplest procedure, you could give respondents one point for each belief to which they agreed, allowing you to score them from 0 to 5 on the index. Notice that this is the same logic by which you may earn one point for each correct answer on an exam, with the total scores being taken as an indication of how well you know the material.

Some social science concepts are implicitly multidimensional. Consider the concept of social class, for example. Typically, this term is used in reference to a combination of education, income, occupation, and sometimes dimensions such as social class identification and prestige. This would be measured for data analysis through the use of multiple indicators.

When it becomes appropriate in the analyses we are going to undertake together below, we'll show you how to create and use some simple composite measures.

3.4 Levels of Measurement

As we convert the concepts in our minds into empirical measurements in the form of variables, we sometimes have options as to their level of statistical sophistication. Specifically, there are a number of different possibilities regarding the relationships among the attributes comprising a variable. Let's look at those alternatives.

Nominal Variables

Some variables simply distinguish different kinds of people. Gender is a good example of this, simply distinguishing men from women. Political party distinguishes Democrats from Republicans and from other parties. Religious affiliation distinguishes Protestants, Catholics, Jews, and so forth. We refer to these measurements as nominal, in that term's sense of "naming." **Nominal variables** simply name the different *attributes* constituting them.

The attributes comprising a nominal variable (e.g., gender, composed of male and female) are simply *different*. Republicans and Democrats are simply different from each other, as are Protestants and Catholics. In other cases, however, we can say more about the attributes making up variables.

Ordinal Variables

Many social scientific variables go a step beyond simply naming the different attributes comprising a variable. **Ordinal variables** arrange those attributes in some order: from low to high, from more to less, and so on. Whereas the nominal variable "religious affiliation" classifies people into different religious groups, "religiosity" might order them in groups, such as very religious, somewhat religious, and not at all religious. And where the nominal variable "political party identification" simply distinguishes different groups (e.g., Democrats and Republicans), an ordinal measure of "political philosophy" might rank order the very liberal, the somewhat liberal, the middle-of-the-road, the somewhat conservative, and the very conservative. Ordinal variables share the nominal variable quality of distinguishing differences among people, and they add the quality of rank ordering those differences.

At the same time, it is not meaningful to talk about the distances separating the attributes that make up an ordinal variable. For example, we have no basis for talking about the "amount of liberalism" separating the very liberal from the somewhat liberal or the somewhat liberal from the middle-of-the-road. We can say that the first group in each comparison is more liberal than the second, but we can't say how much.

Ratio Variables

Some variables allow us to speak more precisely about the distances between the attributes comprising a variable. Consider age for a moment. The distance between 10 years old and 20 years old is exactly the same as that between 60 years old and 70 years old. Thus, it makes sense to talk about the distance between two ages (i.e., they are 10 years apart).

Moreover, **ratio variables** such as age have the additional quality of containing a genuine zero point—no years old in this case. This is what allows us to examine ratios among the categories constituting such variables. Thus, we can say that a 20-year-old is twice as old as a 10-year-old. By comparison, notice that we would have no grounds for saying one person is twice as religious as another.

Ratio variables, then, share all the qualities associated with nominal and ordinal variables, but have additional qualities not applicable to the lower-level measures. Other examples of ratio measures include income, years of schooling, and hours worked per week.

Interval Variables

Rarer in social research are variables that have the quality of standard intervals of measurement but lack a genuine zero point: **interval variables**.

One example is intelligence quotient (IQ). Although it is calculated in such a way as to allow for a score of zero, that would not indicate a complete lack of intelligence, because the person would at least have been able to take the test.

Moving outside the social sciences, consider temperature. The Celsius and Fahrenheit measures of temperature both have 0° marks, but neither represents a total lack of heat, given that it is possible to have temperatures below zero. The Kelvin scale, by contrast, is based on an absolute zero, which does represent a total lack of heat (measured in terms of molecular motion).

Measurement and Information

Knowing a variable's level of measure is important for selecting an appropriate statistic. Variables of different levels of measure contain different amounts of information. The only information we have about nominal variables is the number of cases that share a common attribute. With ordinal variables, in addition to knowing how many cases fall in a category, we know a "greater than, less than" relationship between the cases. Variables measured at the interval level have their points equidistant from each other. With equidistant points, we know how much greater than or less than cases are from each other. Finally, with ratio variables, we have all of the characteristics of nominal, ordinal, and interval variables, plus the knowledge that zero is not arbitrary but means an absence of the phenomena.

The statistics that SPSS has been programmed to compute are designed to make maximum use of the information preserved in a level of measure. Using the mode on a sample of GPAs ignores information used by the mean. Conversely, using the mean for a sample of religious preferences assumes information (equidistant points) not contained in a nominal measure. Responsible use of statistics requires selecting a statistic that matches the data's level of measure. We'll talk about this more later. Right now, we want you to know that being able to tell a variable's level of measure is essential for selecting the right statistical tool. We don't want to see you using a screwdriver when you need a hammer!

Measurement Options

Sometimes, you will have options regarding the levels of measurement to be created in variables. For instance, although age can qualify as a ratio variable, it could be measured as ordinal (e.g., young, middle-aged, old) or even as nominal (baby boomer, not baby boomer).

The significance of these levels of measurement will become more apparent when we begin to analyze the variables in our data set. As you'll discover, some analytic techniques are appropriate to nominal variables, some to ordinal variables, and some to ratio variables. On one hand, you will need to know a variable's level of measurement in order to determine which analytic techniques are appropriate. On the other hand, where you have options for measurement, your choice of measurement level may be determined by the techniques you want to employ.

3.5 Summary

Measurement is a fundamental aspect of social science research. It may be seen as the transition from concepts to variables: from sometimes ambiguous mental images to precise, empirical measures. Whereas we often speak casually about such concepts as prejudice, social class, and liberalism in everyday conversation, social scientists must be more precise in their uses of these terms.

This chapter has given you some of the logical grounding of social scientific measurement. Chapters to follow will continue this discussion, showing you the concrete techniques that allow you to act on that logic.

Chapter 4   Description of Your Data Set

The data we provide for your use here are real. They come from the responses of 2,090 adult Americans selected as a representative sample of the nation in 1996. These data are a major resource for professional social scientists and are the basis of many published books and articles.

The General Social Survey (GSS) is conducted regularly by the National Opinion Research Center (NORC) in Chicago, with financial support from the National Science Foundation and private sources. The purpose of the GSS program is to provide the nation's social scientists with accurate data for analysis. This activity, the brainchild of Jim Davis, one of the most visionary social scientists alive during your lifetime, began in 1972 and has continued more or less annually since then. (For more information about the GSS, see Davis and Smith 1992.)

4.1 Sampling

The data provided by the GSS are representative of American adults. This means that anything we learn about the 2,090 people in our sample can be taken as an accurate reflection of what all (noninstitutionalized, English-speaking) American adults would have said if we could have interviewed them all. This is the case because of a technique known as multistage probability sampling.

The researchers began by selecting a random sample of cities and counties across the country, having grouped them in such a way as to ensure that those selected would reflect all the variations in cities and counties in the nation. At the second stage of sampling, the researchers selected a random sample of city blocks or equivalent units in rural areas within each of the selected cities and counties.

The researchers then visited each of the selected blocks and chose specific households at random on each block. Finally, when interviewers visited each of the selected households, they determined the number of adults living in the household and selected one of them at random as the respondent.

This complex and sophisticated sampling process makes it possible for the responses of 2,090 individuals to provide an accurate reflection of the feelings of all adult Americans. Similar techniques are used by the U.S.

Census Bureau for the purpose of government planning and by polling firms that predict voting behavior with relative accuracy.

We have reduced the size of the sample to 1,500 cases so that the data can be analyzed with the Student Version of SPSS for Windows. Whereas the professional version of SPSS for Windows is virtually unlimited by the size of the computer on which it is installed, the student version is limited to 1,500 cases and 50 variables. The disk included with this book contains a file named GSS.SAV, a subsample of 1,500 cases from the 1996 General Social Survey's 2,090 cases. GSS.SAV may be used with either the student or professional versions of SPSS for Windows.

The data you have at hand, then, can be taken as an accurate reflection of the characteristics, attitudes, and behaviors of Americans 18 and older in 1996. This statement needs to be qualified slightly, however. When you analyze the data and learn that 45.5 percent of the sample said that they supported a woman's unrestricted right to have an abortion for any reason, you are safe in assuming that about 45.5 percent of the entire U.S. adult population feels that way. Because the data are based on a sample rather than on asking everyone, however, we need to anticipate some degree of **sampling error**. It would not be strange, for example, to discover that 43 percent or 47 percent of the total adult population (rather than exactly 45.5 percent) had the opinion in question. It is inconceivable, however, that as little as 10 percent or as much as 90 percent of the population supported unrestricted abortion.

As a rough guideline, you can assume that the sampling error in this data set is plus or minus only a few percentage points. In Chapter 15, we'll see how to calculate the actual sampling error for specific pieces of data.

Even granting the possibility of sampling error, however, our best estimate of what's true among the total U.S. population is what we learned from the probability sample. Thus, if you were to bet on the percentage of the total U.S. population who supported a woman's unrestricted right to an abortion, you should put your money on 45.5 percent. You would be better off, however, to bet that it was, say, between 42.5 percent and 48.5 percent.

4.2 Data Collection

The GSS data were collected in face-to-face household interviews. Once the sample households were selected, professional interviewers were dispatched to call on each. The interviewers asked each of the questions and wrote down the respondents' answers. Each interview took approximately an hour.

To maximize the amount of information that can be collected in this massive interviewing project, NORC asks some questions in only a random subsample of the households, asking other questions in the other households. Some questions are asked of all respondents. When we begin analyzing the GSS data, you will notice that some data items have a substantial number of respondents marked "missing data." For the most part, this refers to respondents who were not asked that particular question.

Although only a subsample was asked some of the questions, you can still take the responses as representative of the U.S. adult population. Only the degree of sampling error, mentioned above, is larger.

4.3   List of Variables

The data set contained on your disk contains the following questionnaire items. You might review the list now to make a note of issues that are of particular interest to you. Before long, you'll be getting much more familiar with them.

Each item in the list has an abbreviated name and the full wording used in the NORC interview. As you analyze survey data, it is important to know exactly how questions were asked if you are to understand the meaning of the answers given in response.

Name	Question
Abortion	
	"Please tell me whether or not you think it should be possible for a pregnant woman to obtain a legal abortion if . . .
ABANY	the woman wants it for any reason?"
ABDEFECT	there is a chance of serious defect in the baby?"
ABHLTH	the woman's own health is seriously endangered by the pregnancy?"
ABNOMORE	she is married and does not want any more children?"
ABPOOR	the family has a very low income and cannot afford any more children?"
ABRAPE	she became pregnant as a result of rape?"
ABSINGLE	she is not married and does not want to marry the man?
Children	
CHLDIDEL	"What do you think is the ideal number of children for a family to have?"
	"If you had to choose, which thing on this list would you pick as the most important for a child to learn to prepare him or her for life?"
OBEY	"To obey"
POPULAR	"To be well-liked or popular"
THNKSELF	"To think for himself or herself"
WORKHARD	"To work hard"
HELPOTH	"To help others when they need help"

Family

MARITAL   "Are you currently—married, widowed, divorced, separated, or have you never been married?"

DIVORCE   "Have you ever been divorced or legally separated?"

SIBS   "How many children have you ever had? Please count all that were born alive at any time (including any you had from a previous marriage)."

Politics

PARTYID   "Generally speaking, do you usually think of yourself as a Republican, Democrat, Independent, or what?"

POLVIEWS   "We hear a lot of talk these days about liberals and conservatives. I'm going to show you a seven-point scale on which the political views that people might hold are arranged from extremely liberal—point 1—to extremely conservative—point 7. Where would you place yourself on this scale?"

Religion

ATTEND   "How often do you attend religious services?"

POSTLIFE   "Do you believe there is a life after death?"

PRAY   "About how often do you pray?"

RELIG   "What is your religious preference? Is it Protestant, Catholic, Jewish, some other religion or no religion?"

Social-Political Opinions

CAPPUN   "Do you favor or oppose the death penalty for persons convicted of murder?"

GETAHEAD   "Some people say that people get ahead by their own hard work; others say that lucky breaks or help from other people are more important. Which do you think is most important?"

GUNLAW   "Would you favor or oppose a law which would require a person to obtain a police permit before he or she could buy a gun?"

[Note: For the following three questions, interviewers were instructed to use the term "Black" or "African American," depending on the customary usage in their area.]

RACDIF4   "On the average (Blacks/African-Americans) have worse jobs, income, and housing than white people. Do you think this difference is . . . because most (Blacks/African-Americans) just don't have the motivation or will power to pull themselves out of poverty?"

RACPRES   "If your party nominated a (Black/African-American) for President, would you vote for him if he were qualified for the job?"

RACSEG   "White people have a right to keep (Blacks/African-Americans) out of their neighborhoods if they want to and (Blacks/African-Americans) should respect that right."

[Possible responses: agree strongly, agree slightly, disagree slightly, disagree strongly]

Sexual Attitudes

HOMOSEX   "What about sexual relations between two adults of the same sex—do you think it is always wrong, almost always wrong, wrong only sometimes, or not wrong at all?"

XMOVIE   "Have you seen an X-rated movie in the last year?"

PREMARSX   "There's been a lot of discussion about the way morals and attitudes about sex are changing in this country. If a man and woman have sex relations before marriage, do you think it is always wrong, almost always wrong, wrong only sometimes, or not wrong at all?"

Additional Demographic Variables

AGE   "What is your date of birth?" [This was recoded into age in years.]

CLASS   "If you were asked to use one of the four names for your social class, which would you say you belong to: the lower class, the working class, the middle class, or the upper class?"

EDUC   "What is the highest grade in elementary school or high school that you finished and got credit for?"

[If high school graduate] "Did you complete one or more years of college for credit—not including schooling such as business college, technical or vocational school?"

[If yes] "How many years did you complete?"

INCOME   "In which of these groups did your total family income, for all sources, fall last year, before taxes, that is?"

SEI   Hodge-Siegel-Rossi socioeconomic ratings for respondents' occupations.

RACE   "What race do you consider yourself?"

RINCOME   "In which of these groups did your earnings from [occupation from a previous question] fall for last year? That is, before taxes or other deductions?"

SEX   [Coded by the interviewers, based on observation.]

Chapter 5   Using SPSS

Like most data analysis programs, SPSS is capable of computing many different statistical procedures with different kinds of data. This makes SPSS a very powerful and useful tool, but because of its generalization, we need to specify what we want SPSS to do for us.

In many ways, SPSS is a vehicle for discovering differences and relationships in data, the same way a car is a vehicle for discovering places we have not yet visited. The car does not know where we want to go or what we wish to see. We, rather than the car, plan the trip and set the direction. Similarly, when we use SPSS, we choose the data we wish to explore and select the statistical procedures we wish to use. Sitting at our computer keyboards, we are in SPSS's driver's seat.

We tell SPSS where to go and what to do in our social research adventure with SPSS commands. These commands instruct SPSS as to where to find our data, ways in which we want to modify the data, and the statistical procedures we want to use.

5.1 Getting Ready

SPSS for Windows has probably already been installed for you by computer center personnel, lab assistants, or your instructor. You need to learn which of the machines available to you are equipped with the system. Your instructor will probably help you get started, but we think you will find it pretty simple.

Once you have run Windows 95, you will probably find yourself looking at something like this:

With your cursor, all you need to do is double-click the SPSS icon. It will take SPSS a little while to respond, with the length of time depending on the kind of computer you are using.

If you do not find the "SPSSwin" icon on the desktop, as shown in the screen above, don't panic. There are other ways of launching SPSS. First, if SPSS has been run recently on this computer, you can reach it again with this shortcut. Click the Start button—probably in the lower left corner of your screen. Move your cursor up the list to Documents. See if "GSS" is listed as a recently used document. If so, move your cursor to highlight it and click. This will load both SPSS and the data file.

Alternatively, move the cursor further up the list to Programs, and look for SPSS among the programs resident on this computer. When you find SPSS, click it.

If neither of these alternatives works, now you can panic if you like. Better yet, ask your instructor for assistance.

Once you locate and launch SPSS, you should see something like what is shown in the screen on the next page.

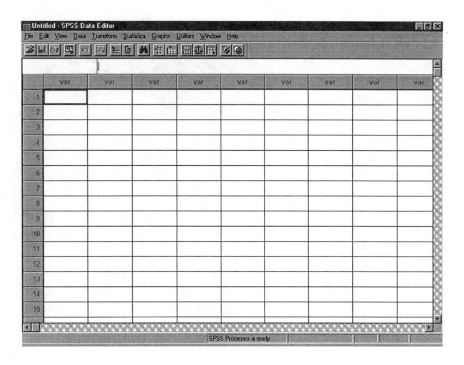

Most of the screen is taken up by the "SPSS Data Editor." You can find that name at the very top of the screen. This matrix is designed to hold data for analysis. If you wished, you could enter data directly into the matrix now and analyze it. Instead, however, we are going to load the GSS data set into the matrix in a moment.

Right beneath the window's title is a set of menus called a menubar, running from File on the left to Help on the right. You are going to become very familiar with these menus, because they are the control system through which you will operate SPSS.

As a preview, click on the word File on the menubar. Notice how a list of commands drops down below the title, some of the commands in dark, black letters and some in faint gray. Whenever you see a list like this, you can execute the black commands (by clicking on them) but the gray ones are not currently available to you. Right now, for example, you could Open a data set, but you can't Save it because there's nothing to be saved just now.

Click on the word File again, and the list disappears. Do that to get rid of the File menu now, and we'll come back to it shortly.

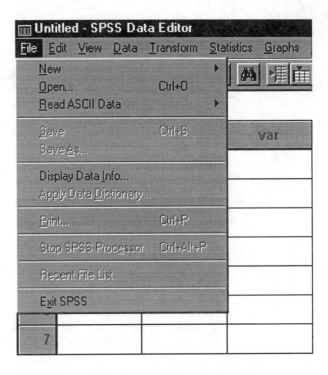

Before continuing with SPSS per se, let's examine a couple of Windows 95 options that will be useful to you. Notice that there are three small buttons in the upper right corner of the screen. Click the leftmost button, the one with heavy underscore on it.

Notice that the window has disappeared! Not to worry. Look now at the task bar at the bottom of the screen and locate a button titled Untitled—SPSS Data Editor. Click it.

Aha! The window didn't exactly disappear; Windows 95 says it was "minimized." That's certainly not an overstatement. This feature will be very useful to you once you have several documents on the screen at once. The minimize option lets you move windows out of the way without actually closing them.

Now click the middle button and notice how the window shrinks. If you click on the window's title bar and hold your mouse button down, you can drag the window around the screen. Sometimes this is a useful alternative to minimizing a window. Click the middle button again, and the window once more fills the screen.

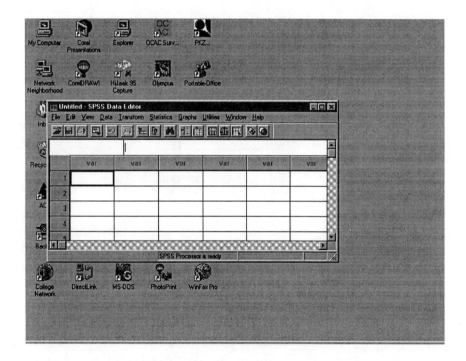

The rightmost button, with an "X," will close the window altogether. If you click it now, you will have to relaunch SPSS to get back here. You choose. We'll wait if you want to shut things down and reopen them.

You should now be looking at the SPSS Data Editor window. As we indicated earlier, this is the window that contains the data for SPSS to analyze, although right now it is empty. If you wanted, you could begin entering data for analysis. In fact, if you decide to conduct your own survey later on (see Chapter 21 and Appendix B), this is how you would enter those data. As a quick preview of this feature, type a 1 and press the Enter key on your keyboard.

You have now created the world's smallest data set: with one piece of information about one person. The "1" on the left of the matrix represents "Person 1." If you entered another number as you did just above, you would have brought "Person 2" into existence—with one piece of information. Why don't you do that now—enter a "2" for that person.

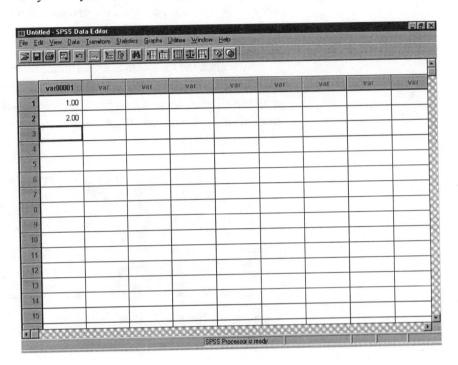

The "var00001" at the head of the column in the matrix represents the specific information we are storing about each person. It might represent his or her gender, for example. Moreover, a value of 1.00 might mean "male" and a value of 2.00 might mean female. Therefore, we would have indicated that Person 1 is a man, Person 2 a woman.

This is the basic structure of the data sets analyzed by SPSS. The good news for you is that we've already prepared a large data set for your use, so you won't have to keep entering data like this.

For our present purposes, however, we are going to load the GSS data that were provided with this book. This is easily done in SPSS for Windows. Click the word File again, and its menu will open up below it. The second command in that menu is the one we want: Open. Click on Open, and a new window will open to assist us in selecting the data set we want. [File → Open]

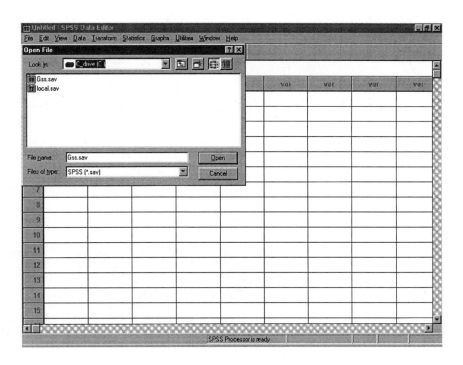

This command will present you with the Open File window. Click on the "Look in" field and select the drive that contains your disk. Next, move the mouse to the "Files of type" dialog box and click on the suffix for SPSS for Windows data files, "SPSS(*.sav)." Now you should see the name of the General Social Survey system file, GSS.SAV in the list of files. Select GSS.SAV by placing the mouse on it and clicking. Click the Open button near the lower right corner of the Open File window. In a few seconds, SPSS will display the GSS data in its data window. Specific instructions on using SPSS with these data are provided in later chapters.

Now you should be looking at the data in the GSS.SAV file, the data used for all of the exercises in this book. Now there are variable names across the top of the matrix and numbers in the cells. These are the GSS data.

Notice that respondent number 1 (the record numbers run down the left side of the matrix) has a "5" in the column for "marital." This variable reflects respondents' marital statuses. As you may recall from the Chapter 4 list of variables, a "5" on "marital" means the respondent is divorced. If you didn't recall that, you could easily find out right inside SPSS.

Under the Utilities menu, select Variables. The screen below is what you should be looking at after that command.

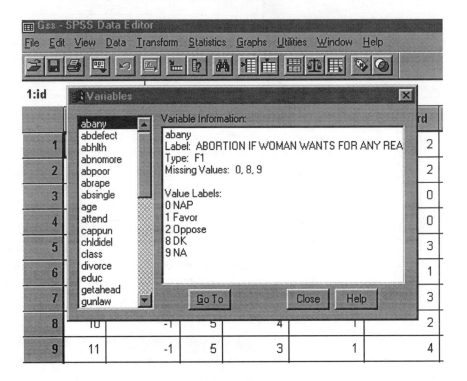

As you can see, the window has opened up with the first (alphabetically) of our variables: "abany." To see "marital," scroll down through the variable list on the left of the window until you reach "marital." Click on the desired variable, and this is what you should see.

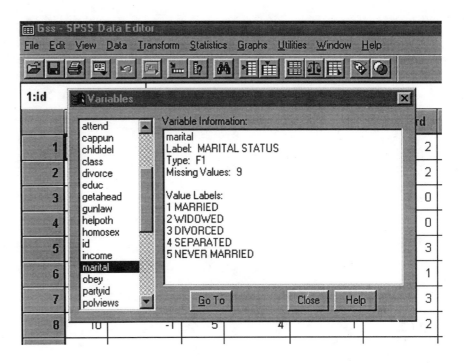

So you can see that anyone with a code of "1" is married, anyone with a "2" is widowed, and so forth. You might want to take a minute to explore some of the other variables in the data set, because it will be useful for you to be familiar with them later on.

When you get bored with the Variables window, there are a couple of ways to leave it. First, you can click the Close button at the bottom of the window. Or, you can click the small button with the "X" in the upper right corner of the window. Either will produce the same result.

Once you return to the data editor window, you might like to browse through more of the data. You can accomplish this by clicking the two arrows at the bottom of the matrix. Why not experiment with this? The two arrows on the right side of the matrix will let you move up and down through the list of respondents, by the way. You could play with that, too. See if you can find the marital status of respondent 10.

When you've finished for this session, open the File menu by clicking it. At the very bottom, you'll see the command Exit. Clicking this will instruct the computer to terminate the SPSS session and return you to the Windows desktop.

Before executing your command, however, the computer will ask if you want to "save contents of data window Newdata." Recall, we've loaded the file "GSS.SAV" into that window. Because the data set is already saved, we can safely click the No button now. If you had entered your own data, you definitely would have wanted to save the data—and the computer would have asked you to name the new data set.

5.2 Summary

So, in this first encounter, you've learned how to launch SPSS for Windows, load a data set, and explore in it. In the next chapter, we'll revisit some of the variables in the data set and see how SPSS lets us explore deeper than we've done in this first incursion.

Part II Univariate Analysis

We are going to begin our data analyses with some basic measurements of variables. Throughout this book, we are going to pay special attention to three concepts: religiosity, political orientations, and attitudes toward abortion. We've chosen these on the basis of general interest and the possibilities they hold for analysis.

In Part II, we are going to engage in **univariate analysis,** the analysis of one variable at a time. This is a basic act of measurement. In Chapter 6, for example, we are going to examine the different ways we might measure the religiosity of the respondents to the GSS, distinguishing the religious from the nonreligious and noting variations in between. In Chapters 7 and 8, we take a first look at differences in political orientations and attitudes toward abortion. Depending on your interest in these topics, we think you may be surprised to learn how Americans in general feel about these issues.

Although these initial univariate analyses will focus on single questions asked in the interview questionnaire, we are going to see in Chapter 9 how social researchers often combine several such responses into more sophisticated measures of the concepts under study. You'll learn a couple of techniques for doing that.

Finally, Chapter 10 suggests a number of other topics you might be interested in exploring: desired family size, child training attitudes, sexual behavior, and prejudice. We'll give you some guidance in approaching these topics, but our main purpose is to give you opportunities to strike out on your own and experience some of the open-endedness of social research.

Chapter 6   **Religiosity**

Let's start analyzing some data now. You'll need to launch the SPSS program as described earlier. Double-click the SPSSwin icon to get things going. Once SPSS has been activated, load your data set by selecting Open under the File menu. Then choose Data, and you'll be given a list of files to choose from. Choose GSS.SAV.

For our first illustration, we're going to look at some aspects of religious behavior. We can get a list of the variables in our data set through the following steps:

Select the Statistics menu
Choose Summarize in that menu
Finally, choose Frequencies in the Summarize menu

We are going to introduce a new notation that will simplify the description of such steps in the future:

Statistics → Summarize → Frequencies

will mean the same as the three separate steps listed above.

Once you've completed these steps, you should be looking at the following screen:

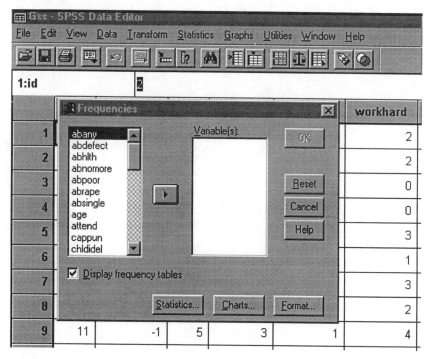

Four of the variables in this data set have to do with religiosity:

RELIG   respondent's religious preference

ATTEND   how often the respondent attends religious services

POSTLIFE   belief in life after death

PRAY   how often the respondent prays

Let's start by looking first at the distribution of religious preferences among the sample. This is easily accomplished as follows. First, move the scroll bar to the right of the list of variable names until RELIG is visible. Click that name so that it's highlighted. Then click the arrow to the right of the list. This will transfer the variable name to the field labeled "Variable(s)."

Once you've moved the name RELIG, click the "OK" button. This will set SPSS off on its assigned task. Depending on the kind of computer you are using, this operation may take a few seconds to complete. Eventually, however, a new window—the SPSS Output Navigator—will be brought to the front of the screen, and you should see the following information:

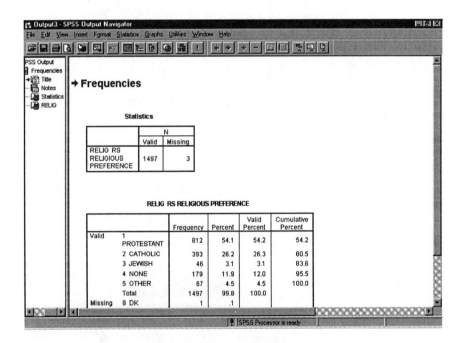

The small box titled "Statistics" tells us that of the 1,500 respondents in our subsample of the 1996 GSS, 1,497 gave valid answers to this question, whereas the remaining 3 have missing data. The box marked "RS RELIGIOUS PREFERENCE" contains the data we were really looking for. Scroll down the using the window bar or arrows on the right side. Now it should look like this:

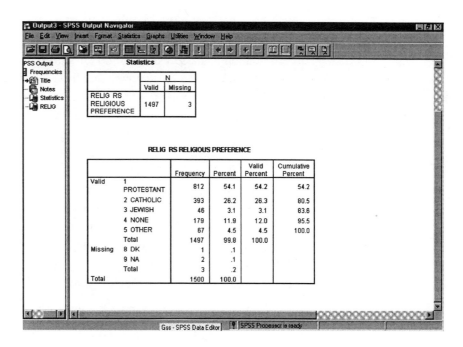

Let's go through this table piece by piece. The first line identifies the variable, presenting both its abbreviated variable label and its full name. Variable names are limited to eight characters and are the key to identifying variables in SPSS commands. Sometimes, it is possible to express the name of a variable clearly in eight or fewer characters (e.g., SEX, RACE), and sometimes the task requires some ingenuity (e.g., RINCOME for the respondent's annual income).

The leftmost column in the table lists the five numeric codes and VALUE LABELS of the several categories constituting the variable: Protestant, Catholic, Jewish, None, and Other. The numeric codes are the actual numbers used to code the data when it was entered. The VALUE LABELS are short descriptions of the response categories to remind us of the meaning of the categories. As we'll see later on, you can change both kinds of labels if you want.

The column headed "Frequency" simply tells how many of the 1,500 respondents said they identified with the various religious groups. We see, for example, that the majority—812—said they were Protestants, 393 said they were Catholic, and so forth. Note that in this context, "None" means that some respondents said they had no religious identification, rather than that they didn't answer. Near the bottom of the table, we see one person who answered "don't know" and two people who failed to answer.

The next column tells us what percentage of the whole sample each of the religious groups represents. Thus, 54.1 percent are Protestants, for example, calculated by dividing the 812 Protestants by the total sample, 1,500.

Usually, you will want to work with the "valid percentage," presented in the next column. As you can see, this percentage is based on the elimination of those who gave no answer, so the first number here means that 54.2 percent *of those giving an answer* said they were Protestant.

The final column presents the cumulative percentage, adding the individual percentages of the previous column as you move down the list. Sometimes, this will be useful to you. In this case, for example, you might note that 80.5 percent of those giving an answer were Christians, combining the Protestants and Catholics.

Now that we've examined the method and logic of this procedure, let's use it more extensively. As you may have already figured out, SPSS doesn't limit us to one variable at a time. (If you tried that out on your own before we said you could, you get two points for being adventurous. Hey, this is supposed to be fun as well as useful.)

So, return to the Frequencies window with:

Statistics → Summarize → Frequencies

If you are doing this all in one session, you may find that RELIG is still in the "Variable(s)" field. If so, you should click it, and once it's highlighted, notice that the arrow between the two fields changes direction. Clicking it now returns RELIG to its original location. Do that.

Now, let's get the other religious variables. One at a time, click and transfer ATTEND, POSTLIFE, and PRAY. When all three are in the "Variables(s)" field, click the "OK" button.

After a few seconds of cogitation, SPSS will present you with the Output window again. Click the up-arrow and you should be looking at the results of our latest analysis. Use the scroll bar to move up to the beginning of the newest data. Your screen should look like this:

		Frequency	Percent	Valid Percent	Cumulative Percent
Valid	0 NEVER	222	14.8	15.2	15.2
	1 LT ONCE A YEAR	142	9.5	9.7	24.9
	2 ONCE A YEAR	205	13.7	14.0	38.9
	3 SEVRL TIMES A YR	220	14.7	15.0	53.9
	4 ONCE A MONTH	93	6.2	6.4	60.3
	5 2-3X A MONTH	131	8.7	9.0	69.2
	6 NRLY EVERY WEEK	78	5.2	5.3	74.6
	7 EVERY WEEK	270	18.0	18.5	93.0
	8 MORE THN	102	6.8	7.0	100.0

ATTEND HOW OFTEN R ATTENDS RELIGIOUS SERVICES

Take a few minutes to study the new table. The structure of the table is the same as the one we saw earlier for religious preference. This one presents the distribution of answers to the question concerning the frequency of attendance at religious services. Notice that the respondents were given several categories to choose from, ranging from "never" to "more than once a week." The final category combines those who answered "don't know" (DK) with those who gave no answer (NA).

Notice that church attendance is an ordinal variable. The different frequencies of church attendance can be arranged in order, but the "distances" between categories vary. Had the questionnaire asked, "How many times did you attend church last year?" the resulting data would have constituted a ratio variable. The problem with that measurement strategy, however, is one of reliability: We couldn't bank on all the respondents recalling exactly how many times they had attended church.

The most common response in the distribution is "every week." Just under one-fourth of those giving an answer—18.5 percent—gave that answer. The most common answer is referred to as the **mode.** If we combine the respondents who report attending religious services weekly with the category immediately below them—more than once a week—we might report that 25.5 percent of our sample reports attending religious services *at least once a week.* If we added those who report attending "nearly every week," we see that approximately 30.7 percent attend church about weekly.

Combining adjacent values of a variable in this fashion is called *collapsing categories.* It is commonly done when the number of categories is large and/or some of the values have relatively few cases. In this instance, we might collapse categories further, for example:

About weekly	31%
1-3 times a month	15%
Seldom	39%
Never	15%
Total	100%

Compare this abbreviated table with the original, and be sure you understand how this one was created. Notice that we have rounded off the percentages here, dropping the decimal points. Typically, data such as these do not warrant the precision implied in the use of decimal points, because the answers given are themselves approximations for many of the respondents. Later in this chapter, we'll show you how to tell SPSS to combine categories in this fashion. That will be especially important when we want to use those variables in more complex analyses.

Now let's look at the other three religious variables. Use the scroll bar of the Output window to move to POSTLIFE.

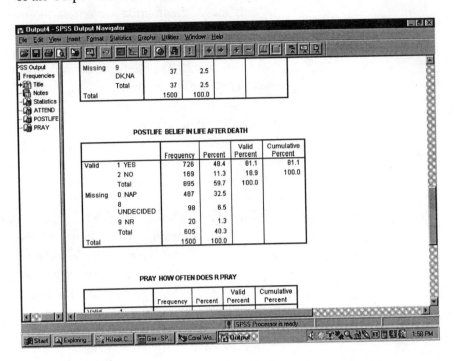

As you can see, there are significantly fewer attributes making up this variable: Yes or No. Notice that 487 respondents are coded "NAP." This stands for "not applicable," meaning that 487 people were not asked this question.

To collect data on a large number of topics, the GSS asks only subsets of the sample some of the questions. Thus, you might be asked whether you believed in an afterlife but not asked for your opinions on abortion. Someone else might be asked about abortion but not about the afterlife. Still other respondents would be asked about both.

Notice that more than four in five American adults believes in an afterlife. Is that higher or lower than you would have predicted? Part of the fun of analyses like these is the discovery of aspects of our society that you might not have known about. We'll have numerous opportunities for that throughout the remainder of the book.

PRAY HOW OFTEN DOES R PRAY

		Frequency	Percent	Valid Percent	Cumulative Percent
Valid	1 SEVERAL TIMES A DAY	136	9.1	26.9	26.9
	2 ONCE A DAY	153	10.2	30.2	57.1
	3 SEVERAL TIMES A WEEK	69	4.6	13.6	70.8
	4 ONCE A WEEK	40	2.7	7.9	78.7
	5 LT ONCE A WEEK	90	6.0	17.8	96.4
	6 NEVER	18	1.2	3.6	100.0
	Total	506	33.7	100.0	
Missing	0 NAP	991	66.1		
	8 DK	1	.1		
	9 NA	2	.1		
	Total	994	66.3		
Total		1500	100.0		

This completes our introduction to frequency distributions. Now that you understand the logic of variables and the values that constitute them, and know how to examine them with SPSS, you should spend some time looking at other variables in the data set. You can see them by using the steps we've just gone through above.

6.1 Bar Chart: A Graphic View

Sometimes, the information in a univariate analysis can be more quickly grasped if it is presented in graphic form rather than in a table of numbers. Take a moment to recall the distribution of religious affiliations examined earlier in this chapter. You may recall the most common affiliation (Protestant), but do you remember the relative sizes of the different groups? Was the Protestant group a little bigger than the others or a lot bigger? Sometimes, a graphic presentation of such data sticks in your mind more than a table of numbers.

SPSS offers an easy method for obtaining a graphic display of a univariate analysis. Under the Graphs menu, select Bar. This will give you the opportunity to select the kind of graph you would like. For now, let's choose the "Simple" type. Probably that's the one already selected, but you can click it again to be sure. Then, click the Define button.

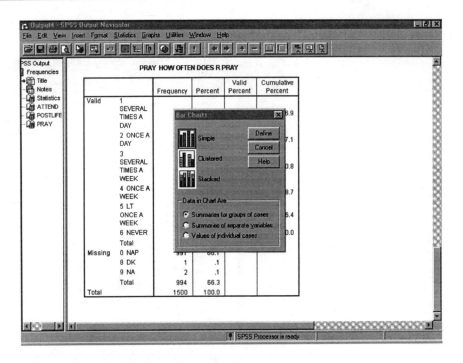

The next window allows you to further specify the kind of bar chart you would like, including a specification of the variable(s) to be graphed. As a start, let's just graph the religious affiliations. Find RELIG in the list and click it. Then click the arrow beside the "Category Axis" box.

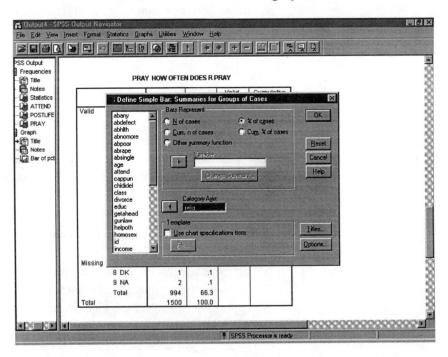

Near the top of the window, let's click "% of cases." We could accept the default of "N of cases," but we can as easily have SPSS calculate the percentage represented by each group. Next, click on Options in the lower right corner. Now you should have a screen that allows you to select how missing values will be treated. Because we are not interested in cases coded as missing, make sure that the check mark is turned off next to the line that says "Display groups defined by missing values." Then click Continue to go back to the Define Bar screen. Now click the "OK" button.

It may take SPSS a few seconds to construct the bar graph, but here's the result you should get eventually.

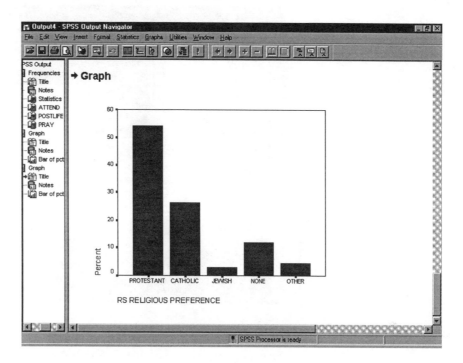

A graphic presentation like this can sometimes communicate the relative sizes of the different groups more powerfully than can a table of numbers. Chances are you'll have a more vivid memory of the distribution of religious groups in the United States from having seen this graph.

6.2 Measuring Central Tendency: Mean

In the previous examples, frequency distributions have been appropriate because of the relatively few categories making up the variables we've examined. If you followed our closing suggestion above that you run Frequencies for all variables, you will have turned up some oddities. You will have discovered, for example, that 0.3 percent of the sample is 18 years of age, 1.2 percent is 19, 1.3 percent is 20, and so forth. This display of AGE is not very useful for analysis.

Age is presented here as a **continuous** variable (in contrast to **discrete** or **categorical** variables). Sometimes, continuous variables like age (and also EDUC in this study) are more appropriately described in terms of their "average" values, such as the **mean.** As you may already know, the mean value in a set is calculated by adding all the individual values and dividing by the number of such values. Add up all the ages in a group and divide by the number of people in that group. This calculation is what people usually have in mind when they use the imprecise term *average*.

In SPSS, we can find the mean value for a variable rather simply, with the menu chain of Statistics → Summarize → Descriptives. SPSS once more offers you the opportunity to specify the variables you want to analyze.

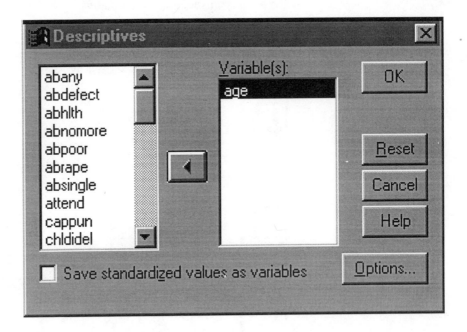

Because we're interested in measuring the central tendency, we should pick an appropriate variable. Let's choose AGE by clicking it. Then, to run Descriptives, click on "OK."

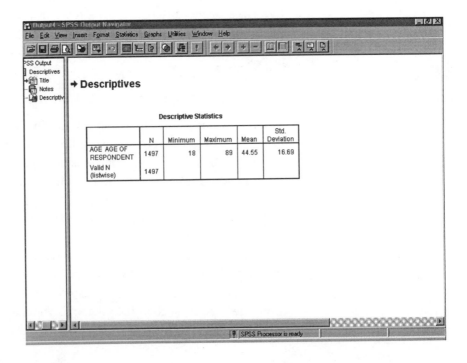

The mean age of respondents in this study is 45.55. This was calculated by adding the individual ages reported by the 1,497 respondents and dividing that total by 1,500.

Skipping a column, we see that the minimum age reported was 18 and the maximum was 89. The distance between these two values—71 years—is known as the **range** of values.

As you may know, the **standard deviation** is a measure of **dispersion,** the extent to which the individual ages are clustered around the mean or spread out away from it. The standard deviation tells us how far we would need to go above and below the mean to include approximately two-thirds of all of the cases. In this instance, two-thirds of the 1,497 respondents have ages between 27.86 and 61.24: (44.55 − 16.69) and (44.55 + 16.69), respectively. Later, we'll discover other uses for the standard deviation.

Now, to practice using the Descriptives command, why don't you examine the variable EDUC? See if you can complete the following sentence:

> The mean education of the respondents is _____, and two-thirds of them have between _____ and _____ years of education.

The answers for this and other exercises in this book are presented in Appendix D.

6.3 Modifying Variables with Recode

You'll recall from earlier in this chapter that we found that the variable ATTEND had so many categories that it was a bit difficult to handle. To simplify matters, we combined some adjacent answer categories.

Now we are going to see how SPSS can be instructed to do that using the Recode command. Under the Transform menu, select Recode. (If you do not see a Transform menu, you are probably looking at the Output window. Go to the Data Editor window.) SPSS now asks if you want to replace the existing values of the variables with the new, recoded ones. Select Into Different Variables, because we are going to assign a new name to the recoded variable.[1] SPSS now presents you with the following screen, in which to describe the recoding you want.

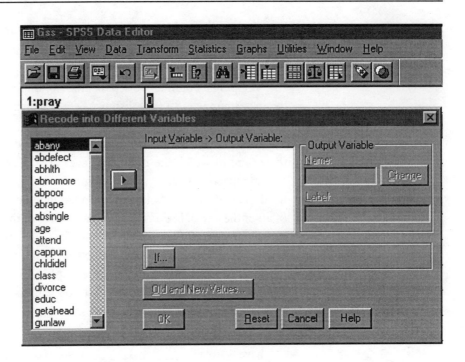

In the variable list at left, find and select ATTEND. Use the arrow to the right of the list to move the variable name to the field in the middle of the window. Notice that you need to tell SPSS what you would like to name the new, recoded variable. You can accomplish this easily in the section of the window called Output Variable.

Let's name the recoded variable CHATT for CHurch ATTendance. Type CHATT into the space provided for the "Output Variable Name." Click the Change button. As you can see in the middle field, SPSS will now modify the entry to read, "ATTEND → CHATT."

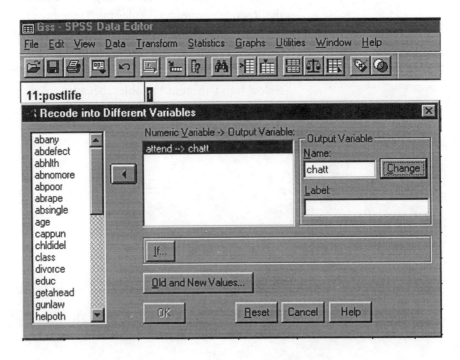

Thus far, we have created a new variable, but we haven't entered any data into it. We initiate this final step by clicking the Old and New Values button. Now SPSS presents you with the following window.

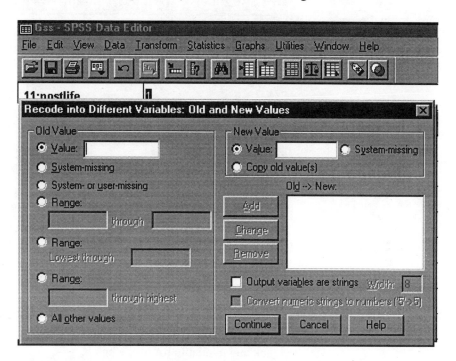

The left side of this window provides us with several options for specifying the old values we want to recode. The first, which SPSS has selected as a default, lets us specify a single value on the old variable—such as 8 ("More than once a week"). A more efficient option, for our present purposes, is found farther down the list, letting us specify a range of values. (To find the numerical codes assigned to ATTEND, you can return to Variables under the Utilities menu.)

In our manual collapsing of categories on this variable earlier, you'll recall that we combined the values 6 ("Nearly every week"), 7 ("Every week"), and 8 ("More than once a week"). We can accomplish the same thing now by clicking the first "Range" button and entering "6" and "8" in the two boxes.

At the top of the right side of the window, notice a space for you to enter the new value for this combination of responses. Let's recode it "1." Enter that number in the box provided, as shown below.

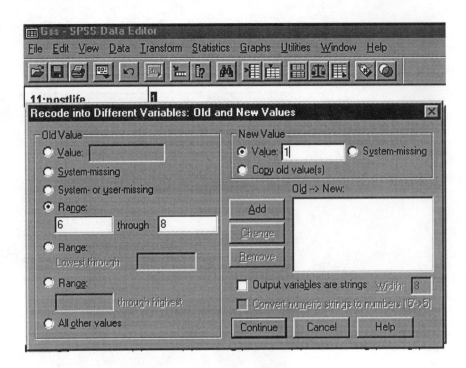

Once you've added the recode value, notice that the Add button just below it is activated. Where it was previously "grayed out," it is now a clear black and available for use. Click it.

This action causes the expression "6 through 8 → 1" to appear in the field. We've given SPSS part of its instructions. Now let's continue.

Click "Range" again, and now, let's combine values 4 ("Once a month") and 5 ("Two to three times a month"). Give this new combined category the value of 2. Click Add to add it to the list of recodes.

Now combine categories 1 ("Less than once a year"), 2 ("Once a year"), and 3 ("Several times a year"). Recode the new category as 3 and Add it to the list.

Finally, let's recode 0 ("Never") as 4. On the left side of the window, use the "Value" button to accomplish this. Enter 0 there, and enter 4 as the new value. Click on Add.

To tidy up our recoding, we could have SPSS maintain the "missing data" values of the original variable. We would accomplish this by clicking "System-missing" as an old value (on the left side) and as the new one (on the right side), and then clicking on Add. Although it is a good practice to consciously recode every category, in this case, it is not necessary. Any cases that were not covered by the range of the old values would be undefined and treated as missing values.

Your recode window should now look like this:

As we wrap up, it should be repeated that there are no hard-and-fast rules for choosing which categories to combine in a recoding process like this. There are, however, two rules of thumb to guide you: one logical, the other empirical.

First, there is sometimes a logical basis for choosing cutting points at which to divide the resulting categories. In recoding AGE, for example, it is often smart to make one break at 21 years (the traditional definition of adulthood) and another at 65 (the traditional age of retirement). In the case of church attendance, our first combined category observes the Christian norm of weekly church attendance.

The second guideline is based on the advantage of having sufficient numbers of cases in each of the combined categories, because a very small category will hamper subsequent analyses. Ideally, each of the combined categories would have roughly the same number of cases.

How do you suppose we'd continue the recoding process? Click Continue, you say? Hey, you may be a natural at this. Do that.

This takes you back to the Recode into Different Variables window. Now that you've completed your specification of the recoding of this variable, all that remains is to click "OK" at the bottom of the window. SPSS may take a few seconds now to accomplish the recoding you've specified.

Go to the Data Editor window again. (You need to minimize the Output Navigator window and enlarge the Data Editor window.) To see your new variable, scroll across the columns of the window until you discover CHATT in the last column used thus far.[2] Notice the values listed in the column. Person number 1 has a value of 3.00 on the new variable.

Now find ATTEND. Notice that person 1 has a *2* in ATTEND as well. That's correct, because everyone with a 1, 2, or 3 in the original variable was recoded a 3 in the new one. You can check a few more people if you want to verify that the coding was accomplished as we instructed. This is a good idea, by the way, to ensure that you haven't made a mistake. (Presumably, SPSS doesn't make mistakes.)

At this point, our recoding could be considered complete. You could now begin using the new variable in your analysis. Let's take one more step in the interests of elegance.

Scroll across the columns again until you find CHATT. Click the variable name at the top of the column and see how SPSS selects the whole column. Now, in the Data menu, select Define Variable. That should present you with the following window.

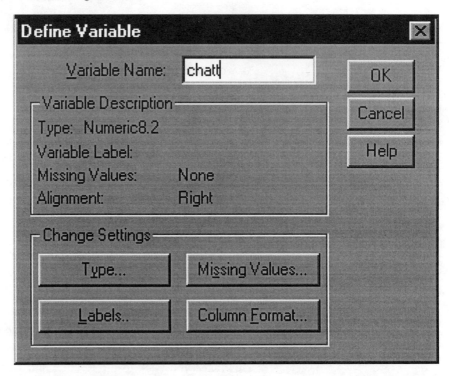

Below the variable name, you'll see a summary of the characteristics currently in effect for this variable. The first line tells us the variable type. In the example above, "Numeric8.2" means that codes on this variable are set up as numbers that are 8 digits wide and there are two digits to the right of the decimal point, so that "1" would be stored as "1.00." Because the decimal points are of no use to us in this situation, let's get rid of them. They only make our output harder to read.

Click on Type.

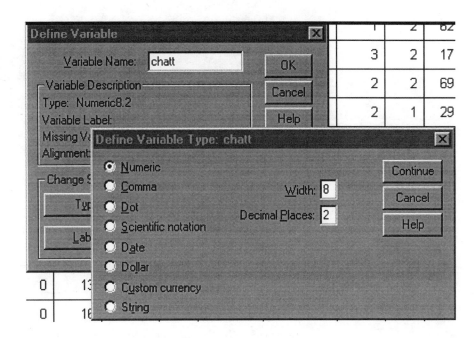

This window shows all the possibilities available to you. For our purposes, however, we want a numeric variable with zero decimal places. Substitute 0 for the 2 in the appropriate field. Then click on Continue.

Finally, the Define Variable window allows us to assign value labels to the recoded, numerical scores on CHATT, so we don't have to remember what a 1 or a 2 represents on the recoded variable.

Click on Labels.

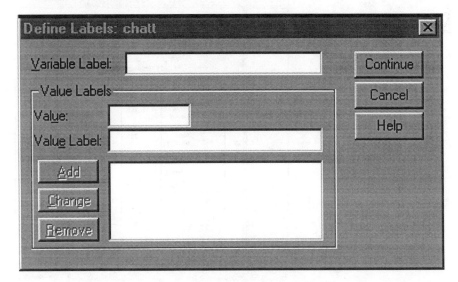

Now SPSS is asking us to give names to the numerical values of the new variable. To start, enter 1 in the "Value" field. Recall that this value represents people who originally scored 6 ("Nearly every week"), 7 ("Every week"), and 8 ("More than once a week"). Let's call this new, combined category "About weekly." Enter that description in the "Value Label" field and click on Add.

Now, enter the remaining value labels as indicated below.

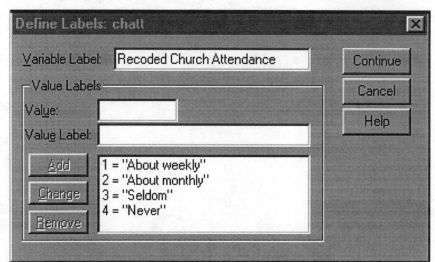

Once your screen looks like this, click Continue. Once you've been returned to the Define Variable window, you can click "OK" to indicate that we've indicated all the changes we want SPSS to make.

Let's review the results of our recoding process now. We can do this most easily through the use of the now-familiar Frequencies command. If you scroll down the variable list, you'll see that CHATT is now included in the list.

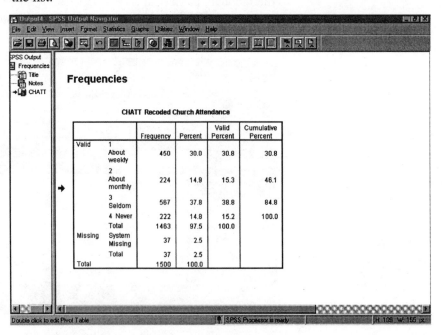

Notice how much more manageable the recoded variable is. Now we can use the recoded variable in our later analyses.

The value of recoding is especially evident in the case of continuous variables such as age and education. Because they have so many answer categories, they are totally unmanageable in some forms of analysis. Fortunately, we can recode continuous variables as easily as we just recoded

ATTEND. In the case of AGE, for instance, we might establish categories "Under 21," "21 to 35," and so on.

You can probably figure out how to do this, but we are going to take advantage of one additional feature in the recoding procedure.

Let's launch Transform → Recode → Into Different Variables again. Notice that the Recode into Different Variables window still has our recoding of ATTEND. Clear the boards by clicking Reset at the bottom of the window. Then, select AGE and move it to the "Input Variable" window.

Let's name the new variable "AGECAT" to represent "AGE CATegories." Once you've named the new variable, click on change to insert the new name. Now click Old and New Variables to tell SPSS how to recode.

In recoding AGE, we want to make use of the "Range" option again, but for our first recode, check the second one: the one that specifies "lowest through _____." This will ensure that our youngest category will include the youngest respondents without our having to know what the youngest age is. Enter 20 in the box, specify the new value as 1, and click on Add.

Beware! Although the "lowest" and "highest" specifications are handy, they must be used with care. If you look at the frequency distribution for EDUC, you will see that the two missing cases were coded "98." If we used 17 through "highest," we would code two people we knew nothing about as being among the most highly educated.

Do what you have to do to create the remaining recode instructions indicated below.

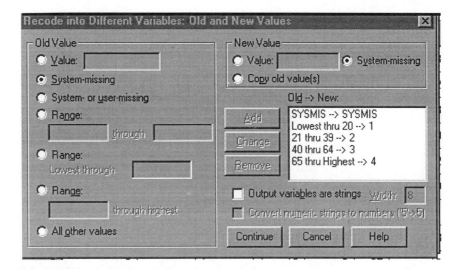

Click Continue to return to the main recode window and then "OK" to make the recoding changes. Once again, you should be looking at the data window, and you have a new variable in the rightmost column. Check it out.

To complete the process, let's tidy up the new variable. In the data window, click the AGECAT column label to select the column. Now activate the Data → Define Variable command. With Type, set the decimal places to 0. With Labels, establish the following labels for the new variable.

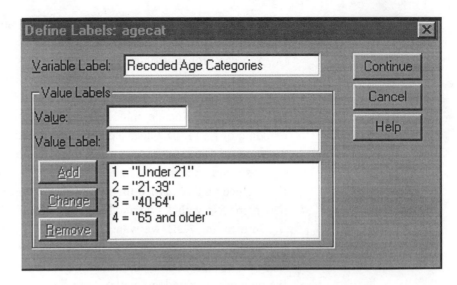

Once you've completed the recoding and labeling, check the results of your labors by running Frequencies on the new variable. Notice that CHATT is still in the list of variables to be analyzed. You can remove it by selecting it and then clicking the arrow that returns it to the main list of variables. If you fail to do this, SPSS will simply calculate and report the frequencies on CHATT again.

Statistics

AGECAT Recoded Age Categories

N	Valid	1500
	Missing	0

AGECAT Recoded Age Categories

		Frequency	Percent	Valid Percent	Cumulative Percent
Valid	1 under 21	55	3.7	3.7	3.7
	2 21-39	612	40.8	40.8	44.5
	3 40-64	613	40.9	40.9	85.3
	4	220	14.7	14.7	100.0
	Total	1500	100.0	100.0	

6.4 Practicing Recodes

To experiment further with this technique, why don't you try changing the age recodes into a somewhat more elaborate coding of age into teens, 20s, 30s, and so on?

For even more practice, recode the variable EDUC . Later on, we are going to want to use it in a recoded form. See if you can create EDCAT with the following categories:

Less than high school graduate

High school graduate

Some college

College graduate

Graduate studies (beyond college)

If you have trouble, the proper commands and results are shown in Appendix D.

6.5 Saving Your Work

That's enough work for now. But before we stop, let's save the work we've done in this session, so we won't have to repeat it all when we start up again.

The recoding you've done so far is being held only in the computer's volatile memory. That means that if you leave SPSS right now, all the recoding changes will disappear. Because we will want to use the recoded variables AGECAT and EDCAT, there's a simple procedure that will save us time at our next session.

First, you may want to save a copy of the output window that you've been accumulating during this session. If you are writing a term paper that will use these results, you can probably copy portions of the output and paste it into your word-processing document. To save the output window, first make sure it is the window frontmost on your screen, then select Save As under the File menu.

SPSS will present you with the following window:

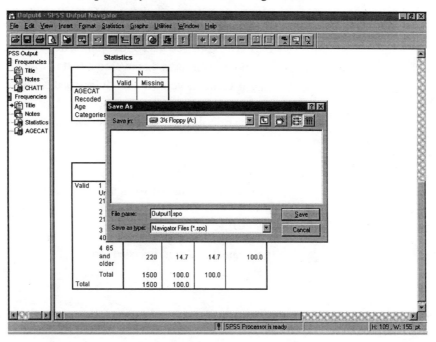

In this example, we've decided to save our output on the Drive A diskette under the name Output1 (which SPSS thoughtfully provided as a default name). As an alternative, you might like to use a name like "Out1022" to indicate it was the output saved on October 22, or use some similar naming convention.

Now, let's save the data file with the recodes we created so painstakingly. Start by selecting the Data Editor window. Then, go to the File menu and select Save again. Now your recodes have been saved, and you can leave SPSS with the File → Exit command. The next time you start an SPSS session and load the data set, it will have all the new, recoded variables.[3]

6.6 Summary

We've now completed your first interaction with data. Even though this is barely the tip of the iceberg, you should have begun to get some sense of the possibilities that exist in a data set such as this. Many of the concepts with which social scientists deal are the subjects of opinions in everyday conversations. A data set such as the one you are using in this book is powerfully different from opinion.

From time to time, you probably hear people make statements like these:

> Almost no one goes to church anymore.

> Americans are pretty conservative by and large.

> Most people are opposed to abortion.

Sometimes, opinions like these are an accurate reflection of the state of affairs; sometimes, they are far from the truth. In ordinary conversation, the apparent validity of such assertions typically hinges on the force with which they are expressed and/or the purported wisdom of the speaker. Already in this book, you have discovered a better way of evaluating such assertions. In this chapter, you've already learned some of the facts about religion in the United States today. The two chapters that follow will take you into the realms of politics and attitudes toward abortion.

Student Version Notes

1. Because the Student Version of SPSS limits the number of variables that can be used to 50, you might need to save the recode under the same name. It's okay to do this if you later save the modified data set under a different name (e.g., GSSR1, GSSR2). That way, you can reopen one of the modified data sets, or you can retrieve the original data in its uncoded form.

2. If you've used the same variable name, look at ATTEND.

3. Because you have written over the earlier forms of some variables, it's a good idea to save your changes using a new file name such as GSSR1, GSSR2, and so on. Then, if you want to use the unrecoded variables, you can always load the original data set for that purpose. To accomplish this, select Save As instead of Save. Then, in the "File Name" field, type in the new name. It can be no longer than 8 characters.

Chapter 7   Political Orientations

Let's turn our attention from religion to politics now. Some people feel so strongly about politics that they joke about it being a "religion." The GSS data set has several items that reflect political issues. Two are key political items: POLVIEWS and PARTYID.

7.1 Political Views: Liberalism versus Conservatism

We'll start our examination of political orientations with POLVIEWS. Let's see what that variable measures. Use the Frequencies command to find out.

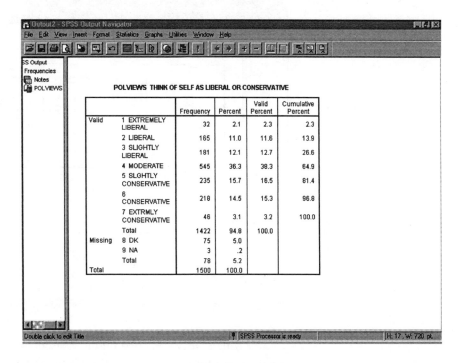

POLVIEWS THINK OF SELF AS LIBERAL OR CONSERVATIVE

		Frequency	Percent	Valid Percent	Cumulative Percent
Valid	1 EXTREMELY LIBERAL	32	2.1	2.3	2.3
	2 LIBERAL	165	11.0	11.6	13.9
	3 SLIGHTLY LIBERAL	181	12.1	12.7	26.6
	4 MODERATE	545	36.3	38.3	64.9
	5 SLGHTLY CONSERVATIVE	235	15.7	16.5	81.4
	6 CONSERVATIVE	218	14.5	15.3	96.8
	7 EXTRMLY CONSERVATIVE	46	3.1	3.2	100.0
	Total	1422	94.8	100.0	
Missing	8 DK	75	5.0		
	9 NA	3	.2		
	Total	78	5.2		
Total		1500	100.0		

As you can see, POLVIEWS taps into basic political philosophy, ranging from extremely liberal to extremely conservative. As you might expect, most people are clustered near the center, with fewer numbers on either extreme.

As we continue to use this variable in our analyses, we will probably want to work with fewer categories. For now, let's recode the variable to just three categories: liberal, moderate, and conservative. Recall from the previous chapter that there are two steps involved in recoding the categories of a variable. First, we combine categories; then we assign names to identify the new groupings.

First, let's create a new variable, POLREC, by recoding POLVIEWS as follows:

1 through 3 → 1

4 → 2

5 through 7 → 3

Then, assign new labels to the values of POLREC:

1 = Liberal

2 = Moderate

3 = Conservative

To see the results of our recoding, we repeat the Frequencies command with the new variable:

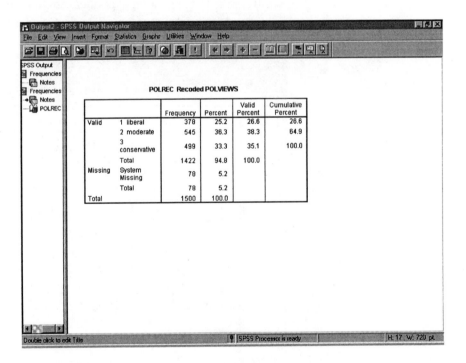

Now that we've recoded political orientations into a form we can use easily in our future analyses, let's turn to the other fundamental measure.

7.2   Political Party Affiliations

Another basic indicator of a person's political orientation is found in the party with which he or she tends to identify. Let's turn now to the variable PARTYID. Get the Frequencies for that variable.

You should get the following result from SPSS.

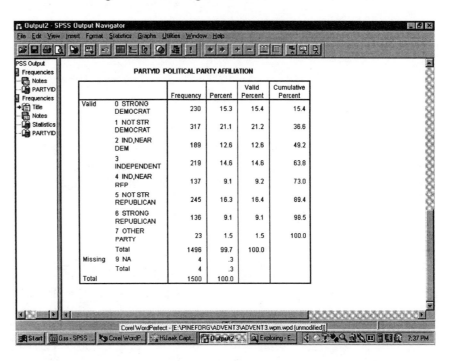

Once again, there are more answer categories here than we will be able to manage easily in our subsequent analyses, so let's consider recoding the variable. Let's call the recoded variable simply PARTY.

It makes sense to combine the first two categories: the "strong" and "not so strong" Democrats. Similarly, we will want to combine the corresponding Republican categories (5 and 6). Two of the categories, however, need a little more discussion: the two Independent groups, who said, when pressed by interviewers, that they were "near" one of the two parties.

Should we combine those near the Democrats with that party, for example, or should we combine them with the other Independents? There are a number of methods for resolving this question. For now, however, we are going to choose the simplest method. As we continue our analyses, it will be useful if we have ample numbers of respondents in each category, so we will recode with an eye to creating roughly equal-sized groups. In this instance, that means combining the three Independent categories into one group. So, let's recode as follows:

0 through 1 → 1

2 through 4 → 2

5 through 6 → 3

7 → 4

Then, label PARTY as follows:

1 = Democrat

2 = Independent

3 = Republican

4 = Other

Enter and execute these commands now. Once you've done so, we'll be ready to look again at the frequency distribution of the new variable. Let's run the Frequencies for PARTY.

That should produce the following result.

PARTY party identification

		Frequency	Percent	Valid Percent	Cumulative Percent
Valid	1 democrat	547	36.5	36.6	36.6
	2 independent	545	36.3	36.4	73.0
	3 republican	381	25.4	25.5	98.5
	4 other	23	1.5	1.5	100.0
	Total	1496	99.7	100.0	
Missing	System Missing	4	.3		
	Total	4	.3		
Total		1500	100.0		

Now we have two basic measures of political orientations. There are other possibilities, however.

7.3 Political Attitudes

The GSS data set contains other variables that also tap into people's political orientations. For instance, GUNLAW measures how people feel about the registration of firearms. This has been a controversial issue in the United States for a number of years, involving, on one hand, Second Amendment guarantees of the right to bear arms, and on the other, high rates of violent crime, often involving firearms. CAPPUN measures whether respondents favor or oppose capital punishment, another topic that is associated with political attitudes.

As you can see, there is no lack of ways to explore people's political outlooks in the data set. We're going to focus on some of these items in later sections of the book. You should take some time now to explore some of them on your own. Take capital punishment, for example. How do you think the American people feel about this issue? Do you think most are in favor of it or most are opposed? This is your chance to find out for yourself.

If you have any interest in political matters, you should enjoy this exercise. You may have your own personal opinion about extramarital sex or homosexuality, but do you have any idea how the general population feels about such things? You have the definitive answers to those questions at your fingertips right now, using the GSS data set and your developing mastery of SPSS.

7.4 Summary

Politics is a favorite topic for many Americans, and it is a realm often marked by the expression of unsubstantiated opinions. Now, you are able to begin examining the facts of political views. In later chapters, we'll move beyond describing political orientations and start explaining why people have the political views they have.

Chapter 8   Attitudes toward Abortion

When we examined the topic of abortion in Chapter 2, we discussed the different degrees of approval represented by the several questions and made some educated guesses as to which ones would receive the most (and least) support. Now that we have gained some proficiency in the use of SPSS to analyze data, let's check on how well we did in our predictions.

Because we want to see the frequency distribution for several variables at once, we can make one request for all of them. In the Frequencies window, you can transfer all of the abortion items into the "Variable(s)" field before clicking "OK." In fact, by holding down the Shift key when you click the name of variables, you can select more than one at once, then click the arrow to transfer them. Experiment with this.

Ultimately, you want to transfer all seven abortion items to the "Variable(s)" field as shown below.

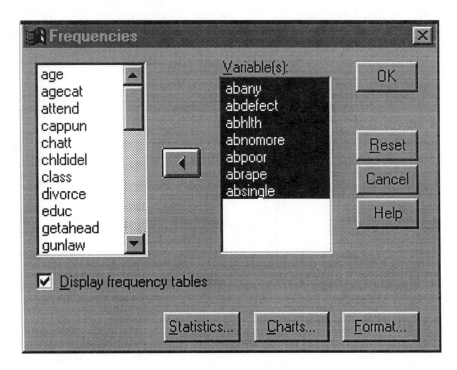

Click "OK" to launch the analysis, and you should get the results in your output window. You may have to expand the size of the window (using the up-arrow) and then scroll up and down through the output to find a specific item. Let's do that now, to check on the different levels of support for abortion under different circumstances.

8.1 Items with the Highest Level of Support

You should now be able to give SPSS the command that will result in the frequency distributions for the various abortion items. Once you've done that, you should get the following tables.

ABDEFECT STRONG CHANCE OF SERIOUS DEFECT

		Frequency	Percent	Valid Percent	Cumulative Percent
Valid	1 Favor	774	51.6	81.2	81.2
	2 Oppose	179	11.9	18.8	100.0
	Total	953	63.5	100.0	
Missing	0 NAP	513	34.2		
	8 DK	30	2.0		
	9 NA	4	.3		
	Total	547	36.5		
Total		1500	100.0		

ABHLTH WOMANS HEALTH SERIOUSLY ENDANGERED

		Frequency	Percent	Valid Percent	Cumulative Percent
Valid	1 Favor	872	58.1	91.2	91.2
	2 Oppose	84	5.6	8.8	100.0
	Total	956	63.7	100.0	
Missing	0 NAP	513	34.2		
	8 DK	27	1.8		
	9 NA	4	.3		
	Total	544	36.3		
Total		1500	100.0		

ABRAPE PREGNANT AS RESULT OF RAPE

		Frequency	Percent	Valid Percent	Cumulative Percent
Valid	1 Favor	809	53.9	85.2	85.2
	2 Oppose	141	9.4	14.8	100.0
	Total	950	63.3	100.0	
Missing	0 NAP	513	34.2		
	8 DK	33	2.2		
	9 NA	4	.3		
	Total	550	36.7		
Total		1500	100.0		

Although we don't have any basis for comparison yet, it would seem at first glance that very high percentages of the general public support a woman's right to an abortion in cases of the danger of birth defects (81 percent), threats to the woman's health (91 percent), and rape (85 percent). Now, let's see how these compare with other reasons.

8.2 Items with Less Support

Let's look at the three items we identified as probably enjoying less support. Here's what you should get in return.

ABNOMORE MARRIED--WANTS NO MORE CHILDREN

		Frequency	Percent	Valid Percent	Cumulative Percent
Valid	1 Favor	455	30.3	48.7	48.7
	2 Oppose	480	32.0	51.3	100.0
	Total	935	62.3	100.0	
Missing	0 NAP	513	34.2		
	8 DK	47	3.1		
	9 NA	5	.3		
	Total	565	37.7		
Total		1500	100.0		

ABPOOR LOW INCOME--CANT AFFORD MORE CHILDREN

		Frequency	Percent	Valid Percent	Cumulative Percent
Valid	1 Favor	455	30.3	48.4	48.4
	2 Oppose	486	32.4	51.6	100.0
	Total	941	62.7	100.0	
Missing	0 NAP	513	34.2		
	8 DK	42	2.8		
	9 NA	4	.3		
	Total	559	37.3		
Total		1500	100.0		

ABSINGLE NOT MARRIED

		Frequency	Percent	Valid Percent	Cumulative Percent
Valid	1 Favor	440	29.3	47.2	47.2
	2 Oppose	492	32.8	52.8	100.0
	Total	932	62.1	100.0	
Missing	0 NAP	513	34.2		
	8 DK	48	3.2		
	9 NA	7	.5		
	Total	568	37.9		
Total		1500	100.0		

The assumption that these reasons would garner less support proves accurate. It is also interesting that virtually the same proportions of respondents—47 percent to 49 percent—support this second set of reasons.

8.3 Support for Unrestricted Choice of Abortion

Finally, let's see what proportion of the population would support a woman having unrestricted freedom to choose an abortion: for any reason.

ABANY ABORTION IF WOMAN WANTS FOR ANY REASON

		Frequency	Percent	Valid Percent	Cumulative Percent
Valid	1 Favor	449	29.9	48.1	48.1
	2 Oppose	484	32.3	51.9	100.0
	Total	933	62.2	100.0	
Missing	0 NAP	513	34.2		
	8 DK	49	3.3		
	9 NA	5	.3		
	Total	567	37.8		
Total		1500	100.0		

Notice that about the same proportion (48 percent) supports a woman's unrestricted freedom to choose abortion as supported the specific situations described in ABNOMORE, ABPOOR, and ABSINGLE.

8.4 Support for Abortion in Overview

Let's construct a table that summarizes those tables we've just examined. It is often useful to bring related tables such as these together in an abbreviated format.

Percentage Who Support a Woman's Right to Choose Abortion because:

the woman's health would be seriously endangered	91
the pregnancy resulted from rape	85
there is a strong chance of a serious defect	81
a family is too poor to afford more children	48
a family wants no more children	49
the woman wants it, for any reason	48
the woman is unmarried	47

The tables we've just examined suggest that attitudes toward abortion fall into three basic groups. There is a small minority of no more than 9 percent who are opposed to abortion under any circumstances. We conclude this because 91 percent would support abortion if the woman's life were seriously endangered.

Another group, just under half the population, would support a woman's free choice of abortion for any reason. The remainder of the population would support abortion in only a few circumstances involving medical danger and/or rape.

In a later chapter, we will return to these three groups and see how we might identify them through recoding our data.

8.5 Summary

In this initial analysis of abortion attitudes, we have had an opportunity to explore the structure of attitudes on this controversial topic. Although abortion is generally discussed as an all-or-nothing proposition, we've seen that relatively few Americans reject abortion completely. A sizable minority appear to have reservations about abortion but are willing to make exceptions in certain circumstances.

We are going to explore this structuring of attitudes further in Chapter 9, where you will learn how to create a new variable in the data set: one that captures the variations of attitudes about abortion.

Chapter 9 Creating Composite Measures

Now that you've had a chance to get familiar with univariate analysis, we're going to add a little more sophistication to that process. As you're about to see, it is not necessary to limit your analysis to single measures of a variable. In this chapter, we're going to create **composite measures** made up of multiple indicators of a single concept.

For purposes of this discussion, let's pick up where we left off in our opening examination of attitudes toward abortion. You'll recall that we examined seven GSS items that reflected people's attitudes, and we tentatively concluded there are three major groups in the population: those who are unalterably opposed; those who support a woman's unrestricted right to choose; and those who support abortion only under certain conditions, such as a threat to the woman's health.

9.1 Using Crosstabs

To explore attitudes toward abortion in more depth, we need to use a new SPSS command: Crosstabs. This command lets us cross-classify people in terms of their answers to more than one question. Let's try a simple example.

The command pathway to this technique is

Statistics → Summarize → Crosstabs

Work your way through those menu selections, and you should reach a window that looks like the following.

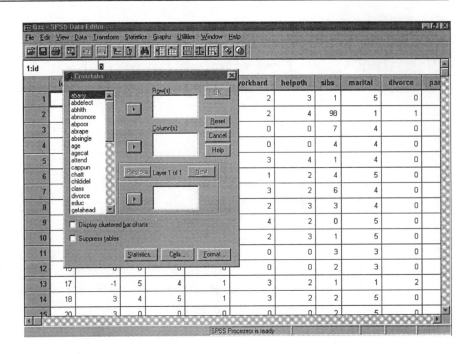

Because the logic of a crosstab will be clearer when we have an example to look at, just follow these steps on faith, and we'll justify your faith in a moment.

Let's analyze the relationship between the answers people gave to the question about whether a woman should be able to have an abortion if (1) her health was seriously endangered (ABHLTH) and (2) if she was too poor to have more children.

In the Crosstabs window, click ABHLTH and then click the arrow pointing toward the "Row(s)" field. Next, click on ABPOOR and transfer it to the "Column(s)" field, producing the result shown below.

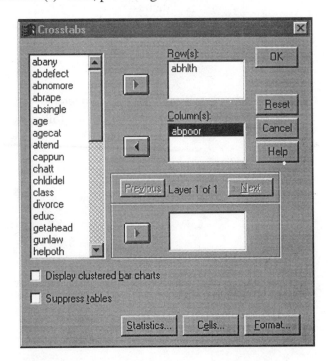

Once your window looks like the one above, click "OK." After a few seconds, you'll be rewarded with the following data in your "Output" window.

ABHLTH WOMANS HEALTH SERIOUSLY ENDANGERED * ABPOOR LOW INCOME--CANT AFFORD MORE CHILDREN Crosstabulation

Count

		ABPOOR LOW INCOME--CANT AFFORD MORE CHILDREN		
		1 Favor	2 Oppose	Total
ABHLTH WOMANS HEALTH SERIOUSLY ENDANGERED	1 Favor	451	387	838
	2 Oppose	4	80	84
Total		455	467	922

Notice that the table demonstrates the logic of the command we asked you to make. By specifying ABPOOR as the "Column" variable, we have caused it to appear across the top of the table with its attributes of "Favor" and "Oppose" representing the two columns of figures.

ABHLTH, as the "Row" variable, appears to the left of the table, and its attributes constitute the rows of the table.

More important, this table illustrates a logic that operates within the system of attitudes that people hold about abortion. First, we notice that 451 people say they would support a woman's right to choose abortion if her health were seriously endangered or if she were poor and felt she couldn't afford more children. At the opposite corner of the table, we find 80 people who would oppose abortion in both cases.

Another 387 respondents said they would support the right to choose if the woman's health were seriously endangered, but not on the basis of poverty. Notice that only 4 respondents would support abortion on the basis of poverty but deny it on the basis of threats to health. There are probably two elements involved in this pattern. On one hand, threats to the woman's life are probably seen as more serious than the suffering presented by another mouth to feed in a poor family. At the same time, few, if any, would hold a woman responsible for having a pregnancy that seriously threatened her health. Some people, however, do blame the poor for their poverty and would likely say that the woman in question should have avoided getting pregnant if she knew that it would be hard for her to feed another child. As a consequence, then, 387 of the respondents oppose abortion under some circumstances but are willing to make an exception in the case of a woman's health being threatened.

What are we to make of the four people who said they would approve an abortion for the poor but not for the woman whose life was threatened? Without ruling out the possibility of some complex point of view that demands such answers, it is most likely that these respondents misunderstood one or both of the questions. Fortunately, they are few enough in number that they will not seriously affect the analysis of this topic.

There is additional information in the SPSS table that will become more useful to us in later analyses. The rightmost column in the table, for example, tells us that a total of 838 of those with an opinion said that they would approve an abortion for a woman whose health was seriously endangered, and 84 would not. The bottom row of numbers in the table gives the breakdown regarding the other variable.

Let's try another example of the same phenomenon. The threat of a birth defect was considered a more compelling reason for abortion by the respondents than was the fact that the woman was not married. Why don't you run that table now? Use Statistics $\rightarrow$ Summarize $\rightarrow$ Crosstabs to get to the Crosstabs window; specify ABDEFECT as the row variable and ABSINGLE as the column variable.

Click "OK," and here's what the output should look like.

ABDEFECT STRONG CHANCE OF SERIOUS DEFECT * ABSINGLE NOT MARRIED Crosstabulation

Count

		ABSINGLE NOT MARRIED		
		1 Favor	2 Oppose	Total
ABDEFECT STRONG CHANCE OF SERIOUS DEFECT	1 Favor	429	309	738
	2 Oppose	8	167	175
Total		437	476	913

This table presents a strikingly similar picture. We see that 429 support the woman's right to choose in both situations, and 167 oppose abortion in both instances. Of those who would approve abortion only in one of the two situations, almost all of them (309) make the exception for the threat of birth defects. Only 8 respondents would allow abortion for a single woman but deny it in the case of birth defects.

We could continue examining tables like these, but the conclusion forthcoming remains the same: There are three major positions regarding abortion. One position approves it unconditionally on the basis of the woman's choice, another position opposes it under all circumstances, and the third position approves abortion only in certain circumstances: involving medical complications or rape.

To explore attitudes toward abortion further, it will be useful for us to have a measure of attitudes that is not limited to a single item. In particular, it might be nice to have a single variable that captures the three groups we have been discussing. We're going to create two such composite measures in this chapter.

9.2 Combining Two Items in an Index

An index is a form of composite measure, composed of more than one indicator of the variable under study. There are two advantages to the use of such measures. First, they include multiple dimensions of the variable. In this case, an index composed of ABDEFECT and ABSINGLE will combine two aspects of the debate over abortion rather than being limited to only one (e.g., the impact of birth defects).

Second, composite measures tap into a greater range of variation between the extremes of a variable. If we were to simply use one of the abortion items, we would distinguish two groups of respondents: the pros and the antis. Combining two items will allow us to distinguish three groups. A later example will extend this range of variation even further.

To illustrate this technique, let's create a simple index based on the two variables we just examined above. Our aim is to create a new measure—we'll call it ABORT—made up of three scores: a score of 2 for those who approve of abortion if birth defects are likely and approve of abortion for a single woman, a score of 1 for those who approve of abortion in one circumstance (primarily birth defects) but not the other, and a score of 0 for those who disapprove of abortion in both cases.

To do this, let's use the Transform → Compute command pathway. That will bring you to the following window.

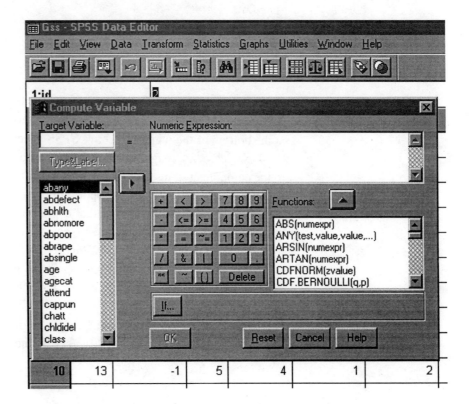

To initiate our index construction, we need to create the new variable so that SPSS will know where to put the results of our work. In the upper left corner of the Compute window, click in the "Target Variable" field and type ABORT. That's the name we'll give to the new variable.

Notice that we've now begun a numeric expression that says "ABORT =," taking account of the equal sign already printed to the right of the "Target Variable" field. Our task from now on is to specify what ABORT equals by filling in the field titled "Numeric Expression." We'll do this in several steps.

Begin by entering the number 0 in that field. You can do this in one of two ways. First, you can simply type it in. Or, you can use the keypad in the center of the window. To use the latter, simply click 0 and then click the period.

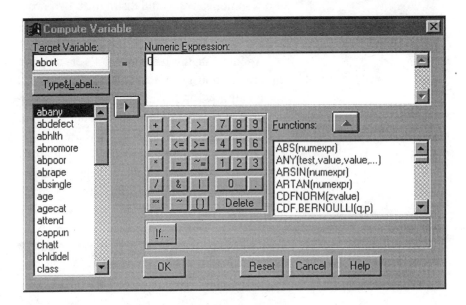

In either case, we've now instructed SPSS to create a new variable named ABORT and to give everyone a score of 0 on it. Click the "OK" button at the bottom of the window to have SPSS execute the command.

Now, let's start assigning index scores based on the answers people gave to the component items. Let's create the index in such a fashion that higher scores on it represent more support for a woman's right to choose an abortion. Thus, if people agreed that a woman should be able to have an abortion in the case of a birth defect (scored 1 on ABDEFECT), we want to give them one point on our index. We do it as follows.

Select Transform → Compute again. You'll see that the Compute window still has your previous work in it. Click Reset at the bottom of the window to clear the boards.

Next, type ABORT into the "Target Variable" field. (Note: As an alternative, you could have left ABORT on the screen and simply erased the earlier instruction in the "Numeric Expression" field instead of clicking Reset.)

In the list of variables, click ABORT and transfer it to the "Numeric Expression" field by clicking the arrow. Then click "+" and "1" on the keypad so that the whole instruction to SPSS is "ABORT = ABORT + 1" at this point.

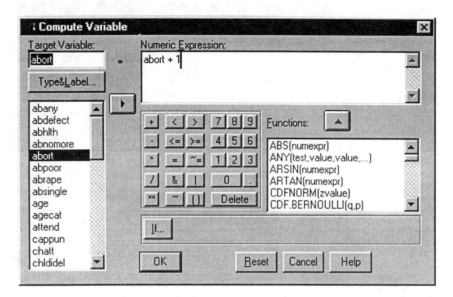

Now, we only want SPSS to take this step for those who agreed that a woman should be able to have an abortion in the case of a birth defect. To make this specification, click the If button near the bottom of the window. Now you should be looking at the following window.

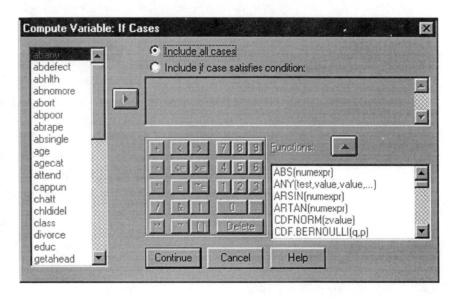

This new window will assist us in specifying our instruction to SPSS. Begin by clicking the button "Include if case satisfies condition," which will engage the variable list.

Transfer ABDEFECT to the open field and then add "= 1" using the keypad. Your screen should look like this:

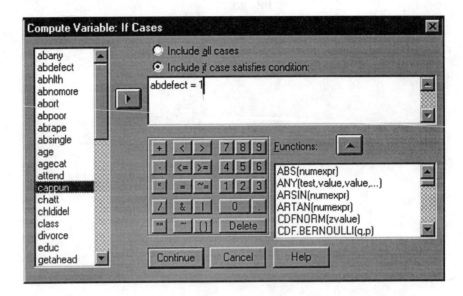

We have now told SPSS that we want it to execute the instruction to add a point to a person's ABORT index score only if their score on ABDEFECT is 1. To continue, click . . . well, you figure it out.

Once you click the Continue button, you will be returned to the Compute window. Take a minute to study the various elements of this window, and be sure you are clear on the logic of what we are asking SPSS to do. Once you are, click "OK." SPSS will ask if you want to "Change the existing variable?" Click "OK."

Now you will be returned to your data window, where you can watch the case counter at the bottom of the window indicate its progress through the data file, making the changes we've asked for. Eventually, you will see that the scores in the ABORT column now contain 0.00's and 1.00's.

Your next step is to repeat this same process, using ABSINGLE in place of ABDEFECT. As you'll see, it's much easier the second time around.

Select Transform → Compute. Notice that "ABORT = ABORT + 1" is still active, as is the conditional statement near the bottom of the window.

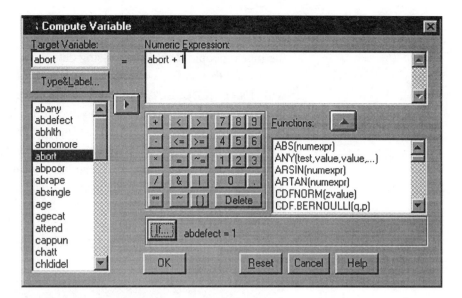

Click on If.

All we need to do now is change the name of the variable we want SPSS to check: from ABDEFECT to ABSINGLE. The easiest way, perhaps, is to delete ABDEFECT from the field in the center of the window, click ABSIN-GLE in the list of variables, and move it with the arrow. Your window should look like this:

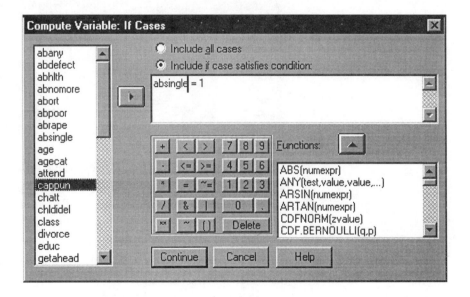

Click Continue, and then click "OK." When asked if you want to change the variable, click "OK."

Our index is nearly complete now. However, we must take account of the people who did not answer either or both of the questions included in the index: people scored as "missing data."

Recall that so far, we gave everyone a score of 0 to begin, then those with 1's on ABDEFECT and/or ABSINGLE were given additional points. Those who had missing data on the two items, however, are still scored 0 on our index. Thus, they look as though they are strongly opposed to abortion, whereas they were actually never asked about it.

To complete our index, then, we must create a missing data code for ABORT and assign that code to the appropriate cases. Let's use –1, because that has no meaning on the index.

Return to Transform → Compute. Put –1 into the "Numeric Expression" field and click on If to tell SPSS when we want the –1 code assigned on ABORT.

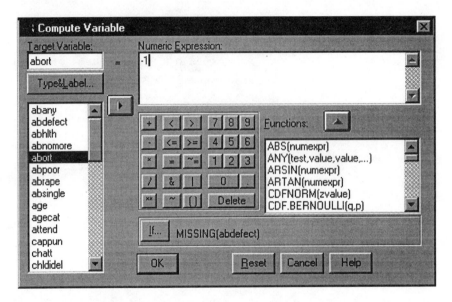

Instead of specifying a numerical value for ABDEFECT and ABSINGLE, we are going to use the list of Functions found on the right side of the window. Scroll down the list until you find "MISSING(variable)." Select it and move it up to the open field using the up-arrow.

Notice that the expression now has a highlighted question mark. Replace the highlighted question mark this time by selecting and transferring the variable name, ABDEFECT.

We have now created the following instruction for SPSS: If a person has a missing data code on ABDEFECT, we want that person scored as –1 on the index, ABORT. Once you understand the logic of this instruction, click Continue, then click "OK" to execute the instruction.

Now repeat the same procedure using ABSINGLE.

Our index is almost complete now, but we want to make two modifications to it.

In the data window, find and select the new variable, ABORT. Once you've done this, select Define Variable under the Data menu.

When you get to the Define Variable window, click Missing Values.

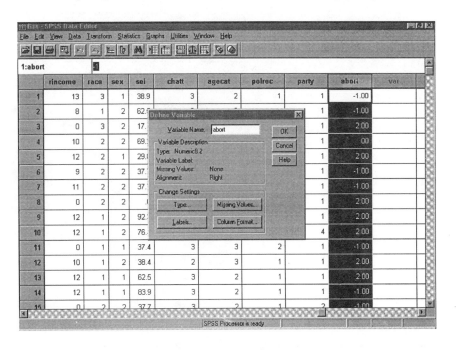

Notice that the index currently has "No missing values." Click "Discrete missing values" and type –1 into the first box underneath it. This tells SPSS that we have assigned that numerical score for those cases who got no index score on ABORT.

Once you are satisfied with the instruction, click Continue to return to the Define Variable window. Then click on Type.

sei	chatt	agecat	polrec	party	abort
38.9	3	2	1	1	-1.00
62.				1	-1.00
17.				1	2.00
69.				1	.00
29.				1	2.00
37.					
37.					
.					
92.					
76.					
37.4					
38.4					
62.5	3	2	1	1	2.00

Define Variable

Variable Name: abort

OK

Cancel

Help

Variable Description

Type: Numeric8.2

Variable Label:

Missing V

Alignment

Change

Typ

Lab

Define Variable Type: abort

- ⦿ Numeric
- ○ Comma
- ○ Dot
- ○ Scientific notation
- ○ Date
- ○ Dollar
- ○ Custom currency
- ○ String

Width: 8

Decimal Places: 2

Continue

Cancel

Help

As we did the last time we were here, we want to set the number of decimal places to zero. So, type 0 in the appropriate box. If it already says 0, of course, you can ignore this change.

Click Continue and then "OK" to complete the procedure. This will bring you back to the data window, where you will see ABORT with its codes of –1, 0, 1, and 2.

Now, let's see if all this really accomplished what we set out to do. Use the Frequencies command to find out. Run the frequency distribution of ABORT and you should see this table on your screen now.

ABORT

		Frequency	Percent	Valid Percent	Cumulative Percent
Valid	0	167	11.1	18.3	18.3
	1	317	21.1	34.7	53.0
	2	429	28.6	47.0	100.0
	Total	913	60.9	100.0	
Missing	-1	587	39.1		
	Total	587	39.1		
Total		1500	100.0		

If you compare the index scores in this table with the crosstabs of the two component variables, you'll see a logical correspondence. In the earlier table, 167 people disapproved of abortion under both of the specified conditions; here, we find 167 people scored 0 on the index. And where we found that 309 people would approve abortion for birth defects but not for a single woman and 8 had the reverse view, the index shows 317 people (309 + 8) with a score of 1. Finally, the 429 people who approved of abortion in both cases previously have a score of 2 on the index. Notice also the 587 people who were excluded on the basis of missing data.

Congratulations! You've just created a composite index. We realize you may still be wondering why that's such good news. After all, it wasn't your idea to create the thing in the first place.

9.3 Validating the Index

To get a clearer idea of the value of such a composite measure, let's move on to the next step in the process we've launched. Let's validate the index; that is, let's make sure it really measures what we are attempting to measure. If you recall the earlier discussion of validity and reliability, you'll see the link to this discussion of index validation.

In creating the simple index, we've tried to put respondents in one of three groups: those very supportive of abortion, those very opposed, and those in the middle. If we've succeeded in that effort, the scores we've assigned people on the new index, ABORT, should help us to predict how people answered other abortion items in the questionnaire. Let's begin with their answers to ABHLTH: approving abortion for a woman whose health is in danger.

To undertake this test of the index's validity, we'll return to the Crosstabs command, introduced earlier in the chapter. As you'll see, it has some additional features that can be used to good effect. In this instance, we want to cross-classify people in terms of their scores on the index and on the variable ABHLTH.

Run the Crosstabs command with ABHLTH as the row variable and ABORT as the column variable. Here's the result you should get.

ABHLTH WOMANS HEALTH SERIOUSLY ENDANGERED * ABORT Crosstabulation

Count

| | | ABORT | | | |
		0	1	2	Total
ABHLTH WOMANS HEALTH SERIOUSLY ENDANGERED	1 Favor	91	303	424	818
	2 Oppose	66	11	5	82
Total		157	314	429	900

You may be able to look at this table and see the relationship between the index and ABHLTH, but the analysis will be much simpler if we convert the data in the table to percentages. Let's express the assumption of validity that we are testing in terms of percentages. If those with a score of 2 on the index are the most supportive of abortion, then we should expect to find a higher percentage of them approving abortion in the case of the woman's health being endangered than would be found among the other groups. Those scored 0 on the index, by contrast, should be the least likely—the smallest percentage—to approve abortion based on the woman's health.

Looking first at those scored 0, in the leftmost column of the table, we would calculate the percentage as follows. Of the 157 people scored 0, we see that 91 approved of abortion in the case of ABHLTH. Dividing 91 by 157 indicates that those 91 people are 57.96 percent of the total 157. Looking to those with a score of 2, in the rightmost column, we find that the 424 who approve represent 98.83 percent of the 429 with that score. These two percentages support the assumption we are making about the index.

Happily, SPSS can be instructed to calculate these percentages for us. In fact, we are going to be looking at percentage tables for the most part in the rest of this book.

Go back to the Crosstabs window. Your previous request should still be in the appropriate fields. Notice a button at the bottom of this window called Cells. Click it. This will take you to a new window, as shown below.

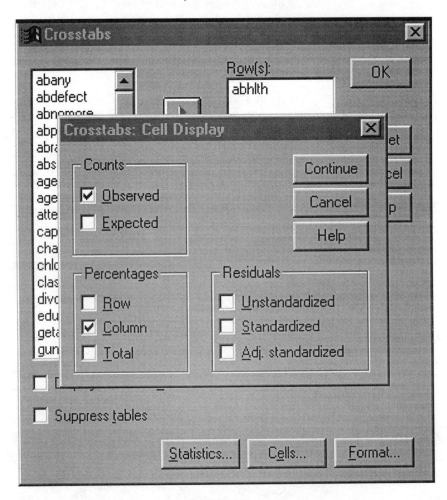

Notice that you can choose to have SPSS calculate percentages for you in one of three ways: using column totals, row totals, or the total number of cases. Click "Columns" and work your way back through the "OKs" to have SPSS run the table for you. Your reward should look like the following.

ABHLTH WOMANS HEALTH SERIOUSLY ENDANGERED * ABORT Crosstabulation

| | | | ABORT | | | |
			0	1	2	Total
ABHLTH WOMANS HEALTH SERIOUSLY ENDANGERED	1 Favor	Count	91	303	424	818
		% within ABORT	58.0%	96.5%	98.8%	90.9%
	2 Oppose	Count	66	11	5	82
		% within ABORT	42.0%	3.5%	1.2%	9.1%
Total		Count	157	314	429	900
		% within ABORT	100.0%	100.0%	100.0%	100.0%

Take a moment to examine the logic of this table. For each score on the index, we have calculated the percentage saying they favor or oppose a woman's right to an abortion if her health is seriously endangered. It is as though we have limited our attention to one of the index-score groups (those scored 0, for example) and described them in terms of their attitudes on the abortion item; then we have repeated the process for each of the index-score groups. Once we've described each of the subgroups, we can compare them.

When you have created a table with the percentages totaling to 100 down each column, the proper way to read the table is across the rows. Rounding off the percentages to simplify matters, we would note, in this case, that

58 percent of those with a score of 0 on the index,

97 percent of those with a score of 1 on the index, and

99 percent of those with a score of 2 on the index

said they would approve of abortion if the woman's health were seriously endangered. This table supports our assumption that the index measures levels of support for a woman's freedom to choose abortion.

Now let's validate the index using the other abortion items not included in the index itself. Repeat the Crosstabs command, substituting the four abortion items—ABNOMORE, ABRAPE, ABPOOR, and ABANY—for ABHLTH.

Run the Crosstabs command now and see what results you get. Look at each of the four tables and see what they say about the ability of the index to measure attitudes toward abortion. Here is an abbreviated table format that you might want to construct from the results of that command. SPSS doesn't create a table like this, but it's a useful format for presenting data in a research report.

	Abortion Index		
Percentage Who Approve of Abortion When	*0*	*1*	*2*
the woman was raped	39	90	99
the couple can't afford more children	3	16	91
a couple doesn't want more children	2	18	91
the woman wants an abortion	4	14	92

Whereas the earlier table showed the percentages who approved and those who disapproved of abortion in a specific situation, this table presents only those who approved. The first entry in the table, for example, indicates that 39 percent of those with a score of 0 on the index would approve of abortion in the case of rape. Of those with a score of 1 on the index, 90 percent approved of abortion for this reason, and 99 percent of those with a score of 2 approved.

As you can see, the index accurately predicts differences in responses to each of the other abortion items. In each case, those with higher scores on the index are more likely to support abortion under the specified conditions than are those with lower scores on the index.

By building this composite index, we've created a more sophisticated measure of attitudes toward abortion. Whereas each of the individual items allows only for approval or disapproval of abortion under various circumstances, this index reflects three positions on the issue: unconditional disapproval (0), conditional approval (1), and unconditional approval (2).

9.4 Creating a More Complex Index with COUNT

Whereas this first index was created from only two of the abortion items, we could easily create a more elaborate index, using more items. This larger index would tap into more of the dimensions of the abortion debate and would also provide a wider range of variation between the extremes.

To illustrate, let's use all the items except for ABANY, supporting a woman's unrestricted choice. While we could create this new index following the same procedures as before, there is also a shortcut that can be used when we want to score several items the same way in creating the index. Suppose, for example, that we want to create a larger index by giving people one point for agreeing to an abortion in each of the six special circumstances.

Under Transform, select Count. This will present you with the following window:

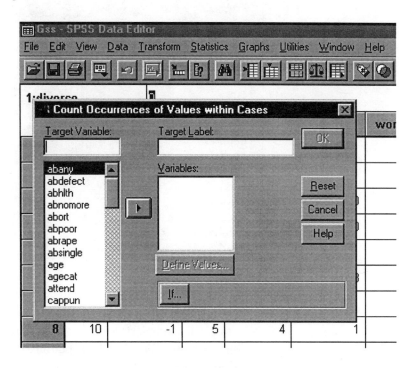

In creating our new index, we will, once more, need to deal with the problem of missing values. In using Count, we are going to handle that matter somewhat differently from before. Specifically, we are going to begin by creating a variable that tells us whether people had missing values on any of the six items we are examining.

To do this, we'll create a variable called MISS. Click on Count and type that name in the "Target Variable" field. Next, we want to specify the items to be considered in the creating MISS. Transfer the following variable names to the "Input Variable" field: ABDEFECT, ABHLTH, ABNO-MORE, ABPOOR, ABRAPE, and ABSINGLE. You can do this by selecting a variable in the list on the left side of the window and clicking the arrow pointing to the "Variables" field or you can simply double-click a variable name. (Where several variables are together in the list, you can drag your cursor across the several names, selecting them all, and then click the arrow.)

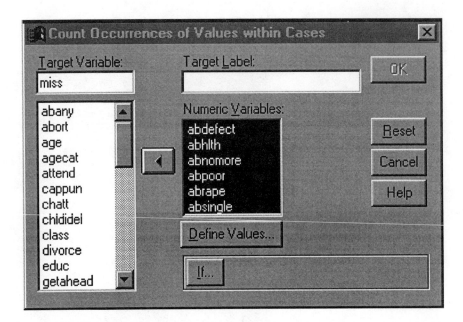

Having selected the variables to be counted, click Define Values.

The left side of the window offers several options for counting, but we want to use the simplest: a single value. Click the button beside "System-or user-missing." Click the "Add" button to transfer the value to the "Values to Count Field."

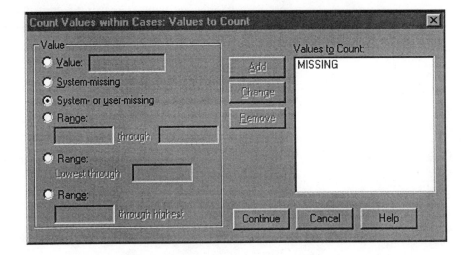

Click "Continue" to return to the "Count Occurrences" window.

Click "OK" to launch the procedure. Once SPSS has completed the procedure, you will find the data window now has a new variable called MISS, with scores ranging from 0 to 6, indicating the number of missing values people had on the six items. (If you are looking at the Output window, you can use the Window menu to shift to the data window.)

Now we are ready to create our new abortion index. Choose Count under the Transform menu again. Replace MISS with ABINDEX in the

"Target Variable" field. Leave the six abortion items where they are in the Numeric Variables field. Click Define Values.

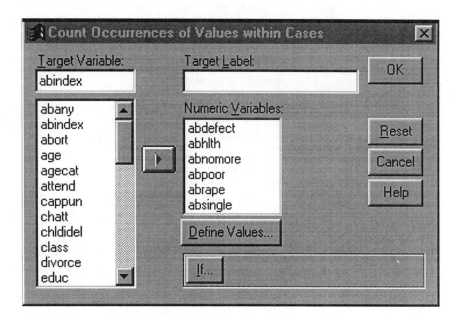

In the "Values to Count" window, you'll notice that MISSING is still showing in the specification field. Click it to select it. Then click Remove. Now the field is empty.

Click the first option on the left, "Value," and type "1" in the field beside it. Click Add to transfer the value to the appropriate field. Then click Continue and "OK."

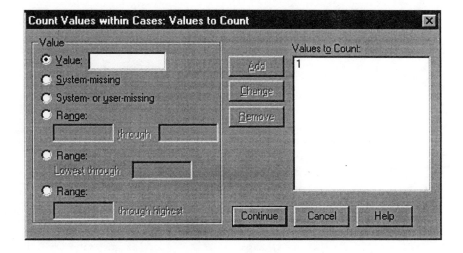

Since we left the six variable names in the "Numeric Values" field, we have now told SPSS to count the number of times a person had a score of "1" on any of those six items.

Before we can use our new ABINDEX variable, we have to inform SPSS which respondents did not answer all 6 abortion questions. We can do that easily using the variable MISS we created a moment ago.

From the Data screen, Transform and the Compute. Identify ABINDEX as the target variables. In the Numeric expression window type "$SYS-MIS". $SYSMIS is a SPSS keyword that causes a case to be eliminated from the analysis.

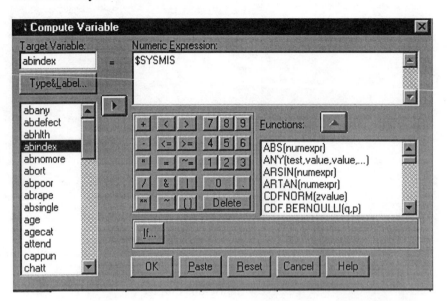

Don't click OK yet! If you did, all of our respondents would be eliminated from further analysis. Instead, click "If." Click the radio button that lightens "Include if case satisfies condition:". In the condition window, type or click in "MISS = 0". (The = means "not equal to") Now you can click your way back to OK.

We have now told SPSS that we want it to count pro-choice answers only for those who had no missing values on any of the six items.

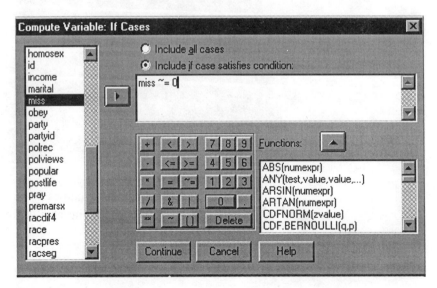

Now, we need to tidy up our new variable. Select ABINDEX in the data window and then select Define Variable under Data.

Click "Type" and change the number of decimal places to 0.

Click "OK" to put SPSS to work.

Once you've entered and executed these commands, let's see what these instructions produced. Get the frequency distribution of ABINDEX. Here's what you should find.

ABINDEX

		Frequency	Percent	Valid Percent	Cumulative Percent
Valid	0	60	4.0	7.0	7.0
	1	38	2.5	4.4	11.5
	2	81	5.4	9.5	20.9
	3	198	13.2	23.2	44.1
	4	63	4.2	7.4	51.5
	5	59	3.9	6.9	58.4
	6	356	23.7	41.6	100.0
	Total	855	57.0	100.0	
Missing	System Missing	645	43.0		
	Total	645	43.0		
Total		1500	100.0		

This table shows the distribution of scores on the new index, ABINDEX. As you can see, there are 356 people, over 40% of those with opinions, who support abortion in all the specified circumstances (score 6 on the index). A total of 60 disapprove of abortion in any of those circumstances. The rest are spread out according to the number of conditions they feel would warrant abortion.

For validation purposes this time, we have only one item not included in the index itself: ABANY. Let's see how well the index predicts respondents' approval of a woman's unrestricted choice of abortion.

Run the Crosstabs procedure specifying:

 ◆ ABANY as the row variable
 ◆ ABINDEX as the column index
 ◆ Cells to be percentaged by column

ABANY ABORTION IF WOMAN WANTS FOR ANY REASON * ABINDEX Crosstabulation

| | | ABINDEX | | | | | | | |
		0	1	2	3	4	5	6	Total
ABANY ABORTION IF WOMAN WANTS FOR ANY REASON	Count	1		6	19	18	36	343	423
	% within ABINDEX	1.7%		7.6%	9.8%	29.0%	62.1%	97.2%	50.2%
	Count	59	37	73	174	44	22	10	419
	% within ABINDEX	98.3%	100.0%	92.4%	90.2%	71.0%	37.9%	2.8%	49.8%
Total	Count	60	37	79	193	62	58	353	842
	% within ABINDEX	100.0%	100.0%	100.0%	100.0%	100.0%	100.0%	100.0%	100.0%

As we can see, answers to ABANY are closely related to scores on ABINDEX. Of those with 0 on the index, one person said a woman had a right to an abortion for any reason. That person may have misunderstood the question. None of the persons who scored 1 on ABINDEX favored a women's right to an abortion for any reason. For scores 2 through 6, the percentage continues increasing across the index until we find that 97.2 percent of those scored 6 on the index say a woman has the unconditional right to an abortion.

Once again, we find the index validated. This means that if we wish to analyze peoples' attitudes toward abortion further (and we will), we have the choice of using a single item to represent those attitudes or using a composite measure. We've seen, moreover, that we can create such an index in different ways.

9.5 Summary

In this chapter, we've seen that it is often possible to measure social scientific concepts in a number of ways. Sometimes, the data set contains a single item that does the job nicely. Measuring gender by asking people for their gender is a good example.

In other cases, the mental images that constitute our concepts (e.g., religiosity, political orientations, prejudice) are varied and ambiguous. Typically, no single item in a data set provides a complete representation of what we have in mind. Often, we can resolve this problem by combining two or more indicators of the concept into a composite index. As we've seen, SPSS offers the tools necessary for such data transformations.

If you continue your studies in social research, you will discover that there are many more sophisticated techniques for creating composite measures. However, the simple indexing techniques you have learned in this chapter will serve you well in the analyses that lie ahead.

Chapter 10   Suggestions for Further Univariate Analyses

In the preceding chapters, we've given you a number of research possibilities to begin exploring, focused on the topics of religion, politics, and abortion. In the event that you've exhausted those possibilities and want to look beyond them, here are some additional topics for you to consider.

10.1   Desired Family Size

One of the major social problems facing the world today is that of over-population. A brief summary of population growth on the planet should illustrate what we mean.

Year	Population	Doubling Time
0	.25 billion	—
1650	.50 billion	1,650 years
1850	1.00 billion	200 years
1930	2.00 billion	80 years
1975	4.00 billion	45 years
1994	5.64 billion	39 years

These data show several things. For example, the world's population has increased more than 20-fold since the beginning of the Christian era. More important, however, the rate of increase has been steadily increasing. This is most easily seen in the rightmost column above, showing what demographers call the "doubling time." It took 1,650 years for the world's population to increase from a quarter of a billion people to half a billion. The time required to double has been shortening ever since; at present, doubling time is about 39 years.

This astounding increase in the pace of population growth has been caused by the fact that during most of human existence, extremely high death rates have been matched by equally high birth rates. During the past few generations, however, death rates have plummeted around the world because of improved public health measures, medical discoveries, and improved food production.

The current pace of population growth simply cannot go on forever. Although scientists may disagree on the number of people the planet can support, there is simply no question that there is some limit. At some point, population growth must be slowed and stopped—perhaps even reversed.

There are two ways to end population growth: Either death rates can be returned to their former high levels or birth rates can be reduced. As most of us would choose the latter solution, demographers have been very interested in the variable Desired Family Size. That's another of the variables with which we're going to be working in this book.

Your data set contains a variable, CHLDIDEL, that presents responses to the question, "What do you think is the ideal number of children for a family to have?" If every family had only two children, then births and deaths would eventually roughly balance each other out, producing a condition of population stabilization, or zero population growth (excluding the effect of migration). What percentage of the population do you suppose chose that as the ideal? Some favored larger families, and others said they thought only one child was the ideal. Why don't you find out what the most common response was?

Later in this book, you may want to explore the causes of people's attitudes about ideal family size.

10.2 Child Training

What do you think are the most important qualities for children to develop as they grow up? Respondents to the General Social Survey were asked that question also. To frame the question more specifically, they were presented with several of the answers people commonly give and were asked how important each was: "If you had to choose, which thing on this list would you pick as the most important for a child to learn to prepare him or her for life?"

The interviewer read the following list (which we've annotated with the GSS variable names):

OBEY	to obey
POPULAR	to be well-liked or popular
THNKSELF	to think for himself or herself
WORKHARD	to work hard
HELPOTH	to help others when they need help

Once the respondents indicated which of these they felt were most important, they were asked:

Which comes next in importance?

Which comes third?

Which comes fourth?

This set of responses allowed the researchers to code the final responses as "least important."

As with earlier topics, take a moment to notice how you feel about such matters. Then see if you can anticipate what public opinion is on these qualities of children. It will be useful, by the way, to observe your reasoning process as you attempt to anticipate public opinion. What observations, clues, or cues prompt you to think OBEY is the most important, or POPU-LAR, or whichever one you picked as the one most people would choose?

Then you can see how people actually responded to the questions. Once you've done that, you should review your earlier reasoning, either to confirm your predictions or to figure out where you went wrong. What can you infer from the differences among your opinions, your predictions, and the actual results?

10.3 Attitudes about Sexual Behavior

As with most other things, Americans differ in their feelings about sexual behavior. We thought you might be interested in this area of public opinion, so we've included three GSS variables dealing with different kinds of sexual behavior.

HOMOSEX asks about homosexual sex relations, PREMARSX focuses on premarital sex, and XMOVIE asks whether the respondent has attended an X-rated movie during the past year. Notice that the last of these measures respondents' own behavior, whereas the first two measure their attitudes toward the behavior of others. Either might be taken as an indication of overall orientation, but it is important always to remember exactly what variables represent.

We realize that you may very well have strong opinions about each of these issues. Your job as a social science researcher, however, is to find out what Americans as a whole think and do. What percentage do you suppose have gone to an X-rated movie? Which do you think people tolerate more: premarital sex or homosexuality? Give it some thought and then check it out.

It's not too early to begin asking yourself what would cause people to be more tolerant or less so in these regards. When we turn to bivariate analysis later on, you'll have a chance to test some of your expectations.

Here's an idea that could take you deeper into this general topic. See if you can use the Transform → Count command to create a composite measure of sexual permissiveness, combining the three items.

10.4 Prejudice

Prejudice is a topic that has concerned social scientists for a long time, and the persistence of the problem keeps it a topic of interest and research. Your disk includes three items from the GSS that deal with two aspects of antiblack prejudice: one political and the other more social.

RACPRES asks respondents if they would vote for an African American candidate for president. RACSEG asks whether whites should have the right to live in segregated neighborhoods, one of the issues of the civil rights movement that has resulted in legislation. You may want to look back at Chapter 4 for the exact wording of the questions. Remember, it's always important to know exactly how survey questions were asked in order to understand what the responses really mean.

As you would no doubt guess, general support for racial segregation has been decreasing in the United States over the years, and support for African American political candidates has increased. Before you look at these variables, however, take a minute to think about the two items, and take a guess at the level of public support for each. Then, see how well you've been able to anticipate American racial opinions.

If this variable really interests you, you might consider the possibility of creating a composite measure of prejudice from these two items. Once you start with the Transform → Compute command, you should be able to construct the If statements and other commands that will result in a measure wherein a score of 2 means that a person was prejudiced on both items, 1 means that he or she was prejudiced on only one item, and 0 means that he or she was unprejudiced on both.

10.5 Summary

There are several other variables in the data set. As you no doubt recall, you can get an overview of the whole thing by the command Utilities → Variables. Once you see the list of variables on the left side of the window, you can click on any of the variable names to get short descriptions and the codes used for categorical responses.

By the time you finish this chapter, you should be feeling fairly comfortable with SPSS and the GSS data set. Now you can add more strength to the facility you are developing. In Part III, you are going to try your hand at bivariate analysis, which lets you start to search for the reasons people are the way they are.

Part III Bivariate Analysis

This set of chapters adds a new dimension to your analyses. By moving from the analysis of one variable, univariate analysis, to the analysis of two variables at a time, **bivariate analysis,** we open the possibility of exploring matters of cause and effect. Thus, in Chapter 11, we'll begin to examine what factors cause some people to be more religious than others. In this analysis, we'll be guided by an earlier analysis, which put forward a "deprivation theory" of church involvement.

In Chapter 12, we'll begin to discover what makes some people liberal and others conservative, as well as what makes some Democrats, others Republicans, and still others Independents. In addition, we'll begin to explore some of the consequences of political orientations. What differences do they make in terms of other attitudes and orientations?

Chapter 13 is going to take us deep inside the hotly controversial issue of abortion. You probably already have some ideas about why some people are supportive of a woman's right to choose an abortion and others are opposed. Now you are going to have an opportunity to test your expectations and learn something about the roots of different points of view in this national debate.

In Chapters 11 through 13, we are going to limit our analyses to percentage tables, a basic format for such investigations in social research. However, there are many other methods for measuring the extent to which variables are related to one another, and we'll examine some of these in Chapter 14: lambda, gamma, Pearson's *r* product-moment correlation coefficient, and regression. You'll learn the logic that lies behind them, and you'll see how to use them through SPSS.

Chapter 15 adds another set of techniques for your use in assessing the associations that you discover among variables. Whenever samples have been chosen from a larger population, as is the case with the GSS data, there is always some danger that the associations we discover among variables in our sample are merely results of sampling error and do not represent a genuine pattern in the larger population. Chapter 15 will demonstrate several techniques used by social researchers to guard against being misled in that fashion.

Finally, as we did in Part II, we conclude our examination of bivariate analysis with suggestions for other lines of inquiry.

Chapter 11 The Sources of Religiosity

So far, we have limited our analyses to single variables. Although we have examined a number of variables, we have looked at them one at a time. This process is appropriate to **description,** but we are going to shift our attention now to **explanation.** Whereas we previously looked at the extent of people's religiosity, for example, we are now going to turn our attention to why: What are the reasons some people are more religious than others?

11.1 The Deprivation Theory of Religiosity

The reading titled "A Theory of Involvement," by Charles Y. Glock, Benjamin B. Ringer, and Earl R. Babbie, in Appendix E of this book, presents one explanation for differing degrees of religiosity. In it, the authors explain their social deprivation theory of religiosity. Simply put, they say that people who are denied gratification within the secular society will be more likely to turn to the church as an alternative source of gratification.

In their analysis, they looked for variables that distinguished those who were getting more gratification from those who were getting less in the secular society. For example, they reasoned that the United States is still a male-dominated society, meaning that women are denied the level of gratification enjoyed by men. Women often earn less for the same work, are denied equal access to prestigious occupations, are underrepresented in politics, and so on. According to the deprivation theory, therefore, women should be more religious than men.

The data analyses done by Glock et al., based on a sample of Episcopalian church members in 1952, confirmed their hypothesis. The question we might now ask is whether the same is true of the general U.S. population in 1991. Our data allow us to test that hypothesis.

11.2 Correlating Religiosity and Gender

This analysis requires us to advance our analytic procedures to what social researchers call **bivariate analysis,** involving two variables: a cause and an effect. In this case, religiosity would be the effect and gender the cause. This means that your gender causes—to some degree—your degree of religiosity. You are more likely to be religious if you are a woman than if you are a man.

To test this hypothesis, we need measures of both variables. Gender is easy: The variable SEX handles that nicely. But what about religiosity? As you'll recall from our earlier discussion, there are several measures available to us. For the time being, let's use church attendance as our measure, even though we've noted that it is not a perfect indicator of religiosity in its most general meaning.

You will remember that when we looked at ATTEND in Chapter 6, it had nine categories. If we were to cross-tabulate ATTEND and SEX without recoding ATTEND, we would expect a table with 18 (9 × 2) cells. To make our table more manageable, we are going to use the recoded CHATT as our measure of church attendance.

Now we can request the Crosstab, specifying:

- CHATT as the row variable

- SEX as the column variable

- Cells to be percentages by columns

Execute this command and you should get the following result.

CHATT Recoded Church Attendance * SEX RESPONDENTS SEX Crosstabulation

			SEX RESPONDENTS SEX		
			1 MALE	2 FEMALE	Total
CHATT Recoded Church Attendance	1 About weekly	Count	176	274	450
		% within SEX RESPONDENTS SEX	26.7%	34.1%	30.8%
	2 About monthly	Count	92	132	224
		% within SEX RESPONDENTS SEX	14.0%	16.4%	15.3%
	3 Seldom	Count	282	285	567
		% within SEX RESPONDENTS SEX	42.8%	35.4%	38.8%
	4 Never	Count	109	113	222
		% within SEX RESPONDENTS SEX	16.5%	14.1%	15.2%
Total		Count	659	804	1463
		% within SEX RESPONDENTS SEX	100.0%	100.0%	100.0%

The first row of percentages in the table tells us that 26.7 percent of the men reported attending church about weekly, contrasted to 34.1 percent of the women. If we want, we can also note that 40.7 percent of the men attend church at least monthly (combining the first two categories). Note also that 50.5 percent of the women attend at least monthly.

Epsilon is a simple statistic often used to summarize percentage differences such as these. In comparing men and women in terms of weekly church attendance, for example, the percentage difference (epsilon) is 7.4 points. This simple statistic gives us a tool for comparing sex differences on other measures of religiosity.

These data make it clear that women are more likely than men to attend church frequently. This would seem to support the deprivation theory of religiosity. Let's see if other indicators of religiosity produce the same result.

We can request more than one table in the Crosstabs window. In the "Row Variable" field, replace CHATT with PRAY and POSTLIFE, one below the other in the field.

Execute that command and then let's review each of the tables in turn.

PRAY HOW OFTEN DOES R PRAY * SEX RESPONDENTS SEX Crosstabulation

			SEX RESPONDENTS SEX		
			1 MALE	2 FEMALE	Total
PRAY HOW OFTEN DOES R PRAY	1 SEVERAL TIMES A DAY	Count	46	90	136
		% within SEX RESPONDENTS SEX	20.9%	31.5%	26.9%
	2 ONCE A DAY	Count	54	99	153
		% within SEX RESPONDENTS SEX	24.5%	34.6%	30.2%
	3 SEVERAL TIMES A WEEK	Count	39	30	69
		% within SEX RESPONDENTS SEX	17.7%	10.5%	13.6%
	4 ONCE A WEEK	Count	20	20	40
		% within SEX RESPONDENTS SEX	9.1%	7.0%	7.9%
	5 LT ONCE A WEEK	Count	51	39	90
		% within SEX RESPONDENTS SEX	23.2%	13.6%	17.8%
	6 NEVER	Count	10	8	18
		% within SEX RESPONDENTS SEX	4.5%	2.8%	3.6%
Total		Count	220	286	506
		% within SEX RESPONDENTS SEX	100.0%	100.0%	100.0%

A quick review of this table indicates that women are more likely than men to report that they pray at least once a day. Combining the first two categories, we calculate 45.4 percent for men and 66.1 percent for women. Or, we could look at the other end of the table and note that men are more likely to report infrequency of prayer. This table would also seem to confirm the deprivation thesis. In terms of praying at least daily, the epsilon is 20.7 percentage points, pointing to a greater sex difference than we observed in the case of church attendance.

Finally, let's consider beliefs in life after death: the variable POSTLIFE.

POSTLIFE BELIEF IN LIFE AFTER DEATH * SEX RESPONDENTS SEX Crosstabulation

| | | | SEX RESPONDENTS SEX | | |
			1 MALE	2 FEMALE	Total
POSTLIFE BELIEF IN LIFE AFTER DEATH	1 YES	Count	318	408	726
		% within SEX RESPONDENTS SEX	79.3%	82.6%	81.1%
	2 NO	Count	83	86	169
		% within SEX RESPONDENTS SEX	20.7%	17.4%	18.9%
Total		Count	401	494	895
		% within SEX RESPONDENTS SEX	100.0%	100.0%	100.0%

The epsilon is smallest in this case, but we note nonetheless that women are slightly more likely to say that they believe in life after death than are men.

Each of these bivariate analyses, therefore, has supported the thesis put forth by Glock and his coauthors, suggesting that people who were deprived of gratification in the secular society would be more likely to turn to religion as an alternative source of gratification. More specifically, we have confirmed the thesis with regard to gender differences—that women are still deprived of gratification in American society in comparison with men.

11.3 Correlating Religiosity and Age

Glock et al. also argue that the United States is a youth-oriented society, with gratification being denied to old people. Whereas some traditional societies tend to revere the elders, this is not the case in the United States. The deprivation thesis, then, would predict that older respondents would be more religious than younger ones. The researchers confirmed this expectation in their 1952 data from Episcopalian church members.

Let's check out the relationship between age and religiosity in 1996. To make the table manageable, we'll use the recoded AGECAT variable created earlier in Chapter 6.

So, request a Crosstab using:

- CHATT, POSTLIFE, and PRAY as row variables
- AGECAT as column variable
- Cells to be percentaged by columns

The resulting tables look like this:

CHATT Recoded Church Attendance * AGECAT Recoded Age Categories Crosstabulation

| | | | AGECAT Recoded Age Categories | | | | |
			1 Under 21	2 21-39	3 40-64	4 65 and older	Total
CHATT Recoded Church Attendance	1 About weekly	Count	6	152	190	102	450
		% within AGECAT Recoded Age Categories	15.0%	24.7%	32.0%	47.7%	30.8%
	2 About monthly	Count	10	106	85	23	224
		% within AGECAT Recoded Age Categories	25.0%	17.2%	14.3%	10.7%	15.3%
	3 Seldom	Count	17	262	231	57	567
		% within AGECAT Recoded Age Categories	42.5%	42.6%	38.9%	26.6%	38.8%
	4 Never	Count	7	95	88	32	222
		% within AGECAT Recoded Age Categories	17.5%	15.4%	14.8%	15.0%	15.2%
Total		Count	40	615	594	214	1463
		% within AGECAT Recoded Age Categories	100.0%	100.0%	100.0%	100.0%	100.0%

POSTLIFE BELIEF IN LIFE AFTER DEATH * AGECAT Recoded Age Categories Crosstabulation

| | | | AGECAT Recoded Age Categories | | | | |
			1 Under 21	2 21-39	3 40-64	4 65 and older	Total
POSTLIFE BELIEF IN LIFE AFTER DEATH	1 YES	Count	21	321	291	93	726
		% within AGECAT Recoded Age Categories	84.0%	85.1%	80.4%	71.0%	81.1%
	2 NO	Count	4	56	71	38	169
		% within AGECAT Recoded Age Categories	16.0%	14.9%	19.6%	29.0%	18.9%
Total		Count	25	377	362	131	895
		% within AGECAT Recoded Age Categories	100.0%	100.0%	100.0%	100.0%	100.0%

PRAY HOW OFTEN DOES R PRAY * AGECAT Recoded Age Categories Crosstabulation

			AGECAT Recoded Age Categories				
			1 Under 21	2 21-39	3 40-64	4 65 and older	Total
PRAY HOW OFTEN DOES R PRAY	1 SEVERAL TIMES A DAY	Count	3	41	59	33	136
		% within AGECAT Recoded Age Categories	25.0%	20.2%	27.3%	44.0%	26.9%
	2 ONCE A DAY	Count	4	58	66	25	153
		% within AGECAT Recoded Age Categories	33.3%	28.6%	30.6%	33.3%	30.2%
	3 SEVERAL TIMES A WEEK	Count	1	34	28	6	69
		% within AGECAT Recoded Age Categories	8.3%	16.7%	13.0%	8.0%	13.6%
	4 ONCE A WEEK	Count	1	19	15	5	40
		% within AGECAT Recoded Age Categories	8.3%	9.4%	6.9%	6.7%	7.9%
	5 LT ONCE A WEEK	Count	3	41	41	5	90
		% within AGECAT Recoded Age Categories	25.0%	20.2%	19.0%	6.7%	17.8%
	6 NEVER	Count		10	7	1	18
		% within AGECAT Recoded Age Categories		4.9%	3.2%	1.3%	3.6%
Total		Count	12	203	216	75	506
		% within AGECAT Recoded Age Categories	100.0%	100.0%	100.0%	100.0%	100.0%

With some slight variations, we can see that older respondents are generally more religious than younger ones. This would tend to confirm the deprivation thesis in terms of age. Interestingly, the oldest group—those 65 and older—are the least likely to believe in life after death, although more than 70 percent do believe in it. You should be aware that some variations like this become more common as the number of groups being compared increases. Looking at the several tables as a whole, however, the general pattern of religiosity increasing with age is supported.

11.4 Continuing the Analysis: Religiosity and Social Class

This completes our initial foray into the world of bivariate analysis. We hope you've gotten a good sense of the potential for detective work in social research.

To continue the present line of analysis, why don't you test the notion from Glock and his colleagues that religiosity decreases with increased social class? This means that upper-class respondents would be less religious than lower-class respondents. The original finding was based on an analysis of Episcopalian church members in 1952, so the relationship might not hold up among the general public (church members and nonmembers) in 1996. You find out.

Once you've tried your hand at the analysis, you can compare your procedures, results, and interpretations with those provided in Appendix D.

11.5 Summary

In this chapter, we made a critical logical advance in the analysis of social scientific data. Up to now, we have focused our attention on description. With this examination of religiosity, we've crossed over into explanation. We've moved from asking *what* to asking *why*.

Much of the excitement in social research revolves around discovering why people think and act as they do. You've now had an initial exposure to the logic and computer techniques that make such inquiries possible.

Let's apply your new capabilities to other subject matter. In the next two chapters, we're going to examine, respectively, the sources of different political orientations and why people feel as they do about abortion.

Chapter 12 Political Orientations as Cause and as Effect

In looking for the sources of religiosity, we worked with a coherent theory. Where possible, that's usually the preferable approach to data analysis. Sometimes, however, it's appropriate to take a less structured route. As we turn our attention to politics in this chapter, we're going to be more inductive than deductive so that you can become familiar with this approach.

In Chapter 7, we examined two GSS variables: POLVIEWS and PARTYID. In the analyses to follow, we'll begin by looking at the relationship between these two variables. You can do that now that you understand the Crosstabs command. Next, we'll explore some of the variables that cause differences in political philosophies and party identification. Finally, we'll look at POLVIEWS and PARTYID as **independent variables**: we'll see what impact they have on other variables.

12.1 The Relationship between POLVIEWS and PARTYID

Let's begin with our two key variables, POLVIEWS and PARTYID, recoded as in Chapter 7. As we indicated earlier, there is a consensus that Democrats are more liberal than Republicans and Republicans are more conservative than Democrats, although everyone recognizes the existence of liberal Republicans and conservative Democrats.

The GSS data allow us to see what the relationship between these two variables actually is. Because neither is logically prior to the other, we could treat either as the independent variable. For present purposes, it is probably useful to explore both possibilities: (a) political philosophy causes party identification and (b) party identification causes political philosophy.

To begin, then, let's see if Democrats are more liberal or more conservative than Republicans. To check this, we'll use the two recoded political variables: You will want to make POLREC the row variable and PARTY the column variable.

POLREC * PARTY party identification Crosstabulation

| | | | PARTY party identification | | | | |
			1 democrat	2 independent	3 republican	4 other	Total
POLREC	1 Liberal	Count	207	134	30	7	378
		% within PARTY party identification	40.0%	26.5%	8.0%	33.3%	26.6%
	2 Moderate	Count	190	226	122	7	545
		% within PARTY party identification	36.7%	44.7%	32.5%	33.3%	38.4%
	3 Conservative	Count	121	146	223	7	497
		% within PARTY party identification	23.4%	28.9%	59.5%	33.3%	35.0%
Total		Count	518	506	375	21	1420
		% within PARTY party identification	100.0%	100.0%	100.0%	100.0%	100.0%

The data in this table confirm the general expectation. Of the Democrats in the GSS sample, 40 percent describe themselves as liberals, in contrast to 8 percent of the Republicans. The Independents fall halfway between the two parties, with 27 percent saying they are liberals. The relationship can also be seen by reading across the bottom row of percentages: 23 percent of the Democrats, versus 60 percent of the Republicans, call themselves conservatives.

We can also turn the table around logically and ask whether liberals or conservatives are more likely to identify with the Democratic party (or which are more likely to say they are Republicans). You can get this table by simply reversing the location of the two variable names in the earlier command. Make PARTY the row variable and POLREC the column variable and rerun the Crosstab request. Here's what you'll get.

PARTY party identification * POLREC Recoded POLVIEWS Crosstabulation

| | | | POLREC Recoded POLVIEWS | | | |
			1 liberal	2 moderate	3 conservative	Total
PARTY party identification	1 demoncrat	Count	207	190	121	518
		% within POLREC Recoded POLVIEWS	54.8%	34.9%	24.3%	36.5%
	2 independent	Count	134	226	146	506
		% within POLREC Recoded POLVIEWS	35.4%	41.5%	29.4%	35.6%
	3 republican	Count	30	122	223	375
		% within POLREC Recoded POLVIEWS	7.9%	22.4%	44.9%	26.4%
	4 other	Count	7	7	7	21
		% within POLREC Recoded POLVIEWS	1.9%	1.3%	1.4%	1.5%
Total		Count	378	545	497	1420
		% within POLREC Recoded POLVIEWS	100.0%	100.0%	100.0%	100.0%

Again, the relationship between the two variables is evident. Liberals are more likely (55 percent) to say they are Democrats than are moderates (35 percent are Democrats) or conservatives (only 24 percent are Democrats).

Now, why don't you state the relationship between these two variables in terms of the likelihood that they will support the Republican party? Either way of stating the relationship is appropriate.

In summary, then, there is an affinity between liberalism and the Democrats and between conservatism and the Republicans. At the same time, it is not a perfect relationship, and you can find plenty of liberal Republicans and conservative Democrats in the tables.

Now, let's switch gears and see if we can discover some of the reasons people are liberal or conservative, Democrats or Republicans.

12.2 Age and Politics

Often, the search for causal variables involves the examination of **demographic** or background variables, such as age, sex, and race. Such variables often have a powerful impact on attitudes and behaviors. Let's begin with age.

There is a common belief that young people are more liberal than old people—that people get more conservative as they get older. As you can imagine, liberals tend to see this as a trend toward stodginess, whereas conservatives tend to explain it as a matter of increased wisdom. Regardless of the explanation you might prefer, let's see if it's even true that old people are more conservative than young people.

To find out, run a Crosstab using POLREC as the row variable and AGECAT as the column variable. Here's what you should get:

POLREC Recoded POLVIEWS * AGECAT Recoded Age Categories Crosstabulation

			AGECAT Recoded Age Categories				
			1 Under 21	2 21-39	3 40-64	4 65 and older	Total
POLREC Recoded POLVIEWS	1 liberal	Count	8	173	160	37	378
		% within AGECAT Recoded Age Categories	21.1%	29.1%	27.2%	18.4%	26.6%
	2 moderate	Count	19	216	223	87	545
		% within AGECAT Recoded Age Categories	50.0%	36.4%	37.9%	43.3%	38.3%
	3 conservative	Count	11	205	206	77	499
		% within AGECAT Recoded Age Categories	28.9%	34.5%	35.0%	38.3%	35.1%
Total		Count	38	594	589	201	1422
		% within AGECAT Recoded Age Categories	100.0%	100.0%	100.0%	100.0%	100.0%

Which of the following statements is a more accurate interpretation of the above table?

People appear to become more conservative as they grow older.

People appear to become more liberal as they grow older.

If you chose the first answer, you have just won the right to continue with the analysis. (Oh, never mind—you can continue even if you got it wrong.) Notice, however, that the strength of the relationship is not terribly strong.

What would you expect to find in terms of political party identification? If that relationship corresponds to the one we've just examined, we'd expect to find growing strength for Republicans as people grow older. Young people should be more likely to identify themselves as Democrats. Here's an opportunity to test common sense. Why don't you try it out and see what you get? How would you interpret the table?

Once you've done this, you might want to compare your interpretation with what we say in Appendix D.

12.3 Religion and Politics

In the United States, the relationship between religion and politics is somewhat complex, especially with regard to Roman Catholics. Let's begin with political philosophies. Now would be a good time for you to ask SPSS for the Crosstabs connecting RELIG with POLREC. If you do, you should soon be looking at this table.

POLREC Recoded POLVIEWS * RELIG RS RELIGIOUS PREFERENCE Crosstabulation

| | | | RELIG RS RELIGIOUS PREFERENCE | | | | | |
			1 PROTESTANT	2 CATHOLIC	3 JEWISH	4 NONE	5 OTHER	Total
POLREC Recoded POLVIEWS	1 liberal	Count	174	90	21	70	22	377
		% within RELIG RS RELIGIOUS PREFERENCE	22.5%	23.9%	45.7%	42.9%	35.5%	26.5%
	2 moderate	Count	286	158	13	60	28	545
		% within RELIG RS RELIGIOUS PREFERENCE	37.0%	41.9%	28.3%	36.8%	45.2%	38.4%
	3 conservative	Count	312	129	12	33	12	498
		% within RELIG RS RELIGIOUS PREFERENCE	40.4%	34.2%	26.1%	20.2%	19.4%	35.1%
Total		Count	772	377	46	163	62	1420
		% within RELIG RS RELIGIOUS PREFERENCE	100.0%	100.0%	100.0%	100.0%	100.0%	100.0%

To begin, you should pretty much ignore the "other" religions in this table because they are so varied (e.g., Mormons, Buddhists, Moslems)—some liberal, some conservative—that they lack any meaning as a group. If you were to work extensively with RELIG, you might want to recode it to throw the "other" category in with "missing data."

"None," on the other hand, is a very meaningful category that is made up of agnostics and atheists. Notice that those in this category are the most liberal politically. Protestants are the most conservative (40 percent), followed by Catholics (34 percent). Among the three religious categories, Jews (26 percent) are apparently the most liberal.

If you were to make a gross generalization about the relationship between religious affiliation and political philosophy, it would place Protestants and Catholics on the right end of the political spectrum and Jews and "nones" on the left.

Political party identification, however, is a somewhat different matter. Like the Jews, Roman Catholics have been an ethnic minority throughout much of U.S. history, and the Democratic party, in this century at least, has focused more on minority rights than has the Republican party. That would explain the relationship between religion and political party. Why don't you run that table now? Make PARTY the row variable and RELIG the column variable.

PARTY party identification * RELIG RS RELIGIOUS PREFERENCE Crosstabulation

			RELIG RS RELIGIOUS PREFERENCE					
			1 PROTESTANT	2 CATHOLIC	3 JEWISH	4 NONE	5 OTHER	Total
PARTY party identification	1 demoncrat	Count	300	153	24	51	18	546
		% within RELIG RS RELIGIOUS PREFERENCE	36.9%	39.2%	52.2%	28.7%	26.9%	36.6%
	2 independent	Count	257	139	13	97	37	543
		% within RELIG RS RELIGIOUS PREFERENCE	31.7%	35.6%	28.3%	54.5%	55.2%	36.4%
	3 republican	Count	243	95	6	27	10	381
		% within RELIG RS RELIGIOUS PREFERENCE	29.9%	24.4%	13.0%	15.2%	14.9%	25.5%
	4 other	Count	12	3	3	3	2	23
		% within RELIG RS RELIGIOUS PREFERENCE	1.5%	.8%	6.5%	1.7%	3.0%	1.5%
Total		Count	812	390	46	178	67	1493
		% within RELIG RS RELIGIOUS PREFERENCE	100.0%	100.0%	100.0%	100.0%	100.0%	100.0%

As we see in the table, Jews are the most likely to identify themselves with the Democratic party. Although Catholics are the next most likely, they do not differ much from the Protestants in this regard.

If you are interested in these two variables, you might want to explore the relationship between politics and the other religious variables we've examined: POSTLIFE and PRAY.

On the other hand, you could look for other consequences of RELIG. What else do you suppose might be affected by differences of religious affiliation?

12.4 Gender and Politics

Gender is a demographic variable associated with a great many attitudes and behaviors. Take a minute to think about the reasons women might be more liberal or more conservative than men. Once you've formed an expectation in this regard, why don't you look for the actual relationship by using SPSS? You can check your results with our comments in Appendix D.

12.5 Race, Class, and Politics

Given the above comments about politics and minority groups, what relationship do you expect to find between politics and race? The variable available to you for analysis codes only "white," "black," and "other," so it's not possible to examine this relationship in great depth, but you should be able to make some educated guesses about how Caucasians and African Americans might differ politically.

After you've thought about the likely relationship between race and politics, why don't you run the tables and test your ability to predict such matters? Once you've done that, you can check your answers with our comments in Appendix D if you like.

The Democratic party traditionally has also been strong among the working class, whereas the well-to-do have seemed more comfortable as Republicans. Why don't you check to see if this relationship still holds true in the 1990s? You can use the variable CLASS, which is a measure of subjective social class, asking respondents how they view themselves in this regard. Again, we provide some tables and comments regarding this analysis in Appendix D.

12.6 Education and Politics

Education, a common component of social class, is likely to be of interest to you, especially if you are currently a college student. From your own experience, what would you expect to be the relationship between education and political philosophy? Run the Crosstabs for EDCAT (column variable) and POLREC (row variable), and you can find out the facts of the matter.

POLREC Recoded POLVIEWS * EDCAT Categorized Education Crosstabulation

			EDCAT Categorized Education					
			1 less than HS	2 HS grad	3 some college	4 college grad	5 grad studies	Total
POLREC Recoded POLVIEWS	1 liberal	Count	51	88	91	71	77	378
		% within EDCAT Categorized Education	24.2%	22.3%	22.7%	33.5%	38.5%	26.6%
	2 moderate	Count	95	180	151	60	56	542
		% within EDCAT Categorized Education	45.0%	45.6%	37.7%	28.3%	28.0%	38.2%
	3 conservative	Count	65	127	159	81	67	499
		% within EDCAT Categorized Education	30.8%	32.2%	39.7%	38.2%	33.5%	35.2%
Total		Count	211	395	401	212	200	1419
		% within EDCAT Categorized Education	100.0%	100.0%	100.0%	100.0%	100.0%	100.0%

As you can see, there is a consistent pattern of increasing liberalism with higher levels of education. This does not mean that conservatism declines with increasing education, however. Instead, the rise in liberalism is accounted for by a decline in the number of moderates as education increases. But how about political party? You decide how to structure your Crosstab instruction to obtain the following table.

PARTY party identification * EDCAT recoded education Crosstabulation

			EDCAT recoded education					
			1 less than HS	2 HS grad	3 some college	4 college grad	5 grad studies	Total
PARTY party identification	1 democrat	Count	101	150	133	77	84	545
		% within EDCAT recoded education	42.1%	35.9%	31.9%	36.3%	41.4%	36.6%
	2 independent	Count	99	167	153	62	60	541
		% within EDCAT recoded education	41.3%	40.0%	36.7%	29.2%	29.6%	36.3%
	3 republican	Count	38	93	128	68	54	381
		% within EDCAT recoded education	15.8%	22.2%	30.7%	32.1%	26.6%	25.6%
	4 other	Count	2	8	3	5	5	23
		% within EDCAT recoded education	.8%	1.9%	.7%	2.4%	2.5%	1.5%
Total		Count	240	418	417	212	203	1490
		% within EDCAT recoded education	100.0%	100.0%	100.0%	100.0%	100.0%	100.0%

The relationship here is fairly consistent, but it is possibly in the opposite direction from what you expected. We've seen throughout these analyses that the association of liberalism with the Democratic party is hardly a perfect one, and these latest two tables point that out very clearly.

Whereas liberalism increases with rising educational levels, Democratic party identification decreases for all educational categories except graduate studies. Why do you suppose that would be the case? Think about this, and we'll return to this issue in Chapter 18, when you have the ability to analyze multivariate tables.

12.7 Marital Status and Politics

Sometimes, the inductive method of analysis produces some surprises. As an example, you might take a look at the relationship between MARITAL and our political variables. It wouldn't seem as though marital status would relate to political orientations, but your analysis is likely to present you with some odd results.

Once you've run the tables, try to think of any good reasons for the observed differences. Here's a clue: Try to think of other variables that might account for the patterns you've observed. Then, in Chapter 18, when we engage in multivariate analysis, you'll have a chance to check out some of your explanations.

12.8   The Impact of Party and Political Philosophy

Let's shift gears now and consider politics as an independent variable. What impact do you suppose political philosophy and/or political party might have in determining people's attitudes on some of the political issues we looked at earlier?

Ask yourself where liberals and conservatives would stand on the following issues. Then run the tables to find out if your hunches are correct.

GUNLAW   registration of firearms

CAPPUN   capital punishment

Remember, when POLREC is the independent variable, you need to alter its location in the Crosstabs command, making it the column variable.

Once you've examined the relationship between political philosophies and these more specific political issues, consider the impact of political party. In forming your expectations in this latter regard, you might want to review recent political platforms of the two major parties or the speeches of political candidates from the two parties. Then, see if the political party identification of the American public falls along those same lines.

12.9   Summary

We hope this chapter has given you a good look at the excitement possible in the detective work called social science research. We're willing to bet that some of the results you've uncovered in this chapter pretty much squared with your understanding of American politics, whereas other findings came as a surprise.

The skills you are learning in this book, along with your access to SPSS and the GSS data, make it possible for you to conduct your own investigations into the nature of American politics and other issues that may interest you. In the chapter that follows, we're going to return to our examination of attitudes toward abortion. This time, we want to learn what causes differences in attitudes on this hotly controversial topic.

Chapter 13   What Causes Different Attitudes toward Abortion?

One of the most controversial issues of recent years has concerned whether a woman has the right to have an abortion. Partisans on both sides of this issue are often extremely vocal and demonstrative.

As we saw earlier (in Chapter 8), there appear to be three main positions on this issue among the GSS respondents in 1996. Just under half support a woman's right to have an abortion for any reason. Fewer than 10 percent oppose abortion under all circumstances, and the rest are opposed to unrestricted abortions but are willing to make exceptions when pregnancy results from rape or when it risks the mother's health or is likely to result in serious birth defects.

In this chapter, we're going to use your new analytic skills to begin exploring the causes of these different points of view on abortion. Why are some people permissive and others not? As we pursue this question, we can profit from an excellent review of the research on abortion attitudes: Cook, Jelen, and Wilcox's *Between Two Absolutes: Public Opinion and the Politics of Abortion* (1992). Chapter 2 from that book is reprinted in Appendix E to serve as background for the analyses we'll undertake in this chapter and to suggest additional directions of analysis if you would like to pursue your analyses of this topic beyond these first steps.

13.1   Gender and Abortion

As you think about possible causes of different attitudes about abortion, the first one that probably comes to mind is gender, given that abortion affects women more directly than it does men. In a quote that has become a popular pro-choice bumper sticker, Florynce Kennedy put it this way several years ago: "If men could get pregnant, abortion would be a sacrament." There is reason to believe, therefore, that women would be more supportive of abortion than men. Let's see.

Here is a table that summarizes attitudes toward abortion by gender. It is not an SPSS output, but we've created it from several SPSS tables. Your task is to figure out how to get the SPSS tables that would allow you to create this table.

Percentage Approving of Abortion under the Following Conditions		*Men*	*Women*
ABHLTH	woman's health endangered	92	90
ABDEFECT	serious defect likely	80	82
ABRAPE	resulted from rape	86	85
ABPOOR	too poor for more children	49	48
ABSINGLE	woman is unmarried	46	48
ABNOMORE	family wants no more	49	48
ABANY	for any reason	48	49

Contrary to what we expected, women are not more supportive of abortion than are men. Actually, men are consistently a little more supportive, representing a difference of one to two percentage points on the several items.

We used the individual items concerning abortion for this analysis because it was possible that men and women would differ on some but not on others. For example, we might have expected women to be more supportive on the item concerning the woman's health, but this was not the case.

As an alternative strategy for examining the sources of attitudes toward abortion, let's make use of the index, ABORT, that we created in Chapter 9, combining responses to ABDEFECT and ABSINGLE.

Based on the summary table above, we would certainly expect little difference between women and men in their index scores. And our modified expectations are more accurate, as you'll discover when you create the following table.

ABORT * SEX RESPONDENTS SEX Crosstabulation

			SEX RESPONDENTS SEX		Total
			1 MALE	2 FEMALE	
ABORT	0	Count	80	87	167
		% within SEX RESPONDENTS SEX	19.5%	17.3%	18.3%
	1	Count	141	176	317
		% within SEX RESPONDENTS SEX	34.3%	35.1%	34.7%
	2	Count	190	239	429
		% within SEX RESPONDENTS SEX	46.2%	47.6%	47.0%
Total		Count	411	502	913
		% within SEX RESPONDENTS SEX	100.0%	100.0%	100.0%

Recall that a score of 2 on the index represents those who supported a woman's right to have an abortion if her health is threatened by the pregnancy and/or if she is single. Overall, 47 percent of the sample took that position. This table indicates little difference between men and women, with men slightly *less* likely (46 percent) to score 2 on the index than are women (48 percent).

So far, then, we have learned that gender is not the explanation for differences in attitudes toward abortion. Let's see if age has an impact.

13.2 Age and Abortion

As Cook and her colleagues (1992) point out, abortion is somewhat more relevant to young people because they are more likely to experience unwanted pregnancies than are older people. What would that lead you to expect in the way of a relationship between age and support for abortion? Think about that, and then use SPSS to run the tables that answer the question for you.

Recall that we recoded AGE into AGECAT in Chapter 6. We'll want to use AGECAT for our examination of the relationship between age and abortion attitudes.

Now you can request the SPSS tables that relate age to abortion attitudes. Here's a summary of the tables you should have created.

Percentage Approving of Abortion under the Following Conditions		*Under 21*	*21-39*	*40-64*	*Over 64*
ABHLTH	woman's health endangered	81	94	90	87
ABDEFECT	serious defect likely	77	81	81	84
ABRAPE	resulted from rape	72	88	84	80
ABPOOR	too poor for more children	40	50	48	44
ABSINGLE	woman is unmarried	39	47	50	41
ABNOMORE	family wants no more	31	51	50	43
ABANY	for any reason	46	52	48	36

Take a minute to look over the data presented in this summary table. How do the analytic results square with your expectations?

These data suggest that there is little or no relationship between age and attitudes toward abortion. This is confirmed when we use the ABORT index as our measure.

On the whole, then, there appears to be no relationship between age and abortion attitudes. Or, perhaps it is just more complex than we have been

ABORT * AGECAT Recoded Age Categories Crosstabulation

			AGECAT Recoded Age Categories				
			1 Under 21	2 21-39	3 40-64	4 65 and older	Total
ABORT	0	Count	5	75	68	19	167
		% within AGECAT Recoded Age Categories	19.2%	19.0%	18.1%	16.2%	18.3%
	1	Count	12	133	123	49	317
		% within AGECAT Recoded Age Categories	46.2%	33.7%	32.8%	41.9%	34.7%
	2	Count	9	187	184	49	429
		% within AGECAT Recoded Age Categories	34.6%	47.3%	49.1%	41.9%	47.0%
Total		Count	26	395	375	117	913
		% within AGECAT Recoded Age Categories	100.0%	100.0%	100.0%	100.0%	100.0%

allowing for in these analyses. We'll find out once we are able to undertake a multivariate analysis.

13.3   Religion and Abortion

If we began this analysis by asking you what variable you thought might account for attitudes toward abortion, there is a good chance that you would have guessed religion, given the unconditional and public opposition of the Roman Catholic church. Your growing facility with SPSS and the GSS data make it possible for you to test that expectation.

Let's start with the possible impact of religious affiliation. Here's a summary of what you should discover if you run the several abortion items by RELIG.

Percentage Approving of Abortion under the Following Conditions		*Prot*	*Cath*	*Jew*	*None*
ABHLTH	woman's health endangered	92	87	100	95
BDEFECT	serious defect likely	80	78	96	89
ABRAPE	resulted from rape	83	83	96	95
ABPOOR	too poor for more children	44	41	87	67
ABSINGLE	woman is unmarried	43	39	88	66
ABNOMORE	family wants no more	45	41	88	67
ABANY	for any reason	44	42	85	63

There are several observations you might make about these data. To begin with, the expectation that Catholics would be the most opposed to abortion is confirmed. They are the least likely to approve of abortion under any of the conditions asked about.

At the same time, the level of support for abortion among American Catholics is greatly at variance with the church's official position. Under the traumatic conditions summarized at the top of the table, 83 to 87 percent of the Catholics say they would approve abortion. Even under the less traumatic conditions, at least one-third of the Catholics would support a woman's right to an abortion: 44 percent (more than among Protestants) support it "for any reason."

In contrast, Jews and those with no religion are consistently more supportive of a woman's right to an abortion. Those labeled "Other" fall in the middle of the variation in attitudes, because they are a thoroughly mixed group and hard to generalize about.

To examine this relationship further, why don't you use the index ABORT to see if this pattern is reflected in scores on a composite measure. You can refer to Appendix D to compare your results with ours.

In our earlier examinations of religion, we've sometimes gone beyond affiliation to examine the measure of religiosity, or religiousness. How do you suppose church attendance would relate to abortion attitudes? To find out, let's use CHATT, the recoded variable created in Chapter 6.

Run the appropriate tables, and here's a summary of what you should have learned.

Percentage Approving of Abortion under the Following Conditions		Weekly	Monthly	Seldom	Never
ABHLTH	woman's health endangered	81	93	97	93
ABDEFECT	serious defect likely	63	83	91	90
ABRAPE	resulted from rape	66	86	96	92
ABPOOR	too poor for more children	27	46	59	65
ABSINGLE	woman is unmarried	27	46	58	62
ABNOMORE	family wants no more	28	43	61	65
ABANY	for any reason	27	45	60	64

What does this table tell you about religion and abortion attitudes? The overall relationship is pretty clear: Increased church attendance is related to decreased support for abortion. There is a substantial difference, however, between those who attend church about weekly and those who attend less often. Those who attend one to three times per month are more than twice as likely to support unconditional abortion as those who attend church weekly. Even in the case of the traumatic conditions at the top of the table, only those who attend church weekly stand out in their relatively low level of support.

The fact that the other three groups do not differ much from one another, by the way, is a result of what we call a "ceiling effect." Whenever the overall percentage of people agreeing with something approaches 100 percent, it's not possible for there to be much variation among subgroups. In the extreme case, if everyone agreed on something, there would be no way for men and women to differ because 100 percent of both would have to agree. Similarly, there could be no differences among age groups, religions, and so on. When the overall percentage approaches zero, a similar situation occurs that we call a "floor effect."

If you want to check the relationship between CHATT and the abortion index, ABORT, you can compare your results with ours in Appendix D.

The GSS data we've provided for your use permit you to explore this general topic further, if you wish. Why don't you check out the effect of POSTLIFE and PRAY on abortion attitudes? Before running the tables, however, take some time to reflect on what might logically be expected. How should beliefs about an afterlife affect support for or opposition to abortion? You may be surprised by what you learn. Then again, maybe you won't be surprised.

13.4 Politics and Abortion

There is a strong and consistent relationship between political philosophy and abortion attitudes. What do you suppose that relationship is? Who would you expect to be the more supportive of abortion: liberals or conservatives? To carry out this investigation, you'll probably want to use the recoded variable, POLREC.

Now you can examine the relationship between political philosophy and abortion attitudes to see if your hunch is correct. Here's a summary of what you should discover.

Percentage Approving of Abortion under the Following Conditions		*Liberal*	*Moderate*	*Conservative*
ABHLTH	woman's health endangered	96	93	86
ABDEFECT	serious defect likely	87	87	71
ABRAPE	resulted from rape	92	89	76
ABPOOR	too poor for more children	68	47	36
ABSINGLE	woman is unmarried	61	47	37
ABNOMORE	family wants no more	66	48	38
ABANY	for any reason	64	49	36

How would you describe these results? Try your hand at writing up a sentence or two to report on the impact of political philosophy on abortion attitudes. Then, see how your report compares with what we say in Appendix D.

To pursue this relationship further, you may want to use the ABORT index. We haven't included that result in Appendix D, so you're on your own.

Another direction you might want to follow in investigating the relationship between politics and abortion attitudes concerns political party identification. As you no doubt realize, the Democratic party has been generally more supportive of a woman's right to have an abortion than has the Republican party. This difference was dramatically portrayed by the presidential and vice presidential candidates during the 1996 election.

How do you suppose the official differences separating the parties show up in the attitudes of the rank and file? Among the general public, who do you suppose are the most supportive of abortion: Democrats or Republicans? You can find out for yourself. We present our summary of the results in Appendix D, in case you want to compare notes.

13.5 Other Factors to Explore

There are a number of other demographic factors that can affect attitudes toward abortion. We'll suggest a few more for you to check out. You may want to review the excerpt from Cook et al. in Appendix E for further ideas.

Education is strongly related to abortion attitudes. Which direction do you suppose that relationship goes? Why do you suppose that is? We present a partial look at the relationship in Appendix D.

Race is another standard demographic variable that might be related to abortion attitudes. We provide a table using the ABORT index in Appendix D, but you may want to examine the individual abortion items, because race has slightly different effects on different items.

Finally, we suggest that you might like to explore the relationship between abortion attitudes and some family variables. How do you suppose abortion attitudes relate to respondents' views of the ideal number of children to have?

The family variable that may surprise you in its relationship to abortion attitudes is MARITAL. You may recall that we also uncovered a surprising effect of marital status on political philosophy. Check this one out, and we'll take a more in-depth look once we begin our multivariate analyses.

We give you some partial analyses of these topics in Appendix D, but you'll probably want to explore further than we have.

13.6 Sexual Attitudes and Abortion

Recalling that abortion attitudes are related to differences in political philosophy, it might occur to you that other philosophical differences might be relevant as well. As you may recall from Chapter 10, the GSS data set contains three items dealing with sexual permissiveness/restrictiveness:

PREMARSX	attitudes toward premarital sex
HOMOSEX	attitudes toward homosexual sex relations
XMOVIE	attendance at an X-rated movie during the year

Here's the relationship between attitudes toward premarital sex and toward abortion. Notice how permissiveness on one is related to permissiveness on the other.

ABORT * PREMARSX SEX BEFORE MARRIAGE Crosstabulation

			PREMARSX SEX BEFORE MARRIAGE				
			1 ALWAYS WRONG	2 ALMST ALWAYS WRO	3 SOMETIMES WRONG	4 NOT WRONG AT ALL	Total
ABORT	0	Count	40	11	16	12	79
		% within PREMARSX SEX BEFORE MARRIAGE	42.1%	23.4%	15.7%	5.8%	17.6%
	1	Count	32	16	43	56	147
		% within PREMARSX SEX BEFORE MARRIAGE	33.7%	34.0%	42.2%	27.2%	32.7%
	2	Count	23	20	43	138	224
		% within PREMARSX SEX BEFORE MARRIAGE	24.2%	42.6%	42.2%	67.0%	49.8%
Total		Count	95	47	102	206	450
		% within PREMARSX SEX BEFORE MARRIAGE	100.0%	100.0%	100.0%	100.0%	100.0%

Now, why don't you check to see if the same pattern holds for the other sexual attitudes? We give you some tables in Appendix D with which to compare your results.

13.7 Summary

In this chapter, you've had an opportunity to search for explanations for the vast differences in people's feelings about abortion. We've found that religion and politics, for example, are powerful influences. We've also just seen that permissiveness and restrictiveness regarding abortion are strongly related to permissiveness and restrictiveness on issues of sexual behavior.

Thus far, we've only opened up the search for explanations, limiting ourselves to bivariate analyses. In the analyses to come, we'll dig ever deeper into the reasons for differences in the opinions people have. Ultimately, you should gain a well-rounded understanding of the logic of social scientific research as well as master some of the fundamental techniques for acting on that logic through SPSS.

Chapter 14   Measures of Association

In the preceding analyses, we've depended on percentage tables as our format for examining the relationships among variables. In this chapter, we are going to explore some other formats for that examination. By and large, these techniques summarize relationships in contrast to the way percentage tables lay out the details before you.

14.1   Lambda

To introduce the logic of statistical association, we would like you to take a minute for a "thought experiment." Imagine that there is a group of 100 people in a lecture hall, and you are standing in the hallway outside the room. The people will come out of the room one at a time, and your task will be to guess the gender of each before he or she comes into view. Take a moment to consider your best strategy for making these guesses.

If you know nothing about the people in the room, there really is no useful strategy for guessing, no way to make educated guesses. But now suppose you know that 60 of the people in the room are women. This would make educated guesses possible: You should guess "woman" every time. By doing this, you would be right 60 times and wrong 40 times.

Now suppose that every time a person prepares to emerge from the room, his or her first name is announced. This would probably improve your guessing substantially. You'd guess "woman" for every Nancy or Joanne and "man" for every Joseph and Wendell. Even so, you probably wouldn't be totally accurate, given the ambiguity of names like Pat, Chris, and Leslie.

It is useful to notice that we could actually calculate how much knowing first names improved your guessing. Let's say you would have made 40 errors out of 100 guesses without knowing names and only 10 errors when you knew the names. You would have made 30 fewer mistakes. Out of an original 40 mistakes, that's a 75% improvement. Statisticians refer to this as a "proportionate reduction of error," which they abbreviate as PRE.

Lambda is a measure of association appropriate for use with nominal variables, and it operates on the PRE logic. Essentially, this means that the two variables are related to one another to the extent that knowing a person's attribute on one will help you guess his or her attribute on the other.

Here's a very simple example of lambda. Suppose that we have data on the employment status of 1,000 people. Half are employed; half are unemployed. If we were to begin presenting you with person after person, asking you to guess whether each was employed or not, you'd get about half wrong and half right by guessing blindly. So, the logic of lambda begins with the assumption that you'd make 500 errors, in this case. Let's call these your "uneducated errors."

Now, take a look at the table below, which gives you additional information: the ages of the subject

	Young	*Old*	*Total*
Employed	0	500	500
Unemployed	500	0	500
Total	500	500	1,000

Suppose now that we were to repeat the guessing exercise. This time, however, you would know whether each person is young or old. What would be your strategy for guessing employment status?

Clearly, you should make an educated guess of "unemployed" for every young person and "employed" for every old person. Do that and you'll make no errors. You will have reduced your errors by 500, in comparison with the first attempt. Given that you will have eliminated all your former errors, we could also say that you have reduced your errors by 100 percent.

Here's the simple equation for lambda that allows you to calculate the reduction of errors:

$$\frac{\text{(uneducated errors)} - \text{(educated errors)}}{\text{(uneducated errors)}} = \frac{500 - 0}{500} = 1.00$$

Notice that the calculation results in 1.00, which we treat as 100 percent in the context of lambda.

To be sure the logic of lambda is clear to you, let's consider another hypothetical example, similar to the previous example:

	Young	*Old*	*Total*
Employed	250	250	500
Unemployed	250	250	500
Total	500	500	1,000

In this new example, we still have half young and half old, and we have half employed and half unemployed. Notice the difference in the relationship between the two variables, however. Just by inspection, you should be able to see that they are independent of one another. In this case, age has no impact on employment status.

The lack of a relationship between age and employment status here is reflected in the "educated" guesses you would make about employment status if you knew a person's age. It wouldn't help you at all, and you would get half the young people wrong and half the old people wrong. You would have made 500 errors in uneducated guesses, and you wouldn't have improved by knowing their ages.

Lambda reflects this new situation:

$$\frac{(\text{uneducated errors}) - (\text{educated errors})}{(\text{uneducated errors})} = \frac{500 - 500}{500} = 0.00$$

Knowing age would have reduced your errors by zero percent.

The real relationships between variables are seldom this simple, of course, so let's look at a real example using SPSS and the General Social Survey data. You'll be pleased to discover that you won't have to calculate the errors or the proportion of reduction, because SPSS does it for you.

Set up a Crosstabs request using ABANY as the row variable and RELIG as the column variable. This time, it will be useful to request no percentaging of the cells in the table. Click on Cells, and turn off "Column" if that's still selected. Return to the Crosstabs window. Before executing the Crosstabs command, however, click the Statistics button. Here's what you should see:

Click the button for Lambda. Leave the Statistics window and execute the Crosstabs command. Here's the result that should show up in your output window.

ABANY ABORTION IF WOMAN WANTS FOR ANY REASON * RELIG RS RELIGIOUS PREFERENCE Crosstabulation

Count

		RELIG RS RELIGIOUS PREFERENCE					
		1 PROTESTANT	2 CATHOLIC	3 JEWISH	4 NONE	5 OTHER	Total
ABANY ABORTION IF WOMAN WANTS FOR ANY REASON	1 Favor	223	103	22	75	25	448
	2 Oppose	279	142	4	44	15	484
Total		502	245	26	119	40	932

We've omitted the request for percentages in this table because it will be useful to see the actual number of cases in each cell of the table. At the far right of the table, notice that 448 people supported the idea of a woman being able to get an abortion just because she wanted one; 484 were opposed. If we were to make uneducated guesses about people's opinion on this issue, we'd do best always to guess "opposed." But by doing that, we would make 448 errors.

If we knew each person's religion, however, we would improve our record somewhat. Here's what would happen.

Religion	Guess	Errors
Protestant	oppose	223
Catholic	oppose	103
Jewish	favor	4
None	favor	44
Other	favor	15
Total		389

To calculate lambda, then,

$$\frac{(\text{uneducated errors}) - (\text{educated errors})}{(\text{uneducated errors})} = \frac{448 - 389}{448} = .13169$$

This indicates, therefore, that we have improved our guessing of abortion attitudes by 13 percent as a result of knowing religious affiliation. Here's how SPSS reports this result:

Directional Measures

			Value	Asymp. Std. Error[a]	Approx. T[b]	Approx. Sig.
Nominal by Nominal	Lambda	Symmetric	.067	.015	4.382	.000
		ABANY ABORTION IF WOMAN WANTS FOR ANY REASON Dependent	.132	.028	4.382	.000
		RELIG RS RELIGIOUS PREFERENCE Dependent	.000	.000	c	c
	Goodman and Kruskal tau	ABANY ABORTION IF WOMAN WANTS FOR ANY REASON Dependent	.037	.011		.000[d]
		RELIG RS RELIGIOUS PREFERENCE Dependent	.007	.003		.000[d]

SPSS reports more information than we need right now, so let's focus our attention on the second row of numbers. Because we have been testing whether we could predict abortion attitudes (ABANY) by knowing religion, that makes ABANY the dependent variable. As you can see, the value of lambda in that instance is 0.13169, the value we got by calculating it for ourselves.

Knowing a person's religious affiliation, then, allows us to predict their attitude on abortion 13 percent more accurately. The implicit assumption in this analysis is that religious affiliation *causes,* to some degree, attitudes toward abortion. We use the value of lambda as an indication of how strong the causal link is.

However, it is important that you bear in mind that *association alone does not prove causation.* When we observe a statistical relationship between two variables, that strengthens the probability that one causes the other, but it is not sufficient proof. To be satisfied that a causal relationship exists, social scientists also want the link to make sense logically (in this case, the role of churches and clergy in the abortion debate offer that reasoning). And finally, we want to be sure that the observed relationship is not an artifact produced by the effects of a third variable. This latter possibility will be examined in Part IV on multivariate analysis.

For curiosity's sake, notice the second line, which treats RELIG as the dependent variable. This deals with the possibility that we might be able to guess people's religions by knowing where they stand on abortion. Take a moment to look at the cross-tabulation above.

If we were to make uneducated guesses about people's religions, we'd always guess Protestant, because Protestants are by far the largest group. Knowing attitudes toward abortion wouldn't help matters, however. In either case, we'd still guess Protestant, even among those who were in favor of abortion rights.

If RELIG were the dependent variable, then, knowing ABANY would improve our guessing by zero percent, which is the calculation presented by SPSS.

Now, why don't you experiment with lambda on some more nominal variables?

14.2 Gamma

Whereas lambda is appropriate to nominal variables, **gamma** is a measure of association based on the logic of proportionate reduction of error appropriate to ordinal variables. We judge two variables to be related to each other to the extent that knowing what a person is like in terms of one variable helps us guess what he or she is like on the other. Whereas the application of this logic in the case of lambda lets us make predictions for individuals (e.g., if a person is Protestant, we guess he or she is also Republican), the logic is applied to pairs of people in the case of gamma.

To see the logic of gamma, let's consider the following nine people, placed in a matrix that indicates their social class standing and their level of prejudice: two ordinal variables.

Prejudice	Lower Class	Middle Class	Upper Class
Low	Jim	Tim	Kim
Med	Mary	Harry	Carrie
High	Nan	Jan	Fran

Our purpose in this analysis is to determine which of the following best describes the relationship between social class and prejudice:

1. The higher your social class, the more prejudiced you are.

2. The higher your social class, the less prejudiced you are.

3. Your social class has no effect on your level of prejudice.

To begin our analysis, we should note that the only pairs who are appropriate to our question are those who differ in both social class and prejudice. Jim and Harry are an example; they differ in both social class and level of prejudice. Here are the 18 pairs that qualify for analysis:

Jim-Harry	Kim-Mary	Harry-Nan
Jim-Carrie	Kim-Harry	Harry-Fran
Jim-Jan	Kim-Nan	
Jim-Fran	Kim-Jan	
Tim-Mary	Mary-Jan	Carrie-Nan
Tim-Nan	Mary-Fran	Carrie-Jan
Tim-Carrie		
Tim-Fran		

Take a minute to assure yourself that no other pair of people satisfies the criterion that they differ in both social class and prejudice.

If you study the table, you should be able to identify pairs of people who would support conclusions 1 and 2—we'll come back to conclusion 3 a little later.

Suppose now that you have been given the list of pairs, but you've never seen the original table. Your task is to guess which member of each pair is the more prejudiced. Given that you will simply be guessing blind, chances are that you'll get about half right and half wrong: nine correct answers and nine errors. Gamma helps us determine whether knowing how two people differ on social class would reduce the number of errors we'd make in guessing how they differ on prejudice.

Let's consider Jim-Harry for a moment. If they were the only two people you could study, and you had to reach a conclusion about the relationship between social class and prejudice, what would you conclude? Notice that Harry is higher in social class than Jim (middle class versus lower class), and Harry is also higher in prejudice (medium versus low). If you were to generalize from this single pair of observations, there is only one conclusion you could reach: "The higher your social class, the more prejudiced you are."

In the language of social research, we would refer to this as a positive association: The higher on one variable, the higher on the other. In the more specific language of gamma, we'll refer to this as a "same" pair: The direction of the difference between Jim and Harry on one variable is the same as the direction of difference on the other. Harry is higher than Jim on both.

Suppose you had to base your conclusion on the Jim-Jan pair. What would you conclude? Look at the table and you'll see that Jan, like Harry, is higher than Jim on both social class and prejudice. This pair would also lead you to conclude that "the higher your social class, the more prejudiced you are." Jim-Jan, then, is another "same" pair, in the language of gamma.

Suppose, on the other hand, we observed only Tim and Mary. They would lead us to a very different conclusion. Mary is lower than Tim on social class, but she is higher on prejudice. If this were the only pair you could observe, you'd have to conclude that "the higher your social class, the lower your prejudice." In the language of gamma, Tim-Mary is an "opposite" pair: The direction of their difference on one variable is the opposite of their difference on the other.

Now, we hope you've been feeling uncomfortable about the idea of generalizing from only one pair of observations, although that's what many people often do in everyday life. In social research, however, we would never do that.

Moving a little bit in the direction of normal social research, let's assume that you have observed all nine of the individuals in the table. What conclusion would you draw about the association between social class and prejudice? Gamma helps you answer this question.

Let's see how well each of the alternative conclusions might assist you in guessing people's prejudice based on knowing about their social class. If you operated on the basis of the conclusion that prejudice increases with social class, for example, and I told you Fran is of a higher social class than Harry, you would correctly guess that Fran is more prejudiced. If, on the other hand, I told you that Harry is higher in social class than Nan, you would incorrectly guess that he is more prejudiced.

Take a minute to go through the list of pairs above and make notations of which ones are "same" pairs and which ones are "opposite." Once you've done that, count the numbers of same and opposite pairs.

You should get nine of each type of pair. This means that if you assume that prejudice increases with social class, you will get the nine opposite pairs wrong; if you assume prejudice decreases with social class, you will get the nine same pairs wrong. In other words, neither strategy for guessing levels of prejudice based on knowing social class will do you any good in this case. In either case, we make as many errors as we would have made if we didn't know the social class differences in the pairs. Gamma gives us a method for calculating that result.

The formula for gamma is as follows:

$$\frac{same - opposite}{same + opposite}$$

To calculate gamma, you must first count the number of same pairs and the number of opposite pairs. Once you've done that, the mathematics is pretty simple.

Now, you can complete the formula as follows:

$$\frac{9-9}{9+9} = \frac{0}{18} = 0$$

In gamma, this result is interpreted as 0 percent, meaning that knowing how two people differ on social class would improve your guesses as to how they differ on prejudice by 0—or not at all.

Consider the following modified table, however. Suppose for the moment that there are only three people to be studied:

Prejudice	Lower Class	Middle Class	Upper Class
Low	Jim		
Med		Harry	
High			Fran

Just by inspection, you can see how perfectly these three people fit the pattern of a positive association between social class and prejudice. Each of the three pairs—Jim-Harry, Harry-Fran, Jim-Fran—is a "same" pair. There are no "opposite" pairs. If we were to give you each of these pairs, telling you who was higher in social class, the assumption of a positive association between the two variables would let you guess who was higher in social class with perfect accuracy.

Let's see how this situation would look in terms of gamma.

$$\frac{\text{same} - \text{opposite}}{\text{same} + \text{opposite}} = \frac{3-0}{3+0} = 1.00 \text{ or } 100 \text{ percent}$$

In this case, we would say gamma equals 1.00, with the meaning that you have reduced the number of errors by 100 percent. To understand this meaning of gamma, we need to go back to the idea of guessing prejudice differences without knowing social class.

Recall that if you were guessing blind, you'd be right about half the time and wrong about half the time. In this hypothetical case, you'd be wrong 1.5 times (that would be your average if you repeated the exercise hundreds of times). As we've seen, however, knowing social class in this instance lets us reduce the number of errors by 1.5—down to zero. It is in this sense that we say we have reduced our errors by 100 percent.

Now, let's consider a slightly different table.

Prejudice	Lower Class	Middle Class	Upper Class
Low			Nan
Med		Harry	
High	Kim		

Notice that in this case, we could also have a perfect record if we use the assumption of a negative association between social class and prejudice: The higher your social class, the lower your prejudice. The negative association shows up in gamma as follows:

$$\frac{\text{same} - \text{opposite}}{\text{same} + \text{opposite}} = \frac{0 - 3}{0 + 3} = -1.00 \text{ or } -100 \text{ percent}$$

Once again, the gamma indicates we have reduced our errors by 100 percent. The minus sign in this result simply signals that the relationship is negative.

We are finally ready for a more realistic example. Just as you would not want to base a generalization on as few cases as we've been considering so far, neither would it make sense to calculate gamma in such situations. Notice how gamma helps you assess the relationship between two variables when the results are not as obvious to the nonstatistical eye.

Prejudice	Lower Class	Middle Class	Upper Class
Low	200	400	700
Med	500	900	400
High	800	300	100

In this table, the names of individuals have been replaced with the numbers of people having a particular social class and level of prejudice. There are 200 lower-class people in the table, for example, who are low on prejudice. On the other hand, there are 100 upper-class people who are high on prejudice.

Perhaps you can get a sense of the relationship in this table by simple observation. The largest cells are those lying along the diagonal running from lower left to upper right. This would suggest a negative association between the two variables. Gamma lets us determine with more confidence whether that's the case and gives us a yardstick for measuring how strong the relationship is.

In the simpler examples, every pair of cells represented one pair, because there was only one person in each cell. Now it's a little more complex. Imagine for a moment just one of the people in the upper left cell (lower class, low prejudice). If we match that person up with the 900 people in the center cell (middle class, medium prejudice), we'd have 900 pairs. The same would result from matching each of the people in the first cell with all those in the second. We can calculate the total number of pairs produced by the two cells by simple multiplication: 200 times 900 gives us 180,000 pairs. Notice, by the way, that these are "same" pairs.

As a further simplification, notice that there are $900 + 400 + 300 + 100$ people who will match with the upper left cell to form "same" pairs. That makes a total of $1,700 \times 200 = 340,000$. Here's an overview of all the "same" pairs in the table:

$200 \times (900 + 300 + 400 + 100) = 340,000$

$500 \times (300 + 100) = 200,000$

$400 \times (400 + 100) = 200,000$

$900 \times 100 = 90,000$

Total "same" pairs $= 830,000$

Following the same procedure, here are all the "opposite" pairs:

$700 \times (500 + 800 + 900 + 300) = 1,750,000$

$400 \times (800 + 300) = 440,000$

$400 \times (500 + 800) = 520,000$

$900 \times 800 = 720,000$

Total "opposite" pairs $= 3,430,000$

Even though this procedure produces quite a few more pairs than we've been dealing with, the formula for gamma still works the same way:

$$\frac{\text{same} - \text{opposite}}{\text{same} + \text{opposite}} = \frac{830,000 - 3,430,000}{830,000 + 3,430,000} = \frac{-2,600,000}{4,260,000} = -.61$$

The minus sign in this result confirms that the relationship between the two variables is a negative one. The numerical result indicates that knowing the social class ranking in each pair reduces our errors in predicting their ranking in terms of prejudice by 61 percent.

Suppose, for the moment, that you had tried to blindly predict differences in prejudice for each of the 4,260,000 pairs. You would have been wrong about 2,130,000 times. By assuming that the person with higher social class is less prejudiced, you would have made only 830,000 errors, or $(2,130,000 - 830,000 = 1,300,000)$ fewer errors. Dividing the 1,300,000 improvement by the 2,130,000 baseline gives .61, indicating you have reduced your errors by 61 percent.

Now, here's the good news. Although it's important for you to understand the logic of gamma, it is no longer necessary for you to do the calculations by hand. Whenever you run Crosstabs in SPSS, you can request that gamma be calculated by making that request when you set up the table.

Go to Crosstabs. Make CHATT the row variable and AGECAT the column variable. Then click on Statistics.

CHATT * AGECAT Crosstabulation

Count

		AGECAT				Total
		1 under 21	2 21-39	3 40-64	4	
CHATT	1 About weekly	6	152	190	102	450
	2 About monthly	10	106	85	23	224
	3 Seldom	17	262	231	57	567
	4 Never	7	95	88	32	222
Total		40	615	594	214	1463

Symmetric Measures

		Value	Asymp. Std. Error[a]	Approx. T[b]	Approx. Sig.
Ordinal by Ordinal	Gamma	-.149	.034	-4.333	.000
N of Valid Cases		1463			

Notice that gamma is a choice for ordinal data. Click it. Return to the main window and click "OK." You should get the following table and report on gamma.

CHATT * AGECAT Recoded Age Categories Crosstabulation

Count

		AGECAT Recoded Age Categories				Total
		1 under 21	2 21 to 39	3 40 to 64	4 65 and older	
CHATT	1 about weekly	6	152	190	102	450
	2 about monthy	10	106	85	23	224
	3 seldom	17	262	231	57	567
	4 never	7	95	88	32	222
Total		40	615	594	214	1463

Symmetric Measures

		Value	Asymp. Std. Error[a]	Approx. T[b]	Approx. Sig.
Ordinal by Ordinal	Gamma	-.149	.034	-4.333	.000
N of Valid Cases		1463			

Notice that gamma is reported as −.149. This means that knowing a person's age would improve our estimate of his or her church attendance by 15 percent. The minus sign in this case needs extra explanation.

Although you might reasonably think this means there is a negative relationship between age and church attendance, that would be incorrect. In this case, the minus sign results from our choosing to arrange attendance categories from the most frequent at the top to the least frequent at the bottom. If we had arranged the categories in the opposite direction, the gamma would have been positive.

Whenever you ask SPSS to calculate gamma, it is important that you determine the direction of the association by inspection of the table. Looking at the first row in the table above, it is clear that church attendance increases as age increases; hence the relationship between the two variables is a positive one.

To gain some more experience with gamma, why don't you select some ordinal variables that interest you and examine their relationships with one another by using gamma?

14.3 Pearson's *r* Product-Moment Correlation Coefficient

Finally, we are going to work with a measure of association appropriate to continuous ratio data such as age, education, and income. Although this measure also reflects the PRE logic, its meaning in that regard is not quite so straightforward as for the discrete variables analyzed by lambda and gamma. Although it made sense to talk about "guessing" someone's gender or employment status and being either right or wrong, there is little chance that we would ever guess someone's annual income in exact dollars or his or her exact age in days. Our best strategy would be to guess the mean income, and we'd be wrong almost every time. **Pearson's *r*** lets us determine whether knowing one variable would help us come closer in our guesses of the other variable and calculates how much closer we would come.

To understand *r*, also known as a *product-moment correlation,* let's take a simple example of eight young people and see whether there is a correlation between their heights (in inches) and their weights (in pounds). To begin, then, let's meet the eight subjects.

	Height	Weight
Eddy	68	144
Mary	58	111
Marge	67	137
Terry	66	153
Albert	61	165
Larry	74	166
Heather	67	92
Ruth	61	128

Take a minute to study the heights and weights. Begin with Eddy and Mary, at the top of the list. Eddy is both taller and heavier than Mary. If we were forced to reach a conclusion about the association between height and weight based only on these two observations, we would conclude there is a positive correlation: The taller you are, the heavier you are. We might even go a step further and note that every additional inch of height corresponds to about 3 pounds of weight.

On the other hand, if you needed to base a conclusion on observations of Eddy and Terry, see what that conclusion would be. Terry is 2 inches shorter but 9 pounds heavier. Our observations of Eddy and Terry would lead us to just the opposite conclusion: The taller you are, the lighter you are.

Sometimes, it's useful to look at a **scattergram,** which graphs the cases at hand in terms of the two variables. The diagram below presents the eight cases in this fashion. Notice that there seems to be a general pattern of increasing height being associated with increasing weight, although there are a couple of cases that don't fit that pattern.

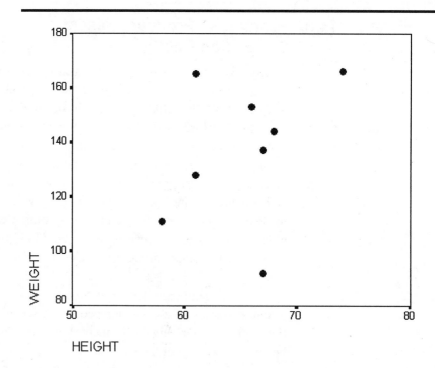

Pearson's *r* allows for the fact that the relationship between height and weight may not be completely consistent, but nevertheless lets us discover any prevailing tendency in that regard. In the gamma logic presented above, we might consider a strategy of guessing who is heavier or lighter on the basis of who is taller or shorter, assuming either a positive (taller means heavier) or negative (taller means lighter) relationship between the two variables. With *r,* however, we'll take account of *how much* taller or heavier.

To calculate *r,* we will need to know the mean value of each variable. As you recall, this is calculated by adding all the values on a variable and dividing by the number of cases. If you do these calculations in the case of height, you'll discover that the eight people, laid end to end, would stretch 522 inches, for a mean height of 65.25 inches. Do the same calculation for their weights, and you'll discover that the eight people weigh a total of 1,096 pounds, for a mean of 137 pounds.

From now on, we are going to focus less on the actual heights and weights of our eight people and deal more with the extent to which they differ from the means. The table below shows how much each person differs from the means for height and weight. Notice that plus and minus signs have been used to indicate whether a person is above or below the mean. (If you want to check your calculations in this situation, you should add all the deviations from height and notice they total 0; the same is true for deviations from mean weight.)

	Height	*Weight*	*H-dev*	*W-dev*
Eddy	68	144	+2.75	+7
Mary	58	111	−7.25	−26
Marge	67	137	+1.75	0
Terry	66	153	+0.75	+16
Albert	61	165	−4.25	+28
Larry	74	166	+8.75	+29
Heather	67	92	+1.75	−45
Ruth	61	128	−4.25	−9
Means	65.25	137		

As our next step, we want to determine the extent to which heights and weights vary from their means overall. Although we have shown the plus and minus signs above, it is important to note that both +2.00 and −2.00 represent deviations of 2 inches from the mean height. For reasons that will become apparent shortly, we are going to capture both positive and negative variations by squaring each of the deviations from the means. The squares of both +2.00 and −2.00 are the same: 4.00. The table below shows the squared deviations for each person on each variable. We've also totaled the squared deviations and calculated their means.

	Height	Weight	H-dev	W-dev	Sq H-dev	Sq W-dev
Eddy	68	144	+2.75	+7	7.5625	49
Mary	58	111	−7.25	−26	52.5625	676
Marge	67	137	+1.75	0	3.0625	0
Terry	66	153	+0.75	+16	0.5625	256
Albert	61	165	−4.25	+28	18.0625	784
Larry	74	166	+8.75	+29	76.5625	841
Heather	67	92	+1.75	−45	3.0625	2,025
Ruth	61	128	−4.25	−9	18.0625	81
Means =	65.25	137		Totals =	179.5000	4,712

Now, we're going to present a couple of steps that would require more complicated explanations than we want to subject you to in this book. So, if you can simply hear what we say without asking why, that's sufficient at this point. (If you are interested in learning the logic of the intervening steps, that's great. You should check discussions of variance and standard deviations in statistics textbooks.)

Dividing the sum of the squared deviations by one less than the number of cases ($N - 1$) yields a quantity statisticians call the *variance*. With a large number of cases, this quantity is close to the mean of the sum of squared deviations.

The variances in this case are 25.643 for height and 673.143 for weight. The square root of the variance is called the *standard deviation*. (Perhaps you are already familiar with these concepts, or perhaps you have heard the terms but haven't known what they mean.) Thus, the standard deviation for height is 5.063891; for weight, 25.94499.

Now, we are ready to put all these calculations to work for us. We are going to express all the individual deviations from mean height and mean weight in units equal to the standard deviations. For example, Eddy was +2.75 inches taller than the average. Eddy's new deviation from the mean height becomes +0.54 (+2.75/5.064). His deviation from the mean weight becomes +0.27 (+7/25.945).

Our purpose in these somewhat complex calculations is to standardize deviations from the means of the two variables, because the values on those variables are of very different scales. Whereas Eddy was 1.75 inches taller than the mean and 7 pounds heavier than the mean, we didn't have a way of knowing whether his height deviation was greater or lesser than his weight deviation. By dividing each deviation by the standard deviation for that variable, we can now see that Eddy's deviation on height is actually greater than his deviation in terms of weight. These new measures of deviation are called *z* **scores.** The table below presents each person's *z* score for both height and weight.

	Height	Weight	zheight	zweight	zcross
Eddy	68	144	.54	.27	.15
Mary	58	111	−1.43	−1.00	1.43
Marge	67	137	.35	.00	.00
Terry	66	153	.15	.62	.09
Albert	61	165	−.84	1.08	−.91
Larry	74	166	1.73	1.12	1.93
Heather	67	92	.35	−1.73	−.60
Ruth	61	128	−.84	−.35	.29
				Total	2.38

You'll notice that there is a final column of the table called "zcross." This is the result of multiplying each person's z score on height by the z score on weight. You'll notice we've begun rounding off the numbers to two decimal places. That level of precision is sufficient for present purposes.

Thanks to your perseverance, we are finally ready to calculate Pearson's r product-moment correlation. By now, it's pretty simple.

r = sum of (z scores for height × z scores for weight) divided by $N - 1$

In our example, this amounts to

r = 2.38 divided by 8 − 1 = .34.

There is no easy, commonsense way to represent the meaning of r. Technically, it has to do with the extent to which variations in one variable can explain variations in the other. In fact, if you square r, .12 in this case, it can be interpreted as follows: 12 percent of the variance in one variable can be accounted for by the variance in the other. Recall that the variance of a variable reflects the extent to which individual cases deviate from the mean value. Reverting to the logic of PRE, this means that knowing a person's height reduces by 12 percent the extent of our errors in guessing how far he or she is from the mean weight.

In large part, r's value comes with use. When you calculate correlations among several pairs of variables, the resulting rs will tell which pairs are more highly associated with one another than is true of other pairs.

Here's the really good news. Your reward for pressing through all the calculations above, in order to gain some understanding of what r represents, is that you'll never have to do it again. SPSS will do it for you.

Let's consider the possible relationship between two of the continuous variables in the data set: AGE and RINCOME. If you think about it, you should expect that people tend to earn more money as they grow older. So, let's check the correlation between age and respondents' incomes. (Note: RINCOME is the respondent's personal income; INCOME is family income.)

You might be reluctant to calculate the deviations, squared deviations, and so on for the 1,372 respondents in your data set (if not, you need a hobby), but computers thrive on such tasks.

Before we tell SPSS to take on the task of computing correlations for us, we need to do a little housekeeping. If you run a frequency distribution on RINCOME, you will see this:

RINCOME RESPONDENTS INCOME

		Frequency	Percent	Valid Percent	Cumulative Percent
Valid	1 LT $1000	15	1.0	1.5	1.5
	2 $1000 TO 2999	46	3.1	4.5	6.0
	3 $3000 TO 3999	17	1.1	1.7	7.7
	4 $4000 TO 4999	16	1.1	1.6	9.3
	5 $5000 TO 5999	23	1.5	2.3	11.5
	6 $6000 TO 6999	15	1.0	1.5	13.0
	7 $7000 TO 7999	19	1.3	1.9	14.9
	8 $8000 TO 9999	38	2.5	3.7	18.6
	9 $10000 - 14999	121	8.1	11.9	30.5
	10 $15000 - 19999	91	6.1	9.0	39.5
	11 $20000 - 24999	128	8.5	12.6	52.1
	12 $25000 OR MORE	487	32.5	47.9	100.0
	Total	1016	67.7	100.0	
Missing	0 NAP	420	28.0		
	13 REFUSED	64	4.3		
	Total	484	32.3		
Total		1500	100.0		

There is a problem in using the codes for RINCOME. The code categories are not equal in width. Code category 8 includes respondents whose incomes were only between $8,000 and $9,999, whereas code category 9 includes incomes between $10,000 and $14,999.

We can use Recode to improve on the coding scheme used for recording incomes. If we simply substitute the midpoints of the interval widths for the codes used in RINCOME, we can rid ourselves of the problems created by the interval widths not being equal. Code 23, $25,000 or more, has no upper limit. We just took a guess that the midpoint would be about $35,000. As SPSS commands, the recoding looks like this:

Transform → Recode → Into Different Variables

Old Variable → New Variable
RINCOME → RINCOME2
Old and New Values
1 → 500
2 → 2000
3 → 4000
4 → 4500
5 → 5500
6 → 6500
7 → 7500
8 → 9000
9 → 12500
10 → 17500
11 → 22500
12 → 35000

Notice that we did not specify new values for code 0 (refused) and code 13 (not applicable). SPSS assigns "SYSMIS," the system missing value, to any of the cases not specifically identified with an old value in the "Old and New Values" list. By ignoring RINCOME's codes 0 and 13, the corresponding cases in RINCOME2 are set to SYSMIS.

Here's what the recoded variable looks like.

RINCOME2

		Frequency	Percent	Valid Percent	Cumulative Percent
Valid	500.00	15	1.0	1.5	1.5
	2000.00	46	3.1	4.5	6.0
	4000.00	17	1.1	1.7	7.7
	4500.00	16	1.1	1.6	9.3
	5500.00	23	1.5	2.3	11.5
	6500.00	15	1.0	1.5	13.0
	7500.00	19	1.3	1.9	14.9
	9000.00	38	2.5	3.7	18.6
	12500.00	121	8.1	11.9	30.5
	17500.00	91	6.1	9.0	39.5
	22500.00	128	8.5	12.6	52.1
	35000.00	487	32.5	47.9	100.0
	Total	1016	67.7	100.0	
Missing	System Missing	484	32.3		
	Total	484	32.3		
Total		1500	100.0		

(The authors greatly appreciate the suggestion of this analysis by Professor Gilbert Klajman, Montclair State College.)

With the housekeeping out of the way, you need only move through this menu path to launch SPSS on the job of computing *r*:

Statistics → Correlate → Bivariate

This will bring you to the following window.

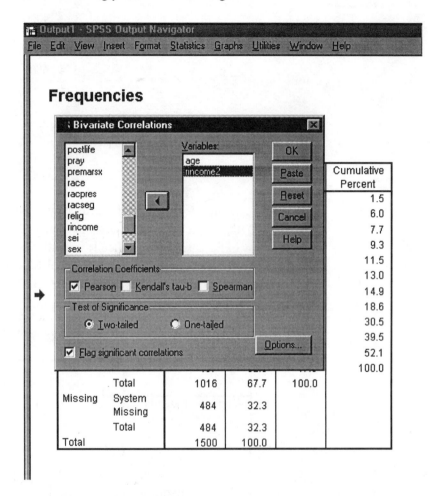

Transfer AGE and RINCOME2 to the "Variables" list. (Be sure to use AGE and not AGECAT, because we want the uncoded variable.)

Below the variable list, you'll see that we can choose from among three forms of correlation coefficients. Our discussion above has described Pearson's *r*, so click "Pearson." Then, click "OK."

Did you ever think about what we would do if we had an AGE for someone, but we did not know his or her RINCOME2? Because we have only one score, we would have to throw that person out of our analysis. But suppose we had three variables and we were missing a score on a case? Would we throw out just the pair that had a missing value, or would we through out the whole case?

SPSS lets us do it either way. Click on Options, and you will see that we can choose to delete cases either "pairwise" or "listwise." If we delete pairwise, we only discard a pair when either score is missing. But with listwise deletion, we discard the entire case if only one pair is missing.

We will use listwise deletion. With a sample as large as ours, it does not hurt to lose a few cases. However, if our sample were small, we would probably want to use pairwise deletion.

Now, click on the "OK"s, and you should be rewarded with the following in your output window.

Correlations

		AGE AGE OF RESPONDENT	RINCOME2
Pearson Correlation	AGE AGE OF RESPONDENT	1.000	.188**
	RINCOME2	.188**	1.000
Sig. (2-tailed)	AGE AGE OF RESPONDENT	.	.000
	RINCOME2	.000	.
N	AGE AGE OF RESPONDENT	1497	1013
	RINCOME2	1013	1016

**. Correlation is significant at the 0.01 level (2-tailed).

The Pearson's r product-moment correlation between AGE and RIN-COME is .188. Notice that the correlation between AGE and itself is perfect (1.000), which makes sense if you think about it.

You now know that the .188 is a measure of the extent to which deviations from the mean income can be accounted for by deviations from the mean of age. By squaring r, we learn that about 3.5 percent of the variance in income can be accounted for by how old people are.

We are going to ignore the references to "Significance" until the next chapter. This indicates the **statistical significance** of the association.

What else do you suppose might account for differences in income? If you think about it, you might decide that education is a possibility. Presumably, the more education you get, the more money you'll make. Your understanding of r through SPSS will let you check it out.

The Correlations command allows you to request several correlation coefficients at once. Go back to the Bivariate Correlations window and add EDUC to the list of variables being analyzed. Execute the command.

Here's what you should get in your output window.

Correlations

		AGE OF RESPONDENT	RINCOME2	HIGHEST YEAR OF SCHOOL COMPLETED
Pearson Correlation	AGE OF RESPONDENT	1.000	.188**	-.139**
	RINCOME2	.188**	1.000	.319**
	HIGHEST YEAR OF SCHOOL COMPLETED	-.139**	.319**	1.000
Sig. (2-tailed)	AGE OF RESPONDENT	.	.000	.000
	RINCOME2	.000	.	.000
	HIGHEST YEAR OF SCHOOL COMPLETED	.000	.000	.
N	AGE OF RESPONDENT	1497	1013	1491
	RINCOME2	1013	1016	1014
	HIGHEST YEAR OF SCHOOL COMPLETED	1491	1014	1494

**. Correlation is significant at the 0.01 level (2-tailed).

This new correlation matrix is a little more complex than the previous one. The fact that each variable correlates perfectly with itself should offer assurance that we are doing something right. The new matrix also tells us that there is a stronger correlation between EDUC and RINCOME: .319. Squaring the r tells us that about 10.2 percent of the variance in income can be accounted for by how much education people have.

We'll be using the Correlations command and related statistics as the book continues. In closing this discussion, we'd like you to recall that Pearson's r is appropriate only for continuous variables. It would not be appropriate in the analysis of nominal variables such as RELIG and MARITAL, for example. But what do you suppose would happen if we asked SPSS to correlate r for those two variables? Let's see.

Correlations

		RS RELIGIOUS PREFERENCE	MARITAL STATUS
Pearson Correlation	RS RELIGIOUS PREFERENCE	1.000	.097**
	MARITAL STATUS	.097**	1.000
Sig. (2-tailed)	RS RELIGIOUS PREFERENCE	.	.000
	MARITAL STATUS	.000	.
N	RS RELIGIOUS PREFERENCE	1497	1496
	MARITAL STATUS	1496	1499

**. Correlation is significant at the 0.01 level (2-tailed).

As you can see, SPSS has no way of knowing that we've asked it to do a stupid thing. It stupidly complies. It tells us there is a significant (see next chapter) relationship between a person's marital status and the religion he or she belongs to, whereas the correlation calculated here has no real meaning.

SPSS has been able to do the requested calculation because it stores "married" as 1 and "widowed" as 2 and stores "Protestant" as 1, "Catholic" as 2, and so on, but these numbers have no numerical meaning in this instance. Catholics are not "twice" Protestants, and widowed people are not "twice" married people.

Here's a thought experiment we hope will guard against this mistake: (a) Write down the telephone numbers of your five best friends; (b) add them up and calculate the "mean" telephone number; (c) call that number and see if an "average" friend answers. Or go to a Chinese restaurant with a group of friends and have everyone in your party select one dish by its number in the menu. Add all those numbers and calculate the mean. When the waiter comes, get several orders of the "average" dish and see if you have any friends left.

Pearson's *r* is designed for the analysis of relationships among continuous ratio variables. We have just entrusted you with a powerful weapon for understanding. Use it wisely. Remember: Statistics don't mislead—those who calculate statistics stupidly mislead.

14.4 Regression

The discussion of Pearson's *r* correlation coefficient opens the door for discussion of a related statistical technique: **regression.** When we looked at the scattergram of weight and height in the hypothetical example that introduced the discussion of correlation, you will recall that we tried to "see" a general pattern in the distribution of cases. Regression makes that attempt more concrete.

To begin, let's imagine an extremely simple example that relates the number of hours spent studying for an examination and the grades students got on the exam. Here are the data in a table:

Student	Hours	Grade
Fred	0	0
Mary	2	25
Sam	4	50
Edith	6	75
Earl	8	100

First question: Can you guess which of us prepared this example? Second question: Can you see a pattern in the data presented?

The pattern, pretty clearly, is this: The more you study, the better the grade you get. Let's look at these data in the form of a graph. (This is something you can do by hand, using graph paper.)

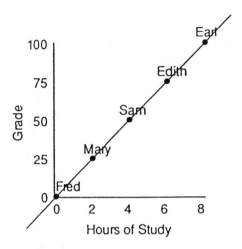

As you can see, the five people in this example fall along a straight line across the graph. This line is called the regression line. As you may recall from plain geometry, it is possible to represent a straight line on a graph in the form of an equation. In this case the equation would be as follows:

$$\text{Grade} = 12.5 \times \text{Hours}$$

To determine a person's grade, using this equation, you need only multiply the number of hours he or she studied by 12.5. Multiply Earl's 8 hours of study by 12.5 and you get his grade of 100. Multiply Edith's 6 hours by 12.5 and you get 75. Multiply Fred's 0 hours by 12.5 and, well, you know Fred.

Whereas correlation considers the symmetrical association between two variables, regression adds the notion of causal direction. One of the variables is the *dependent variable*—grades, in this example—and the other is the *independent variable* or cause—hours of study. Thus, the equation we just created is designed to predict a person's grade based on how many hours he or she studied. If we were to tell you that someone not included in these data studied 5 hours for the exam, you could predict that that person got a 62.5 on the exam (5×12.5).

If all social science analyses produced results as clear as these, you probably wouldn't need SPSS or a book like this one. In practice, however, the facts are usually a bit more complex, and SPSS is up to the challenge.

Given a set of data with an imperfect relationship between two variables, SPSS can discover the line that *comes closest* to passing through all the points on the graph. To understand the meaning of the notion of coming close, we need to recall the squared deviations found in our calculation of Pearson's *r*.

Suppose Sam had gotten 70 on the exam, for example. Here's what he would look like on the graph we just drew.

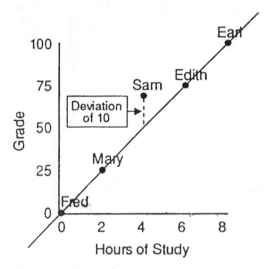

Notice that the improved Sam does not fall on the original regression line: His grade represents a deviation of 10 points. With a real set of data, most people fall to one side or the other of any line we might draw through the data. SPSS, however, is able to determine the line that would produce the smallest deviations overall—measured by squaring all the individual deviations and adding them up. This calculated regression line is sometimes called the **least-squares regression** line.

Requesting such an analysis from SPSS is fairly simple. To use this technique to real advantage, you will need more instruction than is appropriate for this book. However, we wanted to introduce you to regression because it is a popular technique among many social scientists.

To experiment with this technique, let's make use of a new variable: SEI. This variable rates the socioeconomic prestige of respondents' occupations on a scale from a low of 0 to a high of 100, based on other studies that have asked a sample from the general population to rate different occupations.

Here's how we would ask SPSS to find the equation that best represents the influence of EDUC on SEI. You should realize that there are a number of ways to request this information, but we'd suggest you do it as follows. (Just do it this way and nobody gets hurt, okay?)

Under Statistics, select Regression → Linear. Here's what you get.

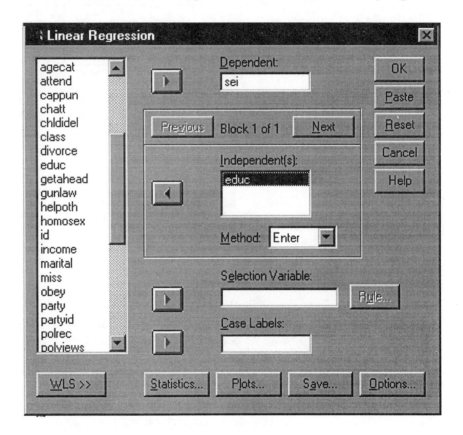

Select SEI as the dependent variable and EDUC as the independent variable. Click "OK," and SPSS is off and running. Here's the output you should get in response to this instruction.

Model Summary

Model	R	R Square	Adjusted R Square	Std. Error of the Estimate
1	.591a	.349	.348	15.347

a. Predictors: (Constant), EDUC HIGHEST YEAR OF SCHOOL COMPLETED

ANOVA[b]

Model		Sum of Squares	df	Mean Square	F	Sig.
1	Regression	179718.328	1	179718.328	763.061	.000a
	Residual	335620.319	1425	235.523		
	Total	515338.647	1426			

a. Predictors: (Constant), EDUC HIGHEST YEAR OF SCHOOL COMPLETED

b. Dependent Variable: SEI RESPONDENT SOCIOECONOMIC INDEX

Coefficients[a]

Model		Unstandardized Coefficients		Standardized Coefficients	t	Sig.
		B	Std. Error	Beta		
1	(Constant)	-4.321	1.969		-2.195	.028
	EDUC HIGHEST YEAR OF SCHOOL COMPLETED	3.917	.142	.591	27.624	.000

a. Dependent Variable: SEI RESPONDENT SOCIOECONOMIC INDEX

The key information we are looking for is contained in the final screen of information: the **intercept** (–4.321) and the **slope** (3.917). These are the data we need to complete our regression equation. Use them as follows:

$$SEI = -4.321 + (EDUC \times 3.917).$$

This means that we would predict the occupation prestige ranking of a high school graduate (12 years of schooling) as follows:

$$SEI = -4.321 + (12 \times 3.917) = 42.683.$$

We would predict the occupational prestige of a college graduate (16 years of schooling), on the other hand, as

$$SEI = -4.321 + (16 \times 3.917) = 58.351.$$

That's enough fun for now. We'll return to regression later, when we discuss multivariate analysis in Chapter 17.

14.5 Summary

In this chapter, we've seen a number of statistical techniques that can be used to summarize the degree of relationship or association between two variables. We've seen that the appropriate technique depends on the level of measurement represented by the variables involved. Lambda is appropriate for nominal variables, gamma for ordinal variables, and Pearson's r product-moment correlation and regression for ratio variables.

We realize that you may have had trouble knowing how to respond to the results of these calculations. How do you decide, for example, if a gamma of .25 is high or low? Should you get excited about it or yawn and continue looking? The following chapter on statistical significance offers one basis for making such decisions.

Chapter 15 **Tests of Significance**

Thus far, in Chapters 11 through 14, we've been looking at the relationships between pairs of variables. In all that, you may have been frustrated over the ambiguity as to what constitutes a "strong" or a "weak" relationship. Ultimately, there is no absolute answer to this question. The strength or significance of a relationship between two variables depends on many things.

If you are trying to account for differences among people on some variable, such as prejudice, the explanatory power of one variable, such as education, needs to be contrasted with the explanatory power of other variables. So you might be interested in knowing whether education, political affiliation, or region of upbringing has the greatest impact on a person's prejudice.

Sometimes, the importance of a relationship is based on practical policy implications. Thus, the impact of some variable in explaining (and potentially reducing) auto theft rates, for example, might be converted to a matter of dollars. Other relationships might be expressed in terms of lives saved, students graduating from college, and so forth.

In this chapter, we're going to address another standard for judging the significance of relationships among variables—one that is commonly used by social scientists. Whenever analyses are based on samples selected from a population rather than on data collected from everyone in that population, there is always the possibility that what we learn from the samples may not truly reflect the whole population. Thus, we might discover that women are more religious than men in a sample, but that could be simply an artifact of our sample: We happened to pick too many religious women and/or too few religious men.

Social scientists often test the *statistical significance* of relationships discovered among variables. Although this does not constitute a direct measure of the *strength* of a relationship, it tells us the likelihood that the observed relationship could have resulted from the vagaries of probability sampling, which we call **sampling error.** These tests relate to the strength of relationships, in that the stronger an observed relationship, the less likely it is that it could be the result of sampling error. Correspondingly, it is more likely that the observed relationship represents something that exists in the population as a whole.

15.1 Chi-Square

To learn the logic of statistical significance, let's begin with a measure, **chi-square,** that is based on the kinds of cross-tabulations we've been examining in previous chapters. For a concrete example, let's return to one of the tables that examines the relationship between religion and abortion attitudes.

Let's reexamine the relationship between religious affiliation and unconditional support for abortion. For present purposes, we'll omit the request for percentages in the cells of the table and let SPSS give us the raw numbers.

Do a Crosstab of ABANY (row variable) and RELIG (column variable).

ABANY ABORTION IF WOMAN WANTS FOR ANY REASON * RELIG RS RELIGIOUS PREFERENCE Crosstabulation

| | | | \multicolumn{5}{c}{RELIG RS RELIGIOUS PREFERENCE} | |
			1 PROTESTANT	2 CATHOLIC	3 JEWISH	4 NONE	5 OTHER	Total
ABANY ABORTION IF WOMAN WANTS FOR ANY REASON	1 Favor	Count	223	103	22	75	25	448
		% within RELIG RS RELIGIOUS PREFERENCE	44.4%	42.0%	84.6%	63.0%	62.5%	48.1%
	2 Oppose	Count	279	142	4	44	15	484
		% within RELIG RS RELIGIOUS PREFERENCE	55.6%	58.0%	15.4%	37.0%	37.5%	51.9%
Total		Count	502	245	26	119	40	932
		% within RELIG RS RELIGIOUS PREFERENCE	100.0%	100.0%	100.0%	100.0%	100.0%	100.0%

The question this table is designed to answer is whether a person's religious affiliation affects his or her attitude toward abortion. You'll recall that we concluded it does: Catholics and Protestants are the most opposed to abortion, and Jews and those with no religion are the most supportive. The question we now confront is whether the observed differences point to some genuine pattern in the U.S. population at large or whether they result from a quirk of sampling.

To assess the observed relationship, we are going to begin by asking what we should have expected to find if there were no relationship between religious affiliation and abortion attitudes. An important part of the answer lies in the rightmost column in the preceding table. It indicates that 48.1 percent of the whole sample supported a woman's unconditional right to an abortion, and 51.9 percent did not.

If there were no relationship between religious affiliation and abortion attitudes, we should expect to find 48.1 percent of the Protestants approving, 48.1 percent of the Catholics approving, 48.1 percent of the Jews approving, and so forth. But we recall that the earlier results did not match this perfect model of no relationship, so the question is whether the disparity between the model and our observations would fall within the normal degree of sampling error.

To measure the extent of the disparity between the model and what's been observed, we need to calculate the number of cases we'd expect in each cell of the table if there were no relationship. The table below shows how to calculate the expected cell frequencies.

ABANY	Protestant	Catholic	Jewish	None	Other
Approve	502	245	26	119	40
	× .481	× .481	× .481	× .481	× .481
Disapprove	502	245	26	119	40
	× .519	× .519	× .519	× .519	× .519

If there were no relationship between religious affiliation and abortion attitudes, we would expect 48.1 percent of the 502 Protestants ($502 \times .481 = 241$) to approve and 51.9 percent of the 502 Protestants ($502 \times .519 = 261$) to disapprove. If you continue this series of calculations, you should arrive at the following set of expected cell frequencies.

ABANY	Protestant	Catholic	Jewish	None	Other
Approve	241	118	13	57	19
Disapprove	261	127	14	62	21

The next step in calculating chi-square is to calculate the difference between expected and observed values in each cell of the table. For example, if religion had no affect on abortion, we would have expected to find 241 Protestants approving; in fact, we observed only 223. Thus, the discrepancy in that cell is –18. The discrepancy for Catholics approving is –15 (observed – expected = 103 – 118). The table below shows the discrepancies for each cell.

ABANY	Protestant	Catholic	Jewish	None	Other
Approve	–18	–15	9	18	4
Disapprove	7	20	–10	–62	–21

Finally, for each cell, we square the discrepancy and divide it by the expected cell frequency. For the Protestants approving of abortion, then, the squared discrepancy is 324 (–18 × –18). Dividing it by the expected frequency of 241 yields 1.34 (rounded off a bit). When we repeat this for each cell, we get the following results.

ABANY	Protestant	Catholic	Jewish	None	Other
Approve	1.34	1.91	6.23	5.68	1.89
Disapprove	1.24	1.77	7.14	5.22	1.71

Chi-square is the sum of all these latest cell figures: 34.13. We have calculated a summary measure of the discrepancy between what we would have expected to observe if religion did not affect abortion and what we actually observed. Now, the only remaining question is whether that resulting number should be regarded as large or small. Statisticians often speak of the "goodness of fit" in this context: How well do the observed data fit a model of two variables being unrelated to each other?

The answer to this latest question takes the form of a probability: the probability that a chi-square this large could occur as a result of sampling error. A probability of .05 in this context would mean that it should happen five times in 100 samples. A probability of .001 would mean it should happen only one time in 1,000 samples.

To evaluate our chi-square of 34.13, we would need to look it up in a table of chi-square values, which you'll find in the back of any statistics textbook. Such tables have several columns marked by different probabilities (e.g., .30, .20, .10, .05, .01, .001). The tables also have several rows representing different **degrees of freedom** (df).

If you think about it, you'll probably see that the larger and more complex a table is, the greater the likelihood that there will be discrepancies from the perfect model of expected frequencies. We take account of this by one final calculation.

Degrees of freedom are calculated from the data table as (rows − 1) × (columns − 1). In our table, there are five columns and two rows, giving us (4 × 1) degrees of freedom. Thus, we would look across the fourth row in the table of chi-square values, which would look, in part, like this:

df	.05	.01	.001
4	9.488	13.277	18.465

These numbers tell us that a chi-square as high as 9.488 from a table like ours would occur only 5 times in 100 samples if there were no relationship between religious affiliation and abortion attitudes among the whole U.S. population. A chi-square as high as 13.277 would happen only once in 100 samples, and a chi-square as high as 18.465 would only happen once in 1,000.

Thus, we conclude that our chi-square of 34.13 could result from sampling error less than once in 1,000 samples. This is often abbreviated as "$p < .001$": The probability is less than 1 in 1,000.

They have no magical meaning, but the .05 and .001 levels of significance are often used by social scientists as a convention for concluding that an observed relationship reflects a similar relationship in the population rather than arising from sampling error. Obviously, if a relationship is significant at the .001 level, we are more confident of our conclusion than if it is significant only at the .05 level.

There you have it: far more than you ever thought you'd want to know about chi-square. By sticking it out and coming to grasp the logical meaning of this statistical calculation, you've earned a reward.

Rather than going through all the preceding calculations, we could have simply modified our Crosstabs request slightly. In the Crosstabs window, click Statistics and select "Chi-Square" in the upper-left corner of the Statistics window. Then run the Crosstab request.

Chi-Square Tests

	Value	df	Asymp. Sig. (2-sided)
Pearson Chi-Square	34.153[a]	4	.000
Likelihood Ratio	35.519	4	.000
Linear-by-Linear Association	19.328	1	.000
N of Valid Cases	932		

a. 0 cells (.0%) have expected count less than 5. The minimum expected count is 12.50.

We are interested primarily in the first row of figures in this report. Notice that the 35.153 value of chi-square is slightly different from our hand calculation. This is because of our rounding off in our cell calculations, and it shouldn't worry you. Notice that we're told that there are four degrees of freedom. Finally, SPSS has calculated the probability of getting a chi-square this high with four degrees of freedom and has run out of space after three zeros to the right of the decimal point. Thus, the probability is far less than .001, as we determined by checking a table of chi-square values.

The reference to a "minimum expected frequency" of 12.50 is worth noting. Because the calculation of chi-square involves divisions by expected cell frequencies, it can be greatly inflated if any of them are very small. By convention, adjustments to chi-square should be made if more than 20 percent of the expected cell frequencies are below 5. You should check a statistics text if you want to know more about this.

While it is fresh in your mind, why don't you have SPSS calculate some more chi-squares for you? You may recall that sex had little impact on abortion attitudes. Why don't you see what the chi-square is?

To experiment more with chi-square, you might rerun some of the other tables relating various demographic variables to abortion attitudes. Notice how chi-square offers a basis for comparing the relative importance of different variables in determining attitudes on this controversial topic.

It bears repeating here that tests of significance are different from measures of association, although they are related to one another. The stronger an association between two variables, the more likely it is that the association will be judged statistically significant, that is, not a simple product of sampling error. Other factors also affect statistical significance, however. As we've already mentioned, the number of degrees of freedom in a table is relevant. So is the size of the sample: The larger the sample, the more likely it is that an association will be judged significant.

Researchers often distinguish between *statistical* significance (examined in this section) and *substantive* significance. The latter refers to the importance of an association, and it can't be determined by empirical analysis alone. As we suggested at the outset of this chapter, substantive significance depends on practical and theoretical factors. All this notwithstanding, social researchers often find statistical significance a useful device in gauging associations.

Whereas chi-square operates on the logic of the contingency table, which you've grown accustomed to through the Crosstabs procedure, we're going to turn next to a test of significance based on means.

15.2 *t* Tests

Who do you suppose lives longer, men or women? Whichever group lives longer should, as a result, have a higher average age at any given time. Regardless of whether you know the answer to this question for the U.S. population as a whole, let's see if our GSS data can shed some light on the issue.

We could find the average ages of men and women in our GSS sample with the simple command path:

Statistics → Compare Means → Means

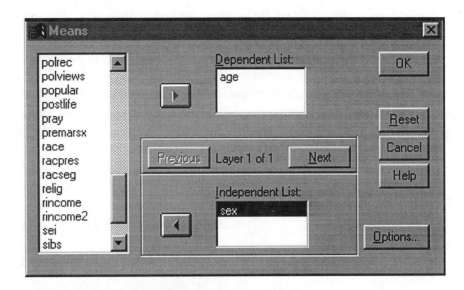

Because age is the characteristic on which we want to compare men and women, AGE is the dependent variable; SEX the independent. Transfer those variables to the appropriate fields in the window. Then click "OK."

Report

AGE AGE OF RESPONDENT

1 MALE	Mean	43.81
	N	677
	Std. Deviation	16.12
2 FEMALE	Mean	45.16
	N	820
	Std. Deviation	17.13
Total	Mean	44.55
	N	1497
	Std. Deviation	16.69

As you can see, our sample reflects the general population in that women have a mean age of 45.16, compared with men's 43.81 mean age. The task facing us now parallels the one pursued in the discussion of chi-square. Does the observed difference reflect a pattern that exists in the whole population, or is it simply a result of a sampling procedure that happened to get too many old women and/or too many young men this time?

Would another sample indicate that men are older than women or that there is no difference?

Given that we've moved very deliberately through the logic and calculations of chi-square, we are going to avoid such details in the present discussion. The *t* test examines the distribution of values on one variable (age) among different groups (men and women) and calculates the probability that the observed difference in means results from sampling error alone.

To request a *t* test from SPSS to examine the relationship between AGE and SEX, you enter the following command path:

Statistics → Compare Means → Independent-Samples T Test

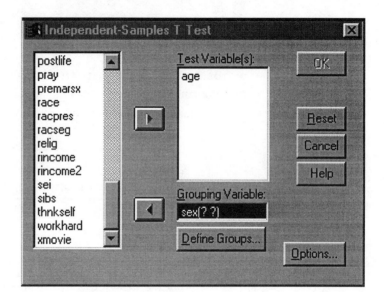

In this window, we want to enter AGE as the "Test Variable" and SEX as the "Grouping Variable." This means that SPSS will group respondents by sex and then examine and compare the mean ages of the two gender groups.

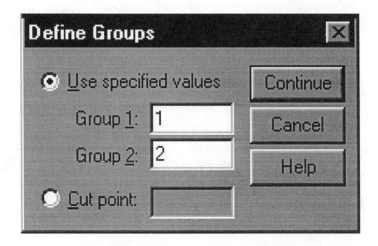

Notice than when you enter the "Grouping Variable," SPSS puts "SEX[??]" in that field. Although the comparison groups are obvious in the case of SEX, it might not be so obvious with other variables—so SPSS wants some guidance. Click Define Groups.

Type 1 into "Group 1" and 2 into "Group 2." Click Continue, then "OK."

Group Statistics

	SEX RESPONDENTS	N	Mean	Std. Deviation	Std. Error Mean
AGE AGE OF RESPONDENT	1 MALE	677	43.81	16.12	.62
	2 FEMALE	820	45.16	17.13	.60

Independent Samples Test

		Levene's Test for Equality of Variances		t-test for Equality of Means						
									95% Confidence Interval of the Difference	
		F	Sig.	t	df	Sig. (2-tailed)	Mean Difference	Std. Error Difference	Lower	Upper
AGE	Equal variances assumed	3.436	.064	-1.561	1495	.119	-1.35	.87	-3.05	.35
	Equal variances not assumed			-1.570	1469.558	.117	-1.35	.86	-3.04	.34

The program gives you much more information than you need for present purposes, so let's identify the key elements. Some of the information is a repeat of what we got earlier from the Means command: means, standard deviations, and standard errors for men and women.

The additional value we want from this table is the .119 under the heading "Sig. (2-tailed)" and in the row designated "Equal" variances. For our purposes, this is the result that we will use from the table.

As you will anticipate, .119 in this context indicates a probability of 119 in 1,000. The "2-tailed" notation requires just a little more explanation.

In our sample, the average age for women is 1.35 years higher than for men. SPSS has calculated that about 119 times in 1,000 samples, sampling error might produce a difference this great in either direction. That is, if the average age of men and the average age of women in the population were exactly the same, and we were to select 1,000 samples like this one, we could expect 119 of those samples to show women at least 1.35 years older than men or men as much as 1.35 years older than women.

When you don't have theoretical reasons to anticipate a particular relationship, it is appropriate for you to use the "2-tailed" probability in evaluating differences in means like these. In some cases—when you have deduced specific expectations from a theory, for example—you might come to the data analysis with a hypothesis that "women are older than men." In such a case, it might be more appropriate to note that there is a probability of 60 in 1,000 ($p = .06$) that sampling error would have resulted in women being as much as 1.35 years older than men. For our purposes in this book, however, we'll stick with the 2-tailed test.

Some of the variables in your GSS data set allow you to explore this issue further. For example, it would be reasonable for better-educated workers to earn more than poorly educated workers. So, if the men in our sample have more education than the women, that might explain the difference in pay. Let's see.

Return to the T Test window and substitute EDUC for AGE as the "Test Variable." Leave "SEX[1 2]" as the "Grouping Variable." Run the new t test.

Group Statistics

	SEX RESPONDENTS	N	Mean	Std. Deviation	Std. Error Mean
EDUC HIGHEST YEAR OF SCHOOL COMPLETED	1 MALE	675	13.73	2.95	.11
	2 FEMALE	819	13.27	2.88	.10

Independent Samples Test

		Levene's Test for Equality of Variances		t-test for Equality of Means						
									95% Confidence Interval of the Difference	
		F	Sig.	t	df	Sig. (2-tailed)	Mean Difference	Std. Error Difference	Lower	Upper
EDUC	Equal variances assumed	2.397	.122	3.011	1492	.003	.46	.15	.16	.75
	Equal variances not assumed			3.004	1424.949	.003	.46	.15	.16	.75

What conclusion do you draw from these latest results? Notice first that the men and women in our sample have very similar mean number of years of education (men = 13.73, women = 13.27). Even though the difference is very small, it is a difference we could expect to find in only 3 of 1,000 samples. As small as it is, the difference probably exists in the population.

With such a small difference between men's and women's educational backgrounds, it is unlikely that education can be used as a "legitimate reason" for women earning less than men. That's not to say that there aren't other legitimate reasons that may account for the difference in pay.

For instance, it is often argued that women tend to concentrate in less prestigious jobs than men: nurses rather than doctors, secretaries rather than executives, teachers rather than principals. Leaving aside the reasons for such occupational differences, that might account for the differences in pay. As you may recall, your GSS data contain a measure of socioeconomic status (SEI). We used that variable in our experimentation with Correlations. Let's see if the women in our sample have lower-status jobs, on average, than the men.

Go back to the T Test window and replace EDUC with SEI. Run the procedure, and you should get the following result.

Group Statistics

	SEX RESPONDENTS SEX	N	Mean	Std. Deviation	Std. Error Mean
SEI RESPONDENT SOCIOECONOMIC INDEX	1 MALE	665	50.455	19.630	.761
	2 FEMALE	767	47.398	18.367	.663

Independent Samples Test

		Levene's Test for Equality of Variances		t-test for Equality of Means						95% Confidence Interval of the Mean	
		F	Sig.	t	df	Sig. (2-tailed)	Mean Difference	Std. Error Difference		Lower	Upper
SEI RESPONDENT SOCIOECONOMIC INDEX	Equal variances assumed	2.691	.101	3.042	1430	.002	3.057	1.005		1.086	5.028
	Equal variances not assumed			3.028	1370.234	.003	3.057	1.010		1.077	5.038

The mean difference in occupational prestige ratings of men and women is 3.1 on a scale from 0 to 100. SPSS tells us that such a difference could be expected just as a consequence of sampling error in only about three samples in 1,000 ($p = .003$). Although it is statistically significant, such a small difference may have little social significance.

To pursue this line of inquiry further, you will need additional analytic skills, which will be covered shortly in the discussion of multivariate analysis.

If you want to experiment more with the t test, you might substitute RACE for SEX in the commands we've been sending to SPSS. If you do that, realize that you have asked SPSS to consider only code categories 1 and 2 on SEX; applied to RACE, that will limit the comparison to whites and blacks, omitting the "other" category.

15.3 Analysis of Variance

The t test is limited to the comparison of two groups at a time. If we wanted to compare the levels of education of different religious groups, we'd have to compare Protestants and Catholics, Protestants and Jews, Catholics and Jews, and so forth. And if some of the comparisons found significant differences and other comparisons did not, we'd be hard-pressed to reach an overall conclusion about the nature of the relationship between the two variables.

The **analysis of variance** (ANOVA) is a technique that resolves the shortcoming of the *t* test. It examines the means of subgroups in the sample and analyzes the variances as well. That is, it examines more than whether the actual values are clustered around the mean or spread out from it.

If we were to ask ANOVA to examine the relationship between RELIG and EDUC, it would determine the mean years of education for each of the different religious groups, noting how they differed from one another. Those "between-group" differences would be compared with the "within-group" differences (variance): how much Protestants differed among themselves, for example. Both sets of comparisons are reconciled by ANOVA to calculate the likelihood that the observed differences are merely the result of sampling error.

To get a clearer picture of ANOVA, ask SPSS to perform the analysis we've been discussing. You can probably figure out how to do that, but here's a hint.

Statistics → General Linear Model → Simple Factorial

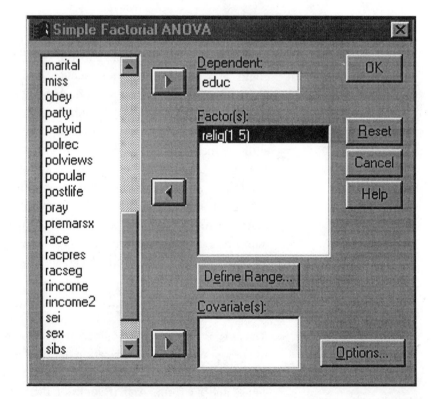

Put EDUC into the "Dependent" field and RELIG in the "Factors" field. As with the *t* test, SPSS wants us to define the values to be considered. Unlike the *t* test, however, ANOVA only wants a *range* of values. In this case, we want everything from 1 (Protestant) to 5 (Other). So enter 1 as the minimum and 5 as the maximum.

When you return to the output, you'll see that the values of the factor have been put in place: RELIG[15]. Launch the procedure.

ANOVA[a,b]

			Unique Method				
			Sum of Squares	df	Mean Square	F	Sig.
EDUC HIGHEST YEAR OF SCHOOL COMPLETED	Main Effects	RELIG RS RELIGIOUS PREFERENCE	240.256	4	60.064	7.168	.000
	Model		240.256	4	60.064	7.168	.000
	Residual		12452.124	1486	8.380		
	Total		12692.380	1490	8.518		

a. EDUC HIGHEST YEAR OF SCHOOL COMPLETED by RELIG RS RELIGIOUS PREFERENCE

b. All effects entered simultaneously

Here's the SPSS report on the analysis. Again, we've gotten more information than we want for our present purposes.

For our immediate purposes, let's look simply at the row titled "Model." This refers to the amount of variance in EDUC that can be explained by variations in RELIG. Because our present purpose is to learn about tests of statistical significance, let's move across the row to the statistical significance of the explained variance. If religion and education were unrelated to each other in the population, we might expect samples that would generate this amount of explained variance less than once in 1,000 samples.

Perhaps you will find it useful to think of ANOVA as something like a statistical broom. We began by noting a lot of variance in educational levels of our respondents; imagine people's educations spread all over the place. In an attempt to find explanatory patterns in that variance, we use ANOVA to sweep the respondents into subgroups based on religious affiliation (stay with us on this). The questions are whether variations in education are substantially less within each of the piles than we originally observed in the whole sample, and whether the mean years of education in each of the subgroups are quite different from one another. Imagine a set of tidy piles that is quite distant from one another. ANOVA provides a statistical test of this imagery.

It is also possible for ANOVA to consider two independent variables, but that goes beyond the scope of this book. We have introduced you to ANOVA because we feel it is useful, and we wanted to open up for you the possibility of your using this popular technique; however, you will need more specialized training in the performance of analysis of variance to use it effectively.

15.4 Summary

This chapter has taken on the difficult question of whether the observed relationship between two variables is important or not. It is natural that you would want to know whether and when you have discovered something worth writing home about. No one wants to shout, "Look what I've discovered!" and have others say, "That's no big thing."

Ultimately, there is no simple test of the substantive significance of a relationship between variables. If we found that women earn less than men, who can say if that amounts to a lot less or just a little bit less? In a more precise study, we could calculate exactly how much less in dollars, but we would still not be in a position to say absolutely whether that amount was a lot or a little. If women made a dollar a year less than men on the average, we'd all probably agree that was not an important difference. If men earned a hundred times as much as women, on the other hand, we'd probably all agree that was a big difference. However, few of the differences we discover in social science research are that dramatic.

In this chapter, we've examined a very specific approach that social scientists often take in addressing the issue of significance. As distinct from notions of *substantive* significance, we have examined *statistical* significance. In each of the measures we've examined—chi-square, *t* test, and analysis of variance—we've asked how likely it would be that sampling error could produce the observed relationship if there were actually no relationship in the population from which the sample was drawn.

This assumption of "no relationship" is sometimes referred to as the **null hypothesis.** The tests of significance we've examined all deal with the probability that the null hypothesis is correct. If the probability is relatively high, we conclude that there is no relationship between the two variables under study in the whole population. If the probability is small that the null hypothesis could be true, then we conclude that the observed relationship reflects a genuine pattern in the population.

Chapter 16 Suggestions for Further Bivariate Analyses

By now, you've amassed a powerful set of analytic tools. In a world where people make casual assertions about sociological topics, you're now in a position to determine the facts. You can determine how the U.S. population feels about a variety of topics, and with your new bivariate skills, you can begin to explain why they feel as they do.

In this chapter, we are going to suggest some additional analyses you might undertake. They will allow you to perfect your skills, and these suggestions open the possibility of your thinking more for yourself. What are you interested in? What would you like to learn more about? Here are some possibilities.

In Chapter 10, we suggested some topics you might pursue with the techniques of univariate analysis. Let's start by returning to those topics.

16.1 Desired Family Size

CHLDIDEL asked respondents what they considered the ideal number of children for a family. A little more than half of the respondents said that two or fewer was best. Because that is also the number of children that would represent population stabilization, you might want to begin by recoding this variable so as to create two response categories. If you have difficulty with this one, we give you a healthy hint in Appendix D.

Once you've gotten CHLDIDEL into a more manageable form, you can start looking for the causes of differences. As a start, you might want to see if the variables we examined in relation to abortion attitudes are related to opinions about ideal family size.

We found that gender was basically unrelated to abortion attitudes; how about ideal family size? Do you think men and women differ in their images of the perfect family? If you think so, which direction do you think that difference goes?

How about age? Support for small families is a fairly recent development in the United States, against a historical backdrop of large farm families. Does this mean that young people would be more supportive of small families than older people? You find out.

The better-educated members of the population are generally more concerned about environmental issues. Are they also more committed to small families?

Religion and race are good candidates for shaping opinions about ideal family size, because the nature of family life is often central to subcultural patterns. We saw that Catholics and Protestants were resistant to abortion; how do they feel about limiting family size in general? You can know the answer in a matter of minutes.

Several family variables may very well relate to attitudes toward ideal family size. Marital status and whether respondents have ever been divorced might be relevant. Can you see why that would be worth exploring? What would you hypothesize?

Of possibly direct relevance, the data set contains SIBS (the number of brothers and sisters the respondent has). You might want to see if the experience of having brothers and sisters has any impact on opinions about what's best in family size.

If you would like to explore the issue of ideal family size further, you might want to look into Judith Blake's *Family Size and Achievement* (1989).

16.2 Child Training

In Chapter 10, we took an initial look at different opinions about what was important in the development of children. The key variables were as follows:

OBEY	to obey
POPULAR	to be well-liked or popular
THNKSELF	to think for himself or herself
WORKHARD	to work hard
HELPOTH	to help others when they need help

If you examined these variables, you discovered some real differences in how people want their children to turn out. Now, let's see what causes those differences, because opinions on this topic can reflect some more general attitudes and worldviews.

Once again, such demographic variables as sex, age, race, and religion might make a difference. OBEY, for example, reflects a certain authoritarian leaning. Perhaps it is related to political variables, such as PARTYID and POLVIEWS; perhaps not. There's only one way to find out.

HELPOTH measures an altruistic dimension. That's something religions often encourage. Maybe there's a relation between this variable and some of the religion variables.

Also consider the variable THNKSELF, which values children's learning to think for themselves. What would you expect to influence this?

Education, perhaps? How about age and sex? Do you think older respondents would be relatively cool to children thinking for themselves? Would men or women be more supportive? Don't rule out religious and political variables. Some of these results are likely to confirm your expectations; some are not.

When it comes to the value of children thinking for themselves, you may find some of the other attitudinal variables in the GSS data set worth looking at. Consider those who have told us they are permissive on premarital sex and homosexuality. Do you think they would be more or less likely to value children's learning to think for themselves?

There are any number of directions you might want to pursue in looking for the causes of different attitudes toward the qualities most valued for children. (For more ideas in this arena, you might want to look at Alwin 1989.)

16.3 Attitudes about Sexual Behavior

You might want to focus on the three sexual variables per se. What do you suppose would cause differences of opinion regarding premarital sexual relations and homosexuality? What do you suppose determines who goes to X-rated movies? You have the ability and the tools to find out for yourself.

Near the end of the movie *Casablanca,* the police chief instructs his officers to "round up the usual suspects." You might do well to round up the usual demographic variables as a way of beginning your examination of sexual attitudes: age, gender, race, religion, education, social class, and marital status, for example.

Before examining each of these relationships, take some time to think about any links you might logically expect. Should men or women be more permissive about homosexuality? Should married, single, or divorced people be more supportive of premarital sex? How do you expect young and old people to differ?

As you investigate these attitudes, be careful about assuming that the three items are just different dimensions of the same orientation. The kinds of people who are permissive about premarital sex are not necessarily the same ones who are permissive about homosexuality.

16.4 Prejudice

Two items in your GSS data set address racial prejudice about African Americans. RACPRES asks respondents if they would vote for an African American candidate for president. RACSEG asks whether whites should have the right to live in segregated neighborhoods.

Certainly, RACE is the most obvious variable to examine, and you probably won't be surprised at what you find. Don't stop there, however. There are other variables that provide even more dramatic relationships.

Education, politics, and social class offer fruitful avenues for understanding the roots of attitudes on these variables. You may be surprised by the impact of religious variables.

As a different approach, you might look at the opinion that homosexuality is morally wrong as is prejudice against gays and lesbians. It's worth checking whether responses to that item are related to prejudice against African Americans.

16.5 Summary

The preceding suggestions should be enough to keep you busy, but you shouldn't feel limited by them. The most fruitful guides to your analyses should be your own personal interests. Which of the topics in the GSS data set most interest or concern you? Now you have a chance to learn something about them on your own. You don't have to settle for polemical statements about "the way things are." You now have the tools you need to find out for yourself.

In examining these bivariate relationships, you may want to begin with Crosstabs, because that technique gives you the most detailed view of the data. At the same time, you should use this exercise as an opportunity to experiment with the other bivariate techniques we've examined. Try chi-squares where appropriate, for example. As you find interesting relationships between variables, you may want to test their statistical significance, to get another window on what they mean.

What you've learned so far may be sufficient for most of your day-to-day curiosities. Now you can learn what public opinion really is on a given topic, and you can determine what kinds of people hold differing views on that topic. In the remaining chapters of this book, however, we are going to show you an approach to understanding that goes much deeper. As we introduce you to multivariate analysis, you're going to have an opportunity to sample a more complex mode of understanding than most people are even aware of.

Part IV Multivariate Analysis

Now that you've mastered the logic and techniques of bivariate analysis, we are going to take you one step further: to the examination of three or more variables at a time, known as **multivariate analysis.** In Chapter 17, we'll delve more deeply into religious orientations to gain a more comprehensive understanding of this variable. Chapter 18 will pick up some loose threads of our bivariate analysis and pursue them further with our new analytic capability.

In Chapter 19, we will set as our purpose the prediction of attitudes toward abortion. We'll progress, step by step, through a number of variables previously found to have an impact on abortion attitudes, and we'll accumulate them in a composite measure that will offer a powerful predictor of opinions.

Finally, Chapter 20 launches you into uncharted areas of social research, which you should now be empowered to chart for yourself.

Chapter 17 Examining Religiosity in Greater Depth

Multivariate analysis is the simultaneous analysis of three or more variables. It is the next step beyond bivariate (two-variable) analysis. In the next few chapters, we are going to see that using more than one independent variable in predicting some dependent variable can yield a variety of outcomes. We are going to start with the simplest of outcomes: multiple causation.

17.1 Age, Sex, and Religiosity

In Chapter 11, we discussed several variables that might affect the levels of respondents' religiosity. Women, we found, were more religious than men. Old people were more religious than young people.

It is often the case with social phenomena that people's attitudes and behaviors are affected by more than one factor. It is the task of the social scientist, then, to discover all those factors that influence the dependent variable under question and discover how those factors work together to produce a result. If both age and gender affect religiosity independently, perhaps a combination of the two would predict even better.

To begin our multivariate analysis, let's see how well we can predict religiosity if we consider AGE and SEX simultaneously. Does religiosity increase with age among both men and women separately? Moreover, do the two variables have a cumulative effect on religiosity? That is, are old women the most religious and young men the least religious?

To begin our exploration of this topic, let's use CHATT as the dependent variable; that is, let's see how well we can predict or explain attendance at worship services. To examine the simultaneous impact of AGECAT and SEX on CHATT, simply make an additional modification to the now-familiar Crosstabs command.

- Enter CHATT as the row variable
- Enter AGECAT as the column variable

Now select SEX in the list of variables. Notice that the arrows activated would let you transfer SEX as a row variable or a column variable—or you can transfer it to the third field, near the bottom of the window. Do that.

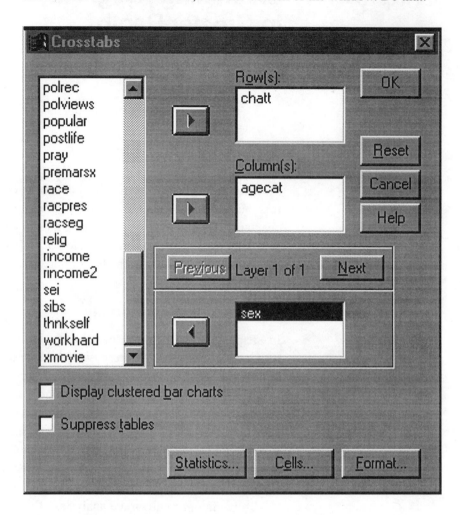

Check that the cells are set to be percentaged by columns, and then execute the command.

This command produces more than one table. We have asked SPSS to examine the impact of AGECAT on CHATT separately for men and women. Thus, we are rewarded with the following three-variable cross-tabulation.

CHATT Recoded Church Attendance * AGECAT Recoded Age Categories * SEX RESPONDENTS SEX Crosstabulation

% within AGECAT Recoded Age Categories

SEX RESPONDENTS SEX			AGECAT Recoded Age Categories				Total
			1 Under 21	2 21-39	3 40-64	4 65 and older	
1 MALE	CHATT Recoded Church Attendance	1 About weekly	13.6%	21.6%	29.4%	37.8%	26.7%
		2 About monthly	18.2%	16.5%	13.5%	6.1%	14.0%
		3 Seldom	50.0%	45.4%	40.4%	40.2%	42.8%
		4 Never	18.2%	16.5%	16.7%	15.9%	16.5%
	Total		100.0%	100.0%	100.0%	100.0%	100.0%
2 FEMALE	CHATT Recoded Church Attendance	1 About weekly	16.7%	27.2%	34.3%	53.8%	34.1%
		2 About monthly	33.3%	17.8%	15.1%	13.6%	16.4%
		3 Seldom	33.3%	40.4%	37.5%	18.2%	35.4%
		4 Never	16.7%	14.6%	13.1%	14.4%	14.1%
	Total		100.0%	100.0%	100.0%	100.0%	100.0%

Notice that the first table is divided into two parts, male and female. For our purposes, we can create a summary table as follows that is easier to read:

Percentage Who Attend Worship Services about Weekly

	Under 21	21-39	40-64	65 and Older
Men	14	22	29	38
Women	17	27	34	54

There are three primary observations to be made regarding this table. First, women are more likely to attend worship services than are men within each age group. Second, with a minor exception, the previously observed relationship between AGE and ATTEND is true for both men and women. Finally, the question we asked earlier about the cumulative effect of the two causal variables is answered with a clear "yes." A mere 14 percent of the youngest men attend worship services weekly, contrasted to 54 percent of the oldest women.

17.2 Family Status and Religiosity

If you read the excerpt by Glock et al. in Appendix E, you will recall that, according to social deprivation theory, "family status" is also related to religiosity. Those who had complete families (spouse and children) were the least religious among the 1952 Episcopal church members, suggesting that those lacking families were turning to the church for gratification.

Using Crosstabs, set CHATT as the row variable and MARITAL as the column variable. Here's what you should get.

CHATT Recoded Church Attendance * MARITAL MARITAL STATUS Crosstabulation

% within MARITAL MARITAL STATUS

		MARITAL MARITAL STATUS					
		1 MARRIED	2 WIDOWED	3 DIVORCED	4 SEPARATED	5 NEVER MARRIED	Total
CHATT Recoded Church Attendance	1 About weekly	35.3%	45.0%	25.3%	20.3%	22.3%	30.8%
	2 About monthly	14.9%	15.3%	18.1%	23.4%	12.9%	15.3%
	3 Seldom	37.6%	24.4%	41.4%	32.8%	45.4%	38.7%
	4 Never	12.2%	15.3%	15.2%	23.4%	19.4%	15.2%
Total		100.0%	100.0%	100.0%	100.0%	100.0%	100.0%

These data certainly do not confirm the earlier finding. Although the widowed are the most religious, those currently married are next. It would not appear that those deprived of conventional family status are turning to the church for an alternative source of gratification. Perhaps the explanation for this lies in historical changes.

In the 44 years separating these two studies, there have been many changes with regard to family life in the United States. Divorce, single-parent families, unmarried couples living together—these and other variations on the traditional family have become more acceptable and certainly more common. It would make sense, therefore, that people who lacked regular family status in 1996 would not feel as deprived as such people may have in the early 1950s.

Before setting this issue aside, however, we should take a minute to consider whether the table we've just seen is concealing anything. In particular, can you think of any other variable that is related to both attendance at worship services and marital status? If so, that variable might be clouding the relations between marital status and religiosity.

The variable we are thinking of is age. We've already seen that age is strongly related to church attendance. It is also probably related to marital status in that young people (low in church attendance) are the most likely to be "never married." And old people (high in church attendance) are the most likely to be widowed. It is possible, therefore, that the widowed are high in church attendance only because they're mostly old, and those never married are low in church attendance only because they're young. This kind of reasoning lies near the heart of multivariate analysis, and the techniques you've mastered allow you to test this possibility.

Return to the Crosstabs window and add AGECAT as the third variable.

Once you've reviewed the resulting tables, see if you can construct the following summary table.

Percentage Who Attend Church about Weekly

	Married	*Widowed*	*Divorced*	*Separated*	*Never Married*
Under 21	—	—	—	—	11
21-39	29	13	28	21	19
40-64	37	43	21	18	31
65 and older	47	49	38	33	69

Dashes in this table indicate that there are too few cases for meaningful percentages. We've required at least 10 cases, a common standard.

As it turns out, the original pattern observed in the relationship between marital status and church attendance is maintained at each age level. The widowed are the most religious in two of the three age groups where there are enough of them for a meaningful comparison. Thus, their high frequency of church attendance cannot be explained as simply a function of their being older. By the same token, those never married have a relatively low level of church attendance regardless of their age.

You can also observe in this table that the effect of age on church attendance is maintained regardless of marital status. Only among the never married does the original relationship partially disappear, and even there, the oldest are the most religious of those never married.

Social scientists often use the term **replication** for the analytic outcome we've just observed. Having discovered that church attendance increases with age overall, we've now found that this relationship holds true regardless of marital status. That's an important discovery in terms of the generalizability of what we have learned about the causes of religiosity.

17.3 Social Class and Religiosity

In the earlier study, Glock and his colleagues found that religiosity increased as social class decreased; that is, those in the lower class were more religious than those in the upper class. This fit nicely into the deprivation thesis, that those deprived of status in the secular society would turn to the church as an alternative source of gratification. The researchers indicated, however, that this finding might be limited to the Episcopalian church members under study. They suggested that the relationship might not be replicated in the general public. You have the opportunity to check it out.

Let's begin with our measure of subjective social class. Run a Crosstabs with CHATT as the row variable and CLASS as the column variable. Here's what you should get.

Case Processing Summary

	Cases					
	Valid		Missing		Total	
	N	Percent	N	Percent	N	Percent
CHATT * CLASS	1454	96.9%	46	3.1%	1500	100.0%

CHATT * CLASS Crosstabulation

% within CLASS

		CLASS				
		1 LOWER CLASS	2 WORKING CLASS	3 MIDDLE CLASS	4 UPPER CLASS	Total
CHATT	1 About weekly	27.8%	26.1%	35.0%	30.6%	30.7%
	2 About monthly	17.7%	15.5%	14.7%	19.4%	15.4%
	3 Seldom	29.1%	42.8%	36.9%	35.5%	38.9%
	4 Never	25.3%	15.6%	13.3%	14.5%	15.0%
Total		100.0%	100.0%	100.0%	100.0%	100.0%

This table suggests there is little relationship between social class and church attendance. To be sure of this conclusion, you might want to rerun the table, controlling for sex and for age. At the same time, you can test the generalizability of the previously observed effects of sex and age on church attendance. Do they hold up among members of different social classes?

To pursue this issue even further, you might want to examine a different measure of social class. Look through the list of variables and decide which ones offer other views of class standing. Once you've done that, see how they relate to church attendance. (If you have trouble deciding which variables to use, check our comments in Appendix D.)

17.4 Other Variables to Explore

Notice that our analyses so far in this chapter have used CHATT as the dependent variable: the measure of religiosity. Recall, however, our earlier comments on the shortcomings of single-item measures of variables. Perhaps our analyses have been misleading by seeking to explain church attendance. Perhaps different conclusions might be drawn if we had studied beliefs in an afterlife, or frequency of prayer. Why don't you test some of the earlier conclusions by using other measures of religiosity? If you are really ambitious, you could create a composite index of religiosity and look for causes.

Similarly, we have limited our preceding investigations in this chapter to the variables examined by Glock and his colleagues. Now that you have gotten the idea about how to create and interpret multivariate tables, you should broaden your exploration of variables that might be related to religiosity. What are some other demographic variables that might affect religiosity? Or you might want to explore the multivariate relationships between religiosity and some of the attitudinal variables we've been exploring: political philosophies, sexual attitudes, and so forth. In each instance, you should examine the bivariate relationships first, then move on to the multivariate analyses.

17.5 Other Analytic Techniques

Thus far, we've introduced the logic of multivariate analysis through the use of Crosstabs. You've already learned some other techniques that can be used in your examination of several variables simultaneously.

First, we should remind you that you may want to use a chi-square test of statistical significance when you use Crosstabs. It's not required, but you may find it useful as an independent assessment of the relationships you discover.

Second, regression can be a powerful technique for exploring multivariate relationships: This is called **multiple regression.** To use regression effectively, you will need more instruction than we propose to offer in this book. Still, we want to give you an introductory look into this technique.

In our previous use of regression, we examined the impact of EDUC on SEI, respondents' socioeconomic status scores. Now we'll open the possibility that other variables in the data set might also affect occupational prestige. AGE is another ratio variable and one we might expect to have an impact. (Be sure to return to its original form, in the event that you have recoded it.)

We are also going to consider SEX, reasoning that men and women are treated very differently in the labor force. Notice that SEX is a nominal variable, not a ratio variable. However, researchers sometimes treat such dichotomies as "dummy variables" appropriate to a regression analysis. The logic used here transforms gender into a measure of "maleness," for example, with men respondents being 100 percent and the women 0 percent male. The following recode statement accomplishes that transformation.

Let's temporarily recode SEX as described above. So take the following steps:

Transform → Recode → Into Different Variables

Select SEX as the "Input Variable." Let's call the new variable SEX2. Using the Old and New Values window, make these assignments.

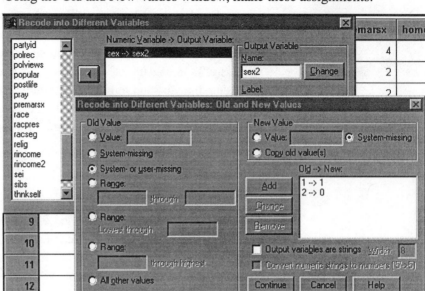

Execute the Recode command, and we are ready to request the multiple regression analysis.

Statistics → Regression → Linear takes us to the window we want. If it still has SEI as the "Dependent Variable" and EDUC as the "Independent Variable," that puts us a step ahead. Add SEX2 and AGE as additional "Independent Variables." Make sure "Stepwise" is visible in the Method Window." In the window labeled method, click the down arrow and select stepwise.

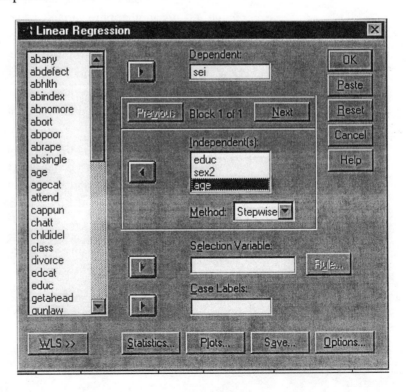

Run this command, and you will receive a mass of output. Without going into all the details, we are simply going to show you how it establishes the equation we asked for. We'll take the output a piece at a time. For our purposes, we'd like you to skip through the output on your screen until you find the following two tables:

Model Summary

Model	R	R Square	Adjusted R Square	Std. Error of the Estimate
1	.591[a]	.349	.349	15.351
2	.600[b]	.360	.359	15.226
3	.602[c]	.362	.361	15.205

a. Predictors: (Constant), HIGHEST YEAR OF SCHOOL COMPLETED

b. Predictors: (Constant), HIGHEST YEAR OF SCHOOL COMPLETED, AGE OF RESPONDENT

c. Predictors: (Constant), HIGHEST YEAR OF SCHOOL COMPLETED, AGE OF RESPONDENT, SEX2

Coefficients[a]

Model		Unstandardized Coefficients B	Unstandardized Coefficients Std. Error	Standardized Coefficients Beta	t	Sig.
1	(Constant)	-4.313	1.969		-2.190	.029
	HIGHEST YEAR OF SCHOOL COMPLETED	3.919	.142	.591	27.624	.000
2	(Constant)	-11.140	2.393		-4.655	.000
	HIGHEST YEAR OF SCHOOL COMPLETED	4.017	.142	.606	28.268	.000
	AGE OF RESPONDENT	.123	.025	.106	4.938	.000
3	(Constant)	-11.826	2.409		-4.909	.000
	HIGHEST YEAR OF SCHOOL COMPLETED	4.000	.142	.603	28.151	.000
	AGE OF RESPONDENT	.124	.025	.107	5.002	.000
	SEX2	1.819	.809	.048	2.247	.025

a. Dependent Variable: RESPONDENT SOCIOECONOMIC INDEX

We have given SPSS *three* variables that it might use to predict occupational prestige. In a stepwise regression, it begins by creating the most effective equation possible with only one independent variable. As you can see, it chose EDUC for that role. In other words, if you had to measure prestige on the basis of only one of the three independent variables, SPSS is telling us we'd do best with EDUC. It also reminds us of the variables not used in this first equation.

To create our equation for Model 1, we take two numbers from the "Unstandardized Coefficients" column: the constant (–4.313) and the B value (called the *slope*) for EDUC (3.919). Locate those in your output. We use these numbers to create the following equation:

$$\text{SEI} = -4.313 + (\text{EDUC} \times 3.919).$$

If someone had 10 years of education, then we would estimate his or her occupational prestige as follows:

$$\text{SEI} = -4.313 + (10 \times 3.919) = 34.877.$$

Model 2 adds AGE as a predictor of occupational prestige. The meaning of this is that if we could use two variables to predict PRESTIGE, we should use EDUC and AGE. Notice that the slope for EDUC changes when we add another independent variable.

$$\text{SEI} = -11.140 + (\text{EDUC} \times 4.017) + (\text{AGE} \times .123).$$

Thus, we would predict the occupational prestige of a 25-year-old with 10 years of education as follows:

$$\text{SEI} = -11.140 + (10 \times 4.017) + (25 \times .123) = 32.105.$$

Model 3, the last row in the chart, uses all three variables. It's your turn to convert these data into a regression equation and experiment with its use. Notice that being a man is worth about an additional one-and-a-half points of prestige—when education and age are held constant.

The column headed "Standardized Coefficients" gives you a guide to the relative impact of the different variables. Take a minute to consider some independent variable that has no impact on the dependent variable. What slope would it be given?

If you think about it, the only proper weight would be zero. That would mean that a person's value on that variable would never make any difference in predicting the dependent variable. By the same token, the larger the slope for any given variable, the larger its part in determining the resulting prediction. But why does AGE have a much smaller scope (.124) than SEX2 (1.819) when AGE is supposed to be a better predictor?

The solution to this puzzle lies in the different scales used in the different variables. SEX2 only goes as high as 1 (male), whereas AGE goes to 89. Slopes must be standardized before they can be compared. Standardized slopes are what the slopes would be if each of the variables used the same scale. SPSS prints standardized slopes under the column "Standardized Coefficients." The data presented above indicate that EDUC (.142) has the greatest impact on SEI, followed distantly by AGE (.107) and SEX2 (.048).

17.6 Summary

In this chapter, we have given you an initial peek into the logic and techniques of multivariate analysis. As you've seen, the difference between bivariate and multivariate analysis is much more than a matter of degree. Multivariate analysis does more than bring in additional variables: It represents a new logic for understanding social scientific relationships.

For this contact, we've looked at how multivariate analysis lets us explore the nature of multiple causation, seeing how two or more independent variables affect a dependent variable. In addition, we've used multivariate techniques for the purpose of testing the generalizability of relationships.

In the latter regard, we have begun using multivariate techniques for the purpose of considering hidden relationships among variables, as when we asked whether the widowed attended church frequently just because they were mostly older people. We'll pursue this kind of detective work further in the chapters to come.

Chapter 18 Dissecting the Political Factor

In Chapter 12, we began exploring some of the causes of political philosophies and party identification. Now you are equipped to dig more deeply.
Let's start with the relationship between political philosophy and party
identification. As you'll recall, our earlier analysis showed a definite
relationship, although it was not altogether consistent. Perhaps we can
clarify it.

18.1 Political Philosophy and Party Identification

On the whole, Democrats in our sample were more liberal than Independents or Republicans, as you'll recall. Also, Republicans were the most
conservative, although there wasn't much distinction between Democrats
and Independents in that regard. Here's the basic table from Chapter 12.

POLREC Recoded POLVIEWS * PARTY party identification Crosstabulation

% within PARTY party identification

		PARTY party identification				Total
		1 democrat	2 independent	3 republican	4 other	
POLREC Recoded POLVIEWS	1 liberal	40.0%	26.5%	8.0%	33.3%	26.6%
	2 moderate	36.7%	44.7%	32.5%	33.3%	38.4%
	3 conservative	23.4%	28.9%	59.5%	33.3%	35.0%
Total		100.0%	100.0%	100.0%	100.0%	100.0%

For purposes of this analysis, let's focus on the percentages who identify
themselves as "conservative." In the table above, the percentage difference
separating the Democrats and Republicans in calling themselves conservative amounts to 36 points. You'll recall, perhaps, that percentage differences
are sometimes designated by the Greek letter epsilon or abbreviated with
the letter e.

If you were to undertake a study of the political party platforms and/or
the speeches of political leaders from the two major parties, you would
conclude that Democrats are, in fact, somewhat more liberal than Republicans, and that Republicans are, in fact, somewhat more conservative than
Democrats. If the relationship between political philosophy and party
identification is not as clear as we might like, then perhaps some of the
respondents simply don't know how the two parties are generally regarded.

Who do you suppose would be the least likely to know the philosophical leanings of the two parties? Perhaps those with the least education would be unaware of this. If that were the case, then we should expect a clearer relationship between political philosophy and party identification among the more educated respondents than among the less educated.

Why don't you run the SPSS command that would let you create the following three-variable summary table?

Percentage Saying They Are Conservative	Less Than High School	HS Grad	Some College	College Grad
Democrat	27	26	24	18
Independent	24	30	31	29
Republican	55	50	65	65
e	28	24	41	47

Our suspicion is confirmed. The clearest relationship between party and political philosophy appears among college graduates, followed by those with some college. Notice that Democrats and Republicans are separated by an epsilon of less than 30 percentage points among the least educated group, and that Democrats and Independents are the reverse of what we would have expected. The epsilon is a little lower (24 percentage points) among high school graduates, and Democrats and Independents are about the same with 41 and 47 percentage points, respectively.

This table reveals something else that relates to our earlier analysis. You may recall that we found only a weak and inconsistent relationship between education and political philosophy in our Chapter 12 analysis. There was a tendency for liberalism to increase with education, although only 14 percentage points separated the least from the most educated groups in that respect. There was no relationship between conservatism and education, with the "moderate" point of view decreasing with education.

This new table clarifies the situation somewhat. The relationship between political philosophy occurs primarily among Democrats. Although the most educated Republicans are the most conservative, there are few differences among the other three educational groups.

This table represents what social scientists call a **specification.** We have specified the relationship between education and political philosophy: It occurs primarily among Democrats. On the other hand, we could say that we have specified the relationship between political philosophy and party identification: It occurs primarily among the better educated.

Specification stands as an alternative to replication. You'll recall that replication indicates that a relationship between two variables can be generalized to all kinds of people. Specification indicates that it cannot.

When we look at the relationship between two variables, such as political philosophy and party identification, among subgroups determined by some other variable, such as education, we often say that we are controlling for that third variable. Social scientists use the expression "controlling for" in the sense of creating controlled conditions: only college graduates, only those with some college, and so on. We also speak of "holding education constant" in the sense that education is no longer a variable (it is a constant) when we look only at one educational group at a time.

Why don't you experiment with this logic, testing the generalizability of the relationship between political philosophy and party identification among other subgroups, formed by holding other variables constant?

18.2 The Mystery of Politics and Marital Status

In Chapter 12, we encouraged you to explore the relationship between marital status and politics. If you took us up on the invitation, you should have found an interesting relationship between marital status and political philosophy. Let's look at the table of marital and POLVIEWS. Because relatively few respondents were separated, we should combine them with some other group. It would seem to make sense to combine the separated with the divorced, reasoning that separation is often experienced as an interim step toward divorce.

Let's recode MARITAL into a new variable, MARITAL2, with

Transform → Recode → Into Different Variables

Once in the Recode window, you should enter MARITAL as the "Input Variable" and MARITAL2 as the "Output Variable." Click on "Change" to move MARITAL2 to the recode list. Then, in the Old and New Values window, carry all the old values, except 4, to MARITAL2 (i.e., 1 → 1, 2 → 2, 3 → 3, 4 → 3, and 5 → 5). Don't forget to use Add to record the instructions. Then, you can Continue and "OK" your way to the recoded variable.

Now create a Crosstab with MARITAL2 as the column variable and POLREC as the row variable. Ask SPSS for column percentages. Here's what you should get:

POLREC Recoded POLVIEWS * MARITAL2 Crosstabulation

% within MARITAL2

		MARITAL2				Total
		1.00	2.00	3.00	5.00	
POLREC Recoded POLVIEWS	1 liberal	21.3%	19.8%	26.4%	39.8%	26.6%
	2 moderate	37.0%	43.8%	42.8%	35.0%	38.3%
	3 conservative	41.7%	36.4%	30.8%	25.2%	35.1%
Total		100.0%	100.0%	100.0%	100.0%	100.0%

If you had run the chi-square test of statistical significance, you would have found this relationship to exceed the .001 level of significance. So, why is it that married and widowed respondents are more conservative than the divorced, separated, or never married? Your multivariate skills will allow you to explore this matter in more depth than was possible before.

Perhaps age is the key. The widowed are likely to be older than others, and the never married are likely to be younger. As we've seen, people tend to become more conservative with age. Here is a summary table created from the results of the Crosstab of POLREC by MARITAL2 by AGECAT. See if you can duplicate this yourself.

Percentage Who Say They Are Conservative	Married	Widowed	Divorced/ Separated	Never Married
Under 21	—	—	—	29
21 to 39	40	38	37	28
40 to 64	43	32	28	15
65 and up	47	38	27	17

This table helps clarify matters. The married are consistently more conservative than the divorced and never married, and the widowed tend to maintain their conservative stance. With the exception of the 21-39 divorced and separated, the never married and divorced and separated are more apt to be liberal.

How about sex? Perhaps it can shed some light on this relationship. Why don't you run the tables that would result in this summary?

Percentage Who Say *They Are Conservative*	*Married*	*Widowed*	*Divorced/* *Separated*	*Never* *Married*
Men	50	50	35	28
Women	34	32	28	22

As before, the married remain relatively conservative, the widowed vary (conservative among men, not so much among women), and the divorced and never married remain relatively less conservative.

To pursue this further, you might want to consider education. Here's the summary table you should generate if you follow this avenue.

Percentage Who Say *They Are Conservative*	*Married*	*Widowed*	*Divorced/* *Separated*	*Never* *Married*
Less than HS	34	33	24	29
HS graduate	36	33	32	22
Some college	51	44	31	28
College graduate	43	43	34	24

Once more, we seem to have dug a dry well. Education does not seem to clarify the relationship we first observed between MARITAL status and political philosophy. This is the point in an analysis where you sometimes wonder if you should ever have considered this line of inquiry.

See what happens when we introduce race as a control.

Percentage Who Say *They Are Conservative*	*Married*	*Widowed*	*Divorced/* *Separated*	*Never* *Married*
White	43	39	32	26
Black	35	25	25	26
Other	—	—	—	24

(As in other tables, the dashes here indicate that there were too few cases for meaningful percentages.)

When we consistently fail to find a clear answer to a question—Why do people of different marital statuses differ in their political philosophies? —it is sometimes useful to reconsider the question itself. Thus far, we have been asking why marital status would affect political philosophy. Perhaps we have the question reversed. What if political philosophy affects marital status? Is that a possibility?

Perhaps those who are politically conservative are also socially conservative. Maybe it would be especially important for them to form and keep traditional families. During the presidential election that followed on the tails of this GSS survey, the political conservatives made "traditional family values" a centerpiece of their campaign. Let's see what the table would look like if we percentaged it in the opposite direction.

MARITAL2 * POLREC Recoded POLVIEWS Crosstabulation

% within POLREC Recoded POLVIEWS

		POLREC Recoded POLVIEWS			
		1 liberal	2 moderate	3 conservative	Total
MARITAL2	1.00	37.8%	45.6%	56.1%	47.2%
	2.00	6.3%	9.7%	8.8%	8.5%
	3.00	20.4%	23.0%	18.0%	20.5%
	5.00	35.4%	21.7%	17.0%	23.7%
Total		100.0%	100.0%	100.0%	100.0%

Look at the first row in this table. The percentage married steadily increases with increasing conservatism across the table. Divorce and singlehood, on the other hand, decrease just as steadily. Perhaps marital status is more profitably seen as a dependent variable in this context: affected to some extent by worldviews such as are reflected in political philosophy.

Sometimes, the direction of a relationship—which is the dependent and which is the independent variable—is clear. If we discover that voting behavior is related to gender, for instance, we can be sure that gender can affect voting, but how you vote can't change your gender. In other situations, such as the present one, the direction of a relationship is somewhat ambiguous. Ultimately, this decision must be based on theoretical reasoning. There is no way the analysis of data can determine which variable is dependent and which is independent.

If you wanted to pursue the present relationship, you might treat marital status as a dependent variable, subjecting its relationship with political philosophies to a multivariate analysis.

18.3 Political Issues

In Chapter 12, we began looking for the causes of opinions on two political issues:

GUNLAW   registration of firearms

CAPPUN   capital punishment

Now that you have the ability to undertake multivariate analysis, you can delve more deeply into the causes of public opinion. Let's think a little about capital punishment for the moment. Here are some variables that might logically affect how people feel about the death penalty.

POLREC and PARTY are obvious candidates. Liberals are generally more opposed to capital punishment than are conservatives. Similarly, Republicans have tended to support it more than have Democrats. You might check to see how these two variables work together on death penalty attitudes.

Given that capital punishment involves the taking of a human life, you might expect some religious effects. How do the different religious affiliations relate to support for or opposition to capital punishment? What about beliefs in an afterlife? Do those who believe in life after death find it easier to support the taking of a life? How do religious and political factors interact in this arena?

Those opposed to capital punishment base their opposition on the view that it is wrong to take a human life. The same argument is made by those who oppose abortion. Logically, you would expect those opposed to abortion to also oppose capital punishment. Why don't you check it out? You may be surprised by what you find.

Another approach to understanding opinions about capital punishment might focus on which groups in society are most likely to be victims of it. Men are more likely to be executed than are women. Blacks are executed disproportionately often, in comparison with their numbers in the population.

18.4 Summary

These few suggestions should launch you on an extended exploration of the nature of political orientations. Whereas people often talk pretty casually about political matters, you are now in a position to check out the facts and to dig deeply into understanding why people feel as they do about political issues.

Multivariate analysis techniques let you uncover some of the complexities that can make human behavior difficult to understand.

Chapter 19 A Powerful Prediction of Attitudes toward Abortion

In previous analyses, we've seen how complex attitudes about abortion are. As we return to our analysis of this controversial topic, you have additional tools for digging deeper. Let's begin with the religious factor. Then we'll turn to politics and other variables.

19.1 Religion and Abortion

In Chapter 13, we found that both religious affiliation and measures of religiosity were related to abortion attitudes. The clearest relationships were observed in terms of the unconditional right to abortion, because only a small minority are opposed to abortion in all circumstances.

Protestants and Catholics are generally less supportive of abortion than Jews and "nones." And on measures of religiosity, opposition to abortion increases with increasing religiosity. The most religious are the most opposed to a woman's right to choose an abortion.

With your multivariate skills, you can examine this more deeply. Consider the possibility, for example, that one of these relationships is an artifact of the other. To explore this possibility, we must first examine the relationship between religious affiliation and church attendance.

CHATT Recoded Church Attendance * RELIG RS RELIGIOUS PREFERENCE Crosstabulation

| | | | RELIG RS RELIGIOUS PREFERENCE | | | | | |
			1 PROTESTANT	2 CATHOLIC	3 JEWISH	4 NONE	5 OTHER	Total
CHATT Recoded Church Attendance	1 About weekly	Count	291	133	7	7	12	450
		% within RELIG RS RELIGIOUS PREFERENCE	37.1%	34.2%	15.2%	4.0%	17.9%	30.8%
	2 About monthly	Count	144	60	6	4	10	224
		% within RELIG RS RELIGIOUS PREFERENCE	18.3%	15.4%	13.0%	2.3%	14.9%	15.3%
	3 Seldom	Count	281	160	28	67	29	565
		% within RELIG RS RELIGIOUS PREFERENCE	35.8%	41.1%	60.9%	38.5%	43.3%	38.7%
	4 Never	Count	69	36	5	96	16	222
		% within RELIG RS RELIGIOUS PREFERENCE	8.8%	9.3%	10.9%	55.2%	23.9%	15.2%
Total		Count	785	389	46	174	67	1461
		% within RELIG RS RELIGIOUS PREFERENCE	100.0%	100.0%	100.0%	100.0%	100.0%	100.0%

As you can see, there is a pretty clear relationship between these two variables. Protestants and Catholics are the most likely to attend worship services weekly or one to three times a month. Those with no religion, of course, attend church seldom or never. If we combine the two most frequent categories, we see that 46 percent of the whole sample attends church at least one to three times a month. There are big differences among the five religious groups, however.

	Percentage Who Attend at Least 1-3 Times a Month
Protestants	55
Catholics	50
Jews	28
None	6
Other	33

Because religious affiliation and church attendance are related to one another and each is related to abortion attitudes, there are two possibilities for us to explore. For example, perhaps church attendance seems to affect abortion attitudes only because Protestants and Catholics (relatively opposed to abortion) attend more often. Or, conversely, perhaps Protestants and Catholics seem more opposed to abortion simply because they attend church more often.

We can test for these possibilities by running a multivariate table, taking account of all three variables. To simplify our analysis, let's recode RELIG into two categories—"Christians" and "others"—and recode ATTEND into two categories as well.

Because we're going to be doing several recodes in this session, let's recode the original variables this time, rather than creating a number of new variables that we may not use again. *Note:* If you save your data set after this exercise, be sure to use Save As and give it a new name, so that you'll still be able to get back to your original, unrecoded data.

So, let's use Transform → Recode → Into Same Variables.

Make the recodes listed below and then go to Data → Define Variables to put labels on the recoded values.

Recode RELIG
1 through 2 → 1
3 through 5 → 2

Label RELIG
1 = "Christian"
2 = "Other"

Recode ATTEND
4 through 8 → 1
0 through 3 → 2

Label ATTEND
1 = "Often"
2 = "Seldom"

Now run a Crosstab with ATTEND as the row variable and RELIG as the column variable.

ATTEND HOW OFTEN R ATTENDS RELIGIOUS SERVICES * RELIG RS RELIGIOUS PREFERENCE Crosstabulation

% within RELIG RS RELIGIOUS PREFERENCE

			RELIG RS RELIGIOUS PREFERENCE		
			1 christian	2 other	Total
ATTEND HOW OFTEN R ATTENDS RELIGIOUS SERVICES	1 often		53.5%	16.0%	46.1%
	2 seldom		46.5%	84.0%	53.9%
Total			100.0%	100.0%	100.0%

As you can see, the relationship between religious affiliation and church attendance is still obvious after categories are collapsed on both variables. Now let's review the relationships between each variable and abortion, again using the recoded variables.

ABORT * RELIG RS RELIGIOUS PREFERENCE * ATTEND HOW OFTEN R ATTENDS RELIGOUS SERVICES Crosstabulation

% within RELIG RS RELIGIOUS PREFERENCE

ATTEND HOW OFTEN R ATTENDS RELIGIOUS SERVICES			RELIG RS RELIGIOUS PREFEREENCE		
			1 christian	2 other	Total
1 often	ABORT	0	31.8%	25.0%	31.4%
		1	35.8%	25.0%	35.2%
		2	32.3%	50.0%	33.4%
	Total		100.0%	100.0%	100.0%
2 seldom	ABORT	0	8.1%	7.9%	8.0%
		1	39.8%	20.4%	33.9%
		2	52.2%	71.7%	58.1%
	Total		100.0%	100.0%	100.0%

ABORT * ATTEND HOW OFTEN R ATTENDS RELIGIOUS SERVICES Crosstabulation

% within ATTEND HOW OFTEN R ATTENDS RELIGIOUS SERVICES

		ATTEND HOW OFTEN R ATTENDS RELIGIOUS SERVICES		
		1 often	2 seldom	Total
ABORT	0	31.4%	8.0%	18.3%
	1	35.2%	33.8%	34.4%
	2	33.4%	58.2%	47.3%
Total		100.0%	100.0%	100.0%

Notice that the relationship between affiliation and abortion is now represented by an epsilon of 26 percentage points. The relationship between church attendance and abortion has an epsilon of 25 percentage points. Now let's look at the three-variable relationship.

ABORT * RELIG RS RELIGIOUS PREFERENCE * ATTEND HOW OFTEN R ATTENDS RELIGIOUS SERVICES Crosstabulation

% within RELIG RS RELIGIOUS PREFERENCE

ATTEND HOW OFTEN R ATTENDS RELIGIOUS SERVICES			RELIG RS RELIGIOUS PREFERENCE		
			1 Christian	2 Other	Total
1 Often	ABORT	0	31.8%	25.0%	31.4%
		1	35.8%	25.0%	35.2%
		2	32.3%	50.0%	33.4%
	Total		100.0%	100.0%	100.0%
2 Seldom	ABORT	0	8.1%	7.9%	8.0%
		1	39.8%	20.4%	33.9%
		2	52.2%	71.7%	58.1%
	Total		100.0%	100.0%	100.0%

To examine the results of this analysis, let's summarize the findings as follows:

Percentage Who Support Abortion Unconditionally	*Christians*	*Others*	*Epsilon*
Attend often	32	50	18
Attend seldom	52	72	20
Epsilon	20	22	

This multivariate analysis suggests a number of conclusions. First, neither of the possibilities we were exploring is confirmed. The opposition to abortion by Protestants and Catholics is not merely a function of their greater church attendance, nor is the effect of church attendance due merely to differences of affiliation. Each variable has an independent impact on attitudes regarding abortion.

At the same time, we can see that the impact of church attendance is less among the non-Christians, and that the impact of affiliation is less among those who attend less often. Putting the two religious variables together, we can see that the Christians who attend church often stand some distance from the other groups in their opposition to abortion. You might like to experiment some more with the religious factor, using some of the other variables included in the GSS data set. In the next section, we are going to examine the impact of political factors as a point of comparison with the religious factor.

19.2 Politics and Abortion

As we saw in Chapter 13, political philosophies have a strong impact on attitudes toward abortion. You might want to refresh your memory by rerunning this table. (You now know how. Wow!)

ABORT * POLREC Recoded POLVIEWS Crosstabulation

% within POLREC Recoded POLVIEWS

		POLREC Recoded POLVIEWS			
		1 liberal	2 moderate	3 conservative	Total
ABORT	0	11.7%	13.2%	29.4%	18.4%
	1	27.5%	39.6%	33.3%	34.1%
	2	60.8%	47.2%	37.3%	47.5%
Total		100.0%	100.0%	100.0%	100.0%

The impact of political philosophy on unconditional support for a woman's right to choose abortion equals 24 percentage points, compared with 26 for religious denomination. As we saw earlier, however, political party identification—despite official party differences on the issue of abortion—does not have much of an effect.

In a multivariate analysis, we might next want to explore the possible interaction of religion and politics on abortion attitudes. For example, in Chapter 13, we found that Protestants and Catholics were somewhat more conservative than were Jews and "nones." Perhaps their political orientations account for the differences that the religious groups have on the issue of abortion.

With your multivariate skills, testing this new possibility is a simple matter. Take a minute to figure out the SPSS command that would provide for such a test. Then enter it and review the results.

Here's a summary table of the results you should have found if you are working with the latest recode for RELIG. Be sure you can replicate this on your own.

Percentage Who Unconditionally Support Right to Abortion	*Liberal*	*Moderate*	*Conservative*
Christian	52	44	34
Other	80	59	66

This table demonstrates the independent impact of religion and politics on abortion attitudes, although the results also describe something of a specification. The religious effect observed earlier occurs only among liberals and moderates, particularly among the former. You can see this by examining the epsilons for each political group: 28, 15, and 32. According to this table, political conservatives are generally opposed to the unconditional right to an abortion when their religious affiliation is Christian.

Overall, the joint impact of politics and religion is represented by an epsilon of 46 percentage points (80 – 34), a powerful degree of prediction for these controversial opinions. To support our continued analysis, let's create a simple index to combine the religious and political factors. For the time being, let's just call it our "prediction index," because we don't really know what it represents except a tool for predicting attitudes toward abortion.

Here's how we might put the index together. Begin with

Transform → Compute

Then, let's create a new "Target Variable" called IND (for index). We'll start by giving everyone a 0.

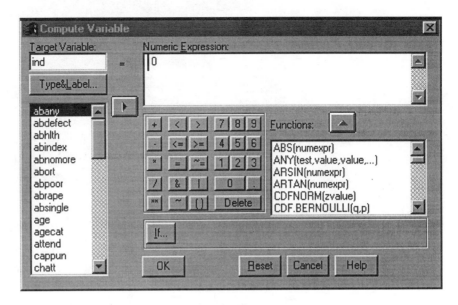

Run this instruction to establish the new index among your variables.

Now we are ready to begin assigning points on our index. Let's start by giving people two points if they have a 1 on POLREC ("Liberal"). Return to the Compute Variable window and make these changes:

* Change the "Numeric Expression" to IND + 2
* Set the "If" statement to POLREC = 1

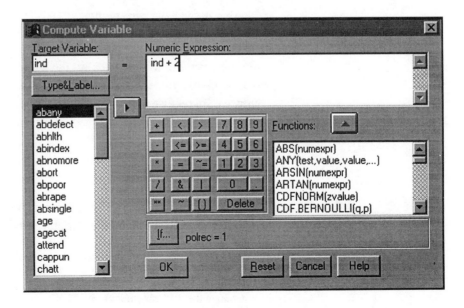

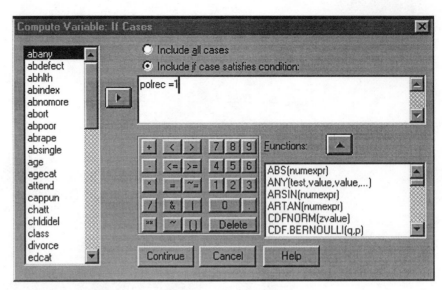

Run this instruction. At this point, the liberals have two points and everyone else (including those with missing data) have zeros.

Now, let's give the "Moderates" one point on the index. Return to the Compute Variable window and make two changes.

- Change the "Numeric Expression" to `IND + 1`
- Change the "If" statement to `POLREC = 2`

Run this instruction.

Now, we have established an index as follows:

Liberals have two points

Moderates have one point

Conservatives have zero points

Those who are none of the above have zero points on the index

You may want to look at `IND` in the data window or run Frequencies at any time in this process to see how the index is shaping up.

Now we are ready to add to the index. Go back to the Compute Variable window and make the following specifications.

- Leave the "Numeric Expression" as `IND + 1`
- Change the "If" statement to `RELIG = 2`

Run this instruction, and we've added one point for each non-Christian.

Finally, return to the Compute Variable window and make these specifications:

- Leave the "Numeric Expression" as `IND + 1`
- Change the "If" statement to `ATTEND = 2`

Run this expression and review the logic of what we have done.

We've now created an index that presumably captures religious and political predispositions to support for a woman's right to an abortion. Scores on the index run from 0 (opposed to abortion) to 4 (supportive). There is one glitch in this index that we need to correct before moving on: those with missing data.

Let's use Count to handle this. Go to the Count window and do the following:

- Enter MISS as the "Target Variable"
- Enter ATTEND, POLREC, and RELIG as "Numeric Variables"
- Define values as "System- or user-missing" (and click on Add)
- Click on Continue to return to the Count screen and then click on "OK" to run the Count command.

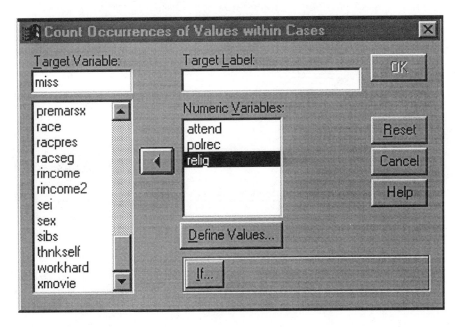

Now, return to the Compute Variable window and make this modification to the index.

- Set the "Numeric Expression" for IND to –1
- Set "If" condition as MISS ~= 0

Run this instruction, and you will have converted those with missing data from 0's to –1's in the index. All that remains is to let SPSS know what we meant by the latest modification to the index.

Select IND in the Data window and go to Data → Define Variable. Set the missing value as –1, and while you're here, you might as well change the number of decimals to 0 in "Types."

Having created such an index, it is always a good practice to check the frequencies. Run Frequencies on IND and you should get this:

IND

		Frequency	Percent	Valid Percent	Cumulative Percent
Valid	0	261	17.4	18.8	18.8
	1	392	26.1	28.3	47.1
	2	408	27.2	29.4	76.6
	3	225	15.0	16.2	92.8
	4	100	6.7	7.2	100.0
	Total	1386	92.4	100.0	
Missing	-1	114	7.6		
	Total	114	7.6		
Total		1500	100.0		

So, let's see how well our index predicts abortion attitudes. Run this table.

ABORT * IND Crosstabulation

% within IND

		IND1					
		0	1	2	3	4	Total
ABORT	0	45.8%	14.6%	15.3%	8.2%	1.6%	18.4%
	1	29.7%	43.3%	34.7%	29.5%	15.9%	33.9%
	2	24.5%	42.1%	50.0%	62.3%	82.5%	47.7%
Total		100.0%	100.0%	100.0%	100.0%	100.0%	100.0%

As you can see, the index provides a very strong prediction of support for the unconditional right to an abortion: from 25 percent to 83 percent, for an epsilon of 58 percentage points. Let's see if we can improve on our ability to predict.

19.3 Sexual Attitudes and Abortion

Earlier, we discovered that attitudes about various forms of sexual behavior were also related to abortion attitudes. As you'll recall, people were asked whether they felt premarital sex and homosexuality were "always wrong," "almost always wrong," "sometimes wrong," or "not wrong at all." In addition, respondents were asked whether they had attended an X-rated movie during the past year. Each of these items was related to abortion attitudes, with those most permissive in sexual matters also being more permissive about abortion.

Because we want to pursue this phenomenon, why don't you recode PREMARSX and HOMOSEX into dichotomies (only two values) of "always or almost always wrong" versus "only sometimes or never wrong"? (Check Appendix D if you have trouble with this.) That will make it easier to conduct the following analysis.

Now, let's see whether the sexual behavior attitudes are related to our political-religious index that predicts abortion attitudes so powerfully. Why don't you run each of those tables now? Here's a summary of what you should find.

Percentage Who Are	Political-Religious Index				
Permissive About	*0*	*1*	*2*	*3*	*4*
Premarital sex	41	66	76	84	91
Homosexuality	16	26	37	63	76

Even though there is a great difference in the overall level of permissiveness on these issues, we can see that the political-religious index is clearly related to each. Why don't you see if the index predicts whether people have taken in an X-rated movie during the past year?

Now, let's see if the previously observed relationship between attitudes about sexual behavior and attitudes about abortion is really just a product of religious and political factors. Here's a summary of one of the tables you might look at.

Percentage Who Support	Political-Religious Index				
Unconditional Abortion	*0*	*1*	*2*	*3*	*4*
Premarital sex wrong	26	27	31	64	—
Premarital sex acceptable	35	45	63	67	59

Obviously, our index—combining religious affiliation, church attendance, and political philosophy—does not explain away the relationship between attitudes on premarital sex and attitudes on abortion. Regardless of their scores on the index, those who find premarital sex somewhat acceptable are more supportive of abortion than are those who disapprove of premarital sex.

Why don't you continue this analysis, focusing on the other sexual attitudes? You could consider expanding the index by including one or two of the items on sexual attitudes. Here's a result you might get. Can you recreate this? (If this exercise gets too aggravating, you'll find a hint in Appendix D.)

ABORT * IND Crosstabulation

% within IND

		IND							Total
		.00	1.00	2.00	3.00	4.00	5.00	6.00	Total
ABORT	0	52.1%	25.0%	25.0%	9.3%	4.5%	5.6%		18.0%
	1	25.0%	45.5%	39.8%	36.0%	25.4%	22.2%	5.3%	31.4%
	2	22.9%	29.5%	35.2%	54.7%	70.1%	72.2%	94.7%	50.6%
Total		100.0%	100.0%	100.0%	100.0%	100.0%	100.0%	100.0%	100.0%

The power of this new composite index is represented by an epsilon of 71 percentage points. Clearly, we have gone a good distance in accounting for people's opinions on the issue of abortion. At the same time, we've moved quickly in order to give you a broad view. If attitudes toward abortion interest you, there are any number of directions you could follow up on in a more focused and deliberate analysis.

19.4 Summary

You've had an opportunity now to see how social scientists might set out to understand people's attitudes toward abortion. We know this is a topic about which you hear a great deal in the popular media, and it may be an issue that concerns you and about which you have strong opinions. The analyses above should give you some insight into the sources of opinions on this topic.

We hope this chapter has also expanded your understanding of the possibilities for multivariate analysis. Whereas bivariate analysis allows for some simple explanations of human thoughts and behaviors, multivariate analysis permits more sophisticated investigations and discoveries.

Chapter 20   Suggestions for Further Multivariate Analyses

In each of the previous analytic chapters, we have tried to leave a large number of "loose ends" for you to pursue on your own. If you are using this book in connection with a college class, you can follow up on some of those leads in the form of a term paper.

This chapter will suggest additional possibilities for your analyses. You should realize, however, that even within this fairly limited data set, there are analytic possibilities we have not considered.

20.1   Ideal Family Size and Abortion

Before leaving the topic of abortion altogether, we'd like to suggest another explanatory variable you might consider: ideal family size. We've seen previously that those who favor small families are more supportive of abortion than are those who favor large families. Now, you are able to pursue this matter further. Here's the basic relationship with which you might start. Notice that you'll have to recode CHLDIDEL if you haven't already done that.

ABORT * CHLDIDEL IDEAL NUMBER OF CHILDREN Crosstabulation

% within CHLDIDEL IDEAL NUMBER OF CHILDREN

		CHLDIDEL IDEAL NUMBER OF CHILDREN			
		1	2	3	Total
ABORT	0	11.7%	21.9%	35.7%	15.9%
	1	31.9%	39.4%	28.6%	34.3%
	2	56.4%	38.7%	35.7%	49.8%
Total		100.0%	100.0%	100.0%	100.0%

Why don't you see whether the index of politics and religion has an impact on the ideal family sizes people reported? If it does, you should see whether the impact of ideal family size on abortion attitude is merely a matter of politics and religion or if it has an independent effect. You could substitute CHLDIDEL for the sexual attitudes in the preceding chapter.

As a somewhat more focused approach, you might review two articles reprinted in Appendix E: Renzi's "Ideal Family Size as an Intervening Variable between Religion and Attitudes towards Abortion" (1975) and D'Antonio and Stack's "Religion, Ideal Family Size, and Abortion: Extending Renzi's Hypothesis" (1980). See if you can replicate portions of the published analyses. Perhaps you can see additional variables that should be taken into account.

20.2 Child Training

In Chapter 16, we began looking into some of the factors that might affect people's views of the qualities most important to develop in children. To review, the qualities were as follows:

OBEY	to obey
POPULAR	to be well-liked or popular
THNKSELF	to think for himself or herself
WORKHARD	to work hard
HELPOTH	to help others when they need help

We suggested that you start your analysis with some basic demographic variables, such as age, sex, and race. We encouraged you to consider relationships you might logically expect, such as that more educated respondents may place higher value on children's thinking for themselves.

Now you are able to explore all the possibilities in greater depth. To stay with the example of education and independence of thought in children, you could see if there are variables that shed more light on that relationship. You might check POLVIEWS, for example. Before you do, ask yourself what you would expect to find. You might also check the effect of gender while you're at it.

Earlier, we suggested you look at the impact of the sexual attitude items. Those who are permissive regarding violations of the established norms for sexual conduct often feel that they are thinking for themselves in those regards. How do such people feel about encouraging that trait in young people? With your multivariate skills, you can examine that matter with some sophistication.

Perhaps you will find it useful to combine some of the "quality" items into an index. On the face of it, OBEY and THNKSELF appear to value opposite traits. Are they negatively related to one another? Would they fit into an index of "conformity-independence," perhaps? If that seems a fruitful index to create, to which other variables does it relate?

20.3 The Protestant Ethic

One of the most famous of all sociology books is Max Weber's *The Protestant Ethic and the Spirit of Capitalism* (1905/1958). In it, Weber traces the religious roots (in Calvinism) of the ethic of hard work and thrift that he found to forge the beginnings of capitalism. This ethic is something you might like to explore.

A central notion of the "Protestant ethic" is the idea of "hard work," the belief that individuals are responsible for their own economic well-being. People's wealth is taken as a sign of how hardworking and diligent they are. In its most extreme form, the Protestant ethic sees poverty as the result of slothfulness and laziness, and wealth as the product of persistence and hard work.

The GETAHEAD item in your GSS data set provides a measure of at least one dimension of the Protestant ethic that you might like to explore. To measure the degree to which people took responsibility for their own economic well-being, respondents were read this statement: "Some people say that people get ahead by their own hard work; others say that lucky breaks or help from other people are more important." Following the statement, they were asked, "Which do you think is most important?"

Why don't you begin by examining how GETAHEAD is related to other variables? It would seem logical that GETAHEAD would be related to WORKHARD. Are people who are in disadvantaged groups or have low incomes more apt to believe their fates are governed by luck rather than hard work? Or, does the belief in luck for success provide a rationalization for people who have little power to control the events that affect their lives? Because these variables are not the ratio measures that Pearson's r assumes, you can't take the results literally, but perhaps they can give you a first glimpse. Do not use this technique as a substitution for other, statistically appropriate, examinations.

If you follow these suggestions, you'll need to be prepared for some surprises—even disappointments. So, it may take some hard work (not inappropriate) for you to create a measure of commitment to the Protestant ethic that you like. Then, you can begin the multivariate search for the causes of this point of view. Be sure to check out the Protestants, but don't expect an easy answer.

20.4 Prejudice

In your analysis of the Protestant ethic, you may have looked at the place of the two prejudice items: RACSEG and RACPRES. If not, you may want to do so now. Logically, the belief that people get ahead by hard work alone would seem to rule out the limits imposed by prejudice and discrimination. Yet you will find that some of the "work ethic" items are associated with the belief that whites should be able to segregate their neighborhoods to keep African Americans out and with refusal to vote for an African American candidate for president.

Some beliefs about African Americans seem to be part and parcel of a racist point of view. Prejudiced images can lead to beliefs that, when turned into action, become discrimination. As part of the 1996 GSS, respondents were read the statement, "On the average, African-Americans have worse jobs, income, and housing than white people." Then, they were asked if "they thought the differences were mainly because African-Americans just don't have the motivation or will power to pull themselves up out of poverty?" Their responses are recorded in the item RACDIF4. See the extent to which prejudicial beliefs are associated with the belief that whites should be able to segregate their neighborhoods and the refusal to vote for an African American presidential candidate.

RACSEG WHITES HAVE RIGHT TO SEG. NEIGHBORHOOD *
RACDIF4 DIFFERENCES DUE TO LACK OF WILL Crosstabulation

% within RACDIF4 DIFFERENCES DUE TO LACK OF WILL

		RACDIF4 DIFFERENCES DUE TO LACK OF WILL		
		1 YES	2 NO	Total
RACSEG WHITES HAVE RIGHT TO SEG. NEIGHBORHOOD	1 AGREE STRONGLY	13.0%	4.7%	8.9%
	2 AGREE SLIGHTLY	12.0%	2.8%	7.5%
	3 DISAGREE SLIGHTLY	24.1%	19.8%	22.0%
	4 DISAGREE STRONGLY	50.9%	72.6%	61.7%
Total		100.0%	100.0%	100.0%

RACPRES WOULD VOTE FOR BLACK PRESIDENT * RACDIF4
DIFFERENCES DUE TO LACK OF WILL Crosstabulation

% within RACDIF4 DIFFERENCES DUE TO LACK OF WILL

		RACDIF4 DIFFERENCES DUE TO LACK OF WILL		
		1 YES	2 NO	Total
RACPRES WOULD VOTE FOR BLACK PRESIDENT	1 YES	87.3%	98.3%	92.8%
	2 NO	11.8%	1.7%	6.7%
	9	.9%		.4%
Total		100.0%	100.0%	100.0%

As you can see, the opinion that poverty is a result of a "lack of motivation and will" is strongly related to the view that whites should be able to live in segregated neighborhoods. Similarly, the belief has the potential of preventing many Americans from voting for an African American presidential candidate, if one should run.

To test the racist quality in the first item further, let's control for RACE. If there is a racist element, we should expect to find the correlation only among whites. Let's check it out.

RACDIF4 DIFFERENCES DUE TO LACK OF WILL * RACSEG WHITES HAVE RIGHT TO SEG. NEIGHBORHOOD * RACE RACE OF RESPONDENT Crosstabulation

% within RACSEG WHITES HAVE RIGHT TO SEG. NEIGHBORHOOD

RACE RACE OF RESPONDENT			RACSEG WHITES HAVE RIGHT TO SEG. NEIGHBORHOOD				
			1 AGREE STRONGLY	2 AGREE SLIGHTLY	3 DISAGREE SLIGHTLY	4 DISAGREE STRONGLY	Total
1 WHITE	RACDIF4 DIFFERENCES DUE TO LACK OF WILL	1 YES	77.8%	85.7%	57.9%	41.2%	52.7%
		2 NO	22.2%	14.3%	42.1%	58.8%	47.3%
	Total		100.0%	100.0%	100.0%	100.0%	100.0%
2 BLACK	RACDIF4 DIFFERENCES DUE TO LACK OF WILL	1 YES			42.9%	52.0%	47.1%
		2 NO	100.0%	100.0%	57.1%	48.0%	52.9%
	Total		100.0%	100.0%	100.0%	100.0%	100.0%
3 OTHER	RACDIF4 DIFFERENCES DUE TO LACK OF WILL	1 YES		100.0%	50.0%	20.0%	30.8%
		2 NO			50.0%	80.0%	69.2%
	Total			100.0%	100.0%	100.0%	100.0%

Looking at the table, we can see that among whites, 16 percent strongly agreed and 14 percent slightly agreed that whites had a right to their own neighborhoods. Among the African Americans and "others," no one strongly agreed that whites had a right to their own neighborhoods. Only 13 "other" responded to these items, too few for a meaningful analysis.

Is the divide as great when voting for an African American presidential candidate? You know what to do. Find out.

Here's how you might summarize these tables in a term paper or journal article:

Percentage Who Say African Americans Lack Will	Strongly Agree	Agree	Disagree	Strongly Disagree
Whites	16	14	25	45
Blacks	—	—	18	81

We've taken you through this complex multivariate analysis to demonstrate the importance of ascertaining the sometimes-hidden meanings that lie behind the responses that people give to survey questions. That's a big part of the *adventure* of social research. (We wanted to call this book *Earl and Fred's Excellent Adventure,* but you know publishers.)

If you would like to continue this line of analysis, why don't you substitute POLREC for RACSEG in the above analysis? We leave that possibility in your able, multivariate hands.

20.5 **Summary**

The National Rifle Association and other proponents of extensive gun distribution (see GUNLAW) are fond of saying, "Guns don't kill people; people kill people." Well, in a more pacific spirit, we'd like to suggest that SPSS doesn't analyze data; analysts analyze data. And the good news is that you are now a bona fide, certifiable data analyst.

We've given you about all the guidance and assistance that we planned when we started this adventure. Remember, we said, "just add you" in Chapter 1; well, it's show time. You're on your own now, although you should have a support network behind you. If you read this book in connection with a college course, you have your instructor. In any event, you can call upon SPSS for assistance, and you have us; you can reach us by calling Fred Halley at Socware, Inc., in Brockport, New York, at (716) 352-1986.

The final chapter of this book expands the horizons of social research even further. It suggests a number of ways that you might reach out beyond the GSS data set we have provided for your introductory experience with the adventure of social research.

Part V The Adventure Continues

Chapter 21 **Further Opportunities for Social Research**

In this concluding chapter, we want to explore several different ideas that may support your continued investigations into the nature of human beings and the societies they create. Among other things, we will talk about other data sources you might explore and other computer programs you might use.

It has struck us that you might be interested in conducting your own survey—perhaps as a class project—and we discuss how to do that in this chapter. Appendixes A and B provide you with further resources for this purpose.

We hope that by the time you finish this chapter, you will have fully realized the two purposes that lay behind our writing this book: to help you learn (a) the logic of social research and (b) how to pursue that logic through the use of SPSS. In addition, we hope you will have experienced some of the excitement and challenge that make social research such a marvelous adventure.

Chapter 21 Further Opportunities for Social Research

Well, we've come to the end of our introduction to SPSS. In this final chapter, we want to suggest ways in which you can expand beyond the scope of this book.

21.1 Doing Your Own Survey

The GSS data set provided with this book is of special interest to researchers because it offers a window on American public opinion. We thought you might be interested in learning about the thoughts and actions of people across the country.

At the same time, we've found that data analysis in a classroom setting is sometimes more meaningful if the data are more personal. Perhaps you would like to analyze the opinions and behaviors of your own class (if it's a large one) or those of students elsewhere in your school. To help you collect your own data, we have included a questionnaire in Appendix A that asks some of the same questions that were asked in the GSS. We've also made provisions for any modifications that you might like to make in the interest of local relevance. You can make copies of the questionnaire and use it to collect your data.

More ambitiously, you might choose to design a totally different questionnaire that deals with whatever variables interest you. There is no need for you to be limited to the GSS variables that we've analyzed in this book or that we've suggested in the sample questionnaire. You have learned a technology that is much more broadly usable than that.

Whatever survey you choose to conduct, Appendix B tells you how to get your data into a form that SPSS will accept for analysis.

21.2 The Unabridged GSS

The GSS data set that accompanies this book is limited to 40 variables in order to accommodate all versions of SPSS. At the same time, you should realize that the data available through the GSS program are vastly more extensive. The 1996 data contain 1,041 variables and 2,090 cases.

Since the first General Social Survey was conducted in 1972, data have been collected on hundreds of variables. The table shown here from Davis and Smith (1996) indicates the topics covered and the years during which data were collected on those topics. Now that you are familiar with the use of GSS data through SPSS, you can probably locate other GSS data sets through your school.

The National Opinion Research Center maintains an Internet site called GSSDIRS, the General Social Survey Data and Information Retrieval System. It provides helpful information about the GSS as well as access to the GSS data back to 1972. GSSDIRS's homepage may be found at http://www.icpsr.umich.edu/gss

The site contains a search engine that locates abstracts of research reports produced from GSS data, an electronic edition of the complete GSS codebook, a GSS bibliography, and a data extraction system that permits downloading GSS data in a format that can be used with any version of SPSS.

An important reference book for your use with GSS data is the annual *Cumulative Codebook* published by the National Opinion Research Center at the University of Chicago. Available both in book and computer forms, it may be obtained from the Roper Center for Public Opinion Research, Box 440, Storrs, CT 06268 (860-486-4440). Here is a sample of the information available to you in this valuable document (this excerpt is from the 1996 edition by Davis and Smith).

```
-209-                          COLS. 786-791
                                                        Qs. 206G-208B
G. The woman wants it for any reason?

[VAR:ABANY]

RESPONSE PUNCH                    YEAR
                 1972-82 1982B 1983-87 1987B 1988-91 1993 1994 1996 COL. 786 ALL
Yes          1    2221     87    2164   129   1523   458  895  819       8,296
No           2    3584    237    3646   207   2230   552 1039 1002      12,497
Don't know   8     209     26     201    14    147    59   56   94         806
No answer    9      22      4      61     3     20     6    6    8         130
Not
  applicable BK   7590      0    1470     0  11987   531  996  981      13,555
```

REMARKS: See Appendix T, GSS Methodological Reports Nos. 19 and 42. In 1983 this question was asked immediately before Qs. 167 and 212 on Form 1. On Form 2 this question was immediately preceded by Qs. 167 and 212. See Q. 248 for a discussion of the split-half *sample design.* See Appendix P.

207. Have you heard or read of the recent Supreme Court decision concerning abortion?

```
[VAR: ABORCTI

RESPONSE PUNCH                          YEAR                            COL. 787
                    1972-82 1982B 1983-87 1987B 1988-91 1993 1994 1996    ALL
Yes              1     1288    0      0     0      0     0    a    0     11288
No               2      204    0      0     0      0     0    0    0       204
Don't know       8       11    0      0     0      0     0    0    0        11
No answer        9        1    0      0     0      0     0    0    0         1
Not applicable BK     12122  354   7542   353  51907  1606 2992 2904   33,780
```

208. As far as you've heard what are the main arguments in favor of abortions? PROBE EACH RESPONSE FOR CLARITY. PROBE FOR ADDITIONAL REASONS.

A. First reason

```
[VAR: ABPROL]

RESPONSE PUNCH                          YEAR                          COL.788-789
                    1972-82 1982B 1983-87 1987B 1988-91 1993 1994 1996    ALL
              1-10      44    8      0     0      0     0    0    0        52
             11-20     345   59      0     0      0     0    0    0       404
             21-30     303   56      0     0      0     0    0    0       359
             31-40     206   38      0     0      0     0    0    0       244
             41-50     284   69      0     0      0     0    0    0        80
None           96      259  107      0     0      0     0    0    0       366
No answer      99        0    2      0     0      0     0    0    0         2
Not applicable BK    12120    0   7542   353  5,907  1606 2992 2904   33,424
```

B. Second reason

```
[VAR: ABPRO2]

RESPONSE PUNCH                          YEAR                          COL. 790-791
                    1972-82 1982B 1983-87 1987B 1988-91 1993 1994 1996    ALL
              1-10      13    3      0     0      0     0    0    0        16
             11-20     101   21      0     0      0     0    0    0       122
             21-30     239   40      0     0      0     0    0    0       279
             31-40     162   30      0     0      0     0    0    0       192
             41-50     277   53      0     0      0     0    0    0       330
             51-60      46    5      0     0      0     0    0    0        51
No answer      99        2    0      0     0      0     0    0    0         2
Not appLicable
(No 2nd response) BK 12788  200   7542   353  5,907  1606 2992 2904   34,292
```

From *General Social Surveys, 1972-1996: Cumulative Codebook* (pp. 72-90) by James A. Davis and Tom W. Smith. September, 1996, Chicago: National Opinion Research Center. Reprinted by permission.

Another very valuable resource document is NORC's annual review of research uses of GSS data sets, the *Annotated Bibliography of Papers Using the General Social Survey* (e.g., see Smith, Arnold, and Lancaster, 1996).

In addition to the advantage of working with many more variables than we've included in the present file, the larger GSS data set permits you to conduct longitudinal research—to analyze changes in opinions and behaviors over the years. The initial experience of the GSS data set in connection with this book has put you in touch with a powerful research resource that we hope you'll be able to use more extensively in the future.

21.3 Other Data Sets

As if the full GSS weren't enough, there are thousands of other data sets in existence that are appropriate for analysis with SPSS. To begin, there is a global network of data archives, or data libraries, that operate somewhat like book libraries. Instead of lending books, these archives lend or sell sets of data that have been collected previously. The National Opinion Research Center, which administers the GSS, is one such archive. Another major archive is the Roper Center for Public Opinion Research (P.O. Box 440, Storrs, CT 06268; 860-486-4440 or www.lib.uconn.edu/RoperCenter). Other data archives are maintained in the survey research centers of major universities, such as the University of California, Berkeley and Los Angeles campuses; the University of Michigan; and the University of Wisconsin.

The data sets available for **secondary analysis** include studies conducted by university faculty researchers, for example, that may have been financed by federal research grants. Thus, the results of studies that may have cost hundreds of thousands of dollars to conduct can be yours now for the nominal cost of copying and shipping the data.

The Roper Center is a repository for all the data collected by the Gallup Organization, including not only American "Gallup Polls" but those done by Gallup in other countries. Survey research is an active enterprise in many countries. In Japan, for example, the major newspapers, such as the *Mainichi Shimbun* and *Yomiuri Shimbun,* conduct countless surveys, and it is possible for you to obtain and analyze some of those survey data through data archives in the United States.

You should realize that the U.S. government also conducts a great many surveys that produce data suitable for analysis with SPSS. The U.S. Census is a chief example, and it is possible for researchers to obtain and analyze data collected in the decennial censuses.

It is worth recalling that when Emile Durkheim set about his major analysis of suicide in Europe, he was forced to work with printed government reports of suicide rates in various countries and regions. Moreover, his reanalyses of those data needed to be done by hand.

With the advent of computers for mass data storage and analytic programs such as SPSS, the possibilities for secondary analysis have been revolutionized. You live at an enviable time in that regard.

21.4 Other Computer Programs

We have organized this book around the use of SPSS because it is so widely used by social scientists. Quite frankly, we spent a fair amount of time considering other programs as the focus for the book, but ultimately decided it would be most useful to the greatest number of students if we used SPSS. And by the way, SPSS's popularity is largely due to its excellence as a tool for social research.

At the same time, we want you to know that there are several other excellent analytic programs available. We'll mention some of these here in the event that you may have access to them. You should realize that the commands and procedures used in other programs will differ from those of SPSS, but the logic of data analysis that we've presented in this book applies across the various programs available.

Probably the program package next most commonly used by social scientists is SAS. Like SPSS, it is an omnibus package of techniques that goes far beyond those to which we've introduced you in this book. Should it be useful to you, SAS functions within a broader set of programs for accounting, management, and other activities.

SYSTAT is another widely used package of programs designed for social science research. Moreover, SYSTAT has an excellent and very inexpensive student version called MYSTAT, which you may be able to obtain through your campus bookstore, computing center, or statistics department.

MicroCase, by Cognitive Development, is another excellent program for social science data analysis. It usually comes with a large GSS data set, data on the states of the United States, data from Canadian provinces, and other data sets as well. ShowCase, by the same company, presents state and province data in a map format. Thus, for example, you can ask for the divorce rates in different U.S. states and see the several states shaded according to a code indicating how high or low the rates are. Unlike the command structure of SPSS, MicroCase operates primarily according to a menu system, wherein you select techniques and options from a list rather than having to remember the forms of particular commands.

Here's just a partial list of other programs that you might use for social science data analysis: ABtab, AIDA, A.STAT, BMDP, Chippendale, CRISP, DAISY, DATA-X, Dynacomp, INTER-STAT, MASS, Microquest, Microstat, Micro-SURVEY, MIDAS, Minitab, POINT FIVE, P-STAT, SAM, SNAP, SOS, Statgraf, Statpak, StatPro, STATS PLUS, Statview, Survey Mate, STAT80, STATA, SURVTAB, TECPACS.

We've seen that SPSS has some capability for presenting data in a graphic form, such as histograms. Other programs, such as Cricket and Harvard Graphics, to name just two, offer much more powerful sets of visual techniques.

21.5 Summary

We hope you've had some fun as you've worked through this book, and that you've learned some important research techniques and some facts about the American public. We hope you have discovered that social research—although very important, especially considering the range of social problems we confront today—is also a fascinating enterprise.

Like the investigative detective, the social researcher must possess large amounts of curiosity and ingenuity. Sit beside a social researcher at work, and you'll hear him or her muttering things like, "Wait a minute. If that's the case, then I'd expect to find . . . "; "Hey, that probably explains why . . . "; "Omigod! That means . . ." Maybe you've overheard yourself practicing these social scientific incantations. If so, congratulations and welcome. If not, you have a delightful adventure waiting for you just around the corner. We'll see you there.

Appendix A **Questionnaire for Class Survey**

ID   ____ ____ ____ (CODE LEADING ZEROS)

____   ____   ____

1   2   3

CHLDIDEL   1. What do you think is the ideal number of children for a family to have?

             ____ ____ (CODE LEADING ZERO IF < 10)

____   ____

4   5

2. If you had to choose, which thing on this list would you say is the most important for a child to learn to prepare him or her for life? (CODE 1)

[INTERVIEWER: READ CHOICES BELOW]

OBEY   ____ A. to obey

____

6

POPULAR   ____ B. to be well liked or popular

____

7

THNKSELF   ____ C. to think for himself or herself

____

8

WORKHARD   ____ D. to work hard

____

9

HELPOTH   ____ E. to help others

____

10

     a. Which comes next in importance? (Code 2)

     b. Which comes third? (Code 3)

     c. Which comes forth? (Code 4)

     d. Which comes fifth? (Code 5)

     (no response: Code 9)

SIBS   3. How many brothers and sisters did you have? Please count those born alive, but no longer living, as well as those alive now. Also include stepbrothers and stepsisters, and children adopted by your parents.

____   ____

11   12

             ____ ____ (CODE NUMBER WITH LEADING ZERO)

MARITAL   4. Are you—married, widowed, divorced, separated,
or have you never been married?   ____
                                                             13

       _____ 1. married
       _____ 2. widowed
       _____ 3. divorced
       _____ 4. separated
       _____ 5. never married
       _____ 9. no answer

[INTERVIEWER: ASK QUESTION 5 ONLY IF MARRIED OR WIDOWED]

DIVORCE   5. Have you ever been divorced or legally separated?   ____
                                                                    14

       _____ 1. yes
       _____ 2. no
       _____ 3. no answer or not applicable

PARTYID   6. Generally speaking, do you usually think of yourself
as a Republican, Democrat, Independent, or what?   ____
                                                             15

       _____ 0. strong Democrat
       _____ 1. not very strong Democrat
       _____ 2. Independent, close to Democrat
       _____ 3. Independent, neither, or no response
       _____ 4. Independent, close to Republican
       _____ 5. not very strong Republican
       _____ 6. strong Republican
       _____ 7. other party, refused to say
       _____ 9. no answer

POLVIEWS   7. We hear a lot of talk these days about liberals and conservatives.
I'm going to read you a set of seven categories of political views
that people might hold, arranged from extremely liberal to extremely
conservative. Which best describes you, or haven't you thought much
about this?   ____
                                                             16

       _____ 1. extremely liberal
       _____ 2. liberal
       _____ 3. slightly liberal
       _____ 4. moderate, middle-of-the-road
       _____ 5. slightly conservative
       _____ 6. conservative
       _____ 7. extremely conservative
       _____ 9. no answer or not applicable

CAPPUN   8. Do you favor or oppose the death penalty for murder?   ____
                                                                                                               17

                  ____ 1. favor
                  ____ 2. oppose
                  ____ 9. don't know, no answer

GUNLAW   9. Would you favor or oppose a law that would require a person   ____
                   to obtain a police permit before he or she could buy a gun?   18

                  ____ 1. favor
                  ____ 2. oppose
                  ____ 9. don't know, no answer

GETAHEAD   10. Some people say that people get ahead by their own hard work;   ____
                   others say that lucky breaks or help from other people is more   19
                   important. Which do you think is most important?

                  ____ 1. hard work most important
                  ____ 2. hard work, luck equally important
                  ____ 3. luck most important
                  ____ 9. other, don't know, no answer

RACDIF4   11. On the average, African Americans have worse jobs, income and   ____
                   housing than white people. Do you think this is because African   20
                   Americans just don't have the motivation or will to pull themselves
                   up out of poverty?

                  ____ 1. yes
                  ____ 2. no

RACSEG   12. Do you agree that white people have a right to keep (Blacks/   ____
                   African Americans) out of their neighborhoods if they want to,   21
                   and (Blacks/African Americans) should respect that right?

                  ____ 1. agree strongly
                  ____ 2. agree slightly
                  ____ 3. disagree slightly
                  ____ 4. disagree strongly
                  ____ 9. no opinion, no answer

RACPRES   13. If your party nominated a black for president, would you   ____
                   vote for him if he was qualified for the job?   22

                  ____ 1. yes
                  ____ 2. no
                  ____ 3. don't know, no answer

14. Please tell me whether or not you think it should be possible for a pregnant woman to obtain a legal abortion if . . .

ABDEFECT   A. If there is a strong chance of serious defect in the baby?

                              _____ 1. yes
                              _____ 2. no
                              _____ 3. don't know, no answer

_____ 23

ABNOMORE   B. If she is married and does not want any more children?

    _____ 1. yes
    _____ 2. no
    _____ 3. don't know, no answer

_____ 24

ABHLTH   C. If the woman's own health is seriously endangered by the pregnancy?

    _____ 1. yes
    _____ 2. no
    _____ 3. don't know, no answer

_____ 25

ABPOOR   D. If the family has a very low income and cannot afford any more children?

    _____ 1. yes
    _____ 2. no
    _____ 3. don't know, no answer

_____ 26

ABRAPE   E. If she became pregnant as a result of rape?

    _____ 1. yes
    _____ 2. no
    _____ 3. don't know, no answer

_____ 27

ABSINGLE   F. If she is not married and does not want to marry the man?

    _____ 1. yes
    _____ 2. no
    _____ 3. don't know, no answer

_____ 28

ABANY   G. If the woman wants it for any reason?

    _____ 1. yes
    _____ 2. no
    _____ 3. don't know, no answer

_____ 29

RELIG   15. What is your religious preference? Is it Protestant, Catholic, Jewish, some other religion, or no religion?

_____ 30

_____ 1. Protestant
_____ 2. Catholic
_____ 3. Jewish
_____ 4. none
_____ 5. other
_____ 9. no answer, no response

ATTEND   16. How often do you attend religious services?   _____
                                                              31

_____ 0. never
_____ 1. less than once a year
_____ 2. about once or twice a year
_____ 3. several times a year
_____ 4. about once a month
_____ 5. 2 or 3 times a month
_____ 6. nearly every week
_____ 7. every week
_____ 8. several times a week
_____ 9. don't know, no answer

POSTLIFE   17. Do you believe there is a life after death?   _____
                                                               32

_____ 1. yes
_____ 2. no
_____ 9. undecided, no answer, not applicable

PRAY   18. About how often do you pray?   _____
                                            33

_____ 1. several times a day
_____ 2. once a day
_____ 3. several times a week
_____ 4. once a week
_____ 5. less than once a week
_____ 6. never
_____ 9. don't know, no answer, not applicable

PREMARSX   19. There has been a lot of discussion about the way morals   _____
                and attitudes about sex are changing in this country.   34
                If a man and woman have sex relations before marriage,
                do you think it is always wrong, almost always wrong,
                wrong only sometimes, or not wrong at all?

_____ 1. always wrong
_____ 2. almost always wrong

_____ 3. wrong only sometimes

_____ 4. not wrong at all

_____ 9. don't know, no answer

HOMOSEX   20. What about sexual relations between two adults of the same   _____
sex—do you think it is always wrong, almost always wrong,   35
wrong only sometimes, or not wrong at all?

_____ 1. always wrong

_____ 2. almost always wrong

_____ 3. wrong only sometimes

_____ 4. not wrong at all

_____ 9. don't know, no answer

XMOVIE   21. Have you seen an X-rated movie in the last year?   _____
                                                                            36

_____ 1. yes

_____ 2. no

_____ 3. don't know, no answer

EDUC   22. What is the highest grade in elementary school or high   _____   _____
school that you finished and got credit for?   37   38

_____

[INTERVIEWER: IF RESPONDENT COMPLETED 12 GRADES,
ASK QUESTION 23.]

23. Did you complete one or more years of college for credit—   _____
not including schooling such as business college or technical   39
or vocational school?

_____ 1. yes

_____ 2. no

[INTERVIEWER: IF YES TO QUESTION 23, GO TO
QUESTION 24; ELSE GO TO QUESTION 30.]

24. How many years did you complete?   _____
                                                                     40

_____

CODING INSTRUCTION: ADD YEARS FROM QUESTION 22
TO YEARS FROM QUESTION 24 AND CODE WITH LEADING
ZERO IF NECESSARY IN COLUMNS 37 AND 38. USE CODE 99
FOR NO RESPONSE.

SEI   25. What is your occupation?   _____   _____
                                                                     41   42

_____ (write in)

[INTERVIEWER: IF RESPONDENT HAS NOT BEEN EMPLOYED
FULL-TIME, RECORD HIS OR HER FATHER'S OCCUPATION.]

CODING INSTRUCTION: LOOK UP OCCUPATION ON HODGE,
SIEGEL, AND ROSSI PRESTIGE SCALE AND RECORD SCORE IN
COLUMNS 41 AND 42. USE CODE 99 FOR NO RESPONSE.

CLASS 26. If you were asked to use one of four names for your social class,   ____
which would you say you belong in: the lower class, the working   43
class, the middle class, or the upper class?

_____ 1. lower class
_____ 2. working class
_____ 3. middle class
_____ 4. upper class
_____ 9. don't know, no answer

AGE 27. In what year were you born?   ____   ____
44   45

_____

CODING INSTRUCTION: SUBTRACT BIRTH YEAR FROM
THIS YEAR TO GET AGE IN YEARS. CODE IN COLUMNS
44 AND 45. CODE 99 FOR NO RESPONSE.

INCOME 28. In which of these groups did your total family income, from   ____   ____
all sources, fall last year, before taxes, that is? Just tell me   46   47
to stop when I say the category that describes your family.

_____ 01. less than $1,000
_____ 02. $1,000 to 2,999
_____ 03. $3,000 to 3,999
_____ 04. $4,000 to 4,999
_____ 05. $5,000 to 5,999
_____ 06. $6,000 to 6,999
_____ 07. $7,000 to 7,999
_____ 08. $8,000 to 9,999
_____ 09. $10,000 to 14,999
_____ 10. $15,000 to 19,999
_____ 11. $20,000 to 24,999
_____ 12. $25,000 or more
_____ 99. don't know, refusal, no response

RINCOME 29. In which of these groups did your earnings fall last year   ____   ____
(that is, before taxes and other deductions)?   48   49

_____ 01. less than $1,000

_____ 02. $1,000 to 2,999

_____ 03. $3,000 to 3,999

_____ 04. $4,000 to 4,999

_____ 05. $5,000 to 5,999

_____ 06. $6,000 to 6,999

_____ 07. $7,000 to 7,999

_____ 08. $8,000 to 9,999

_____ 09. $10,000 to 14,999

_____ 10. $15,000 to 19,999

_____ 11. $20,000 to 24,999

_____ 12. $25,000 or more

_____ 99. don't know, refusal, no response

RACE

30. CODING INSTRUCTION: CODE WITHOUT ASKING
ONLY IF THERE IS NO DOUBT IN YOUR MIND.

_____
50

_____ 1. white

_____ 2. black

_____ 3. other

SEX

31. CODING INSTRUCTION: CODE RESPONDENT'S SEX.

_____
51

_____ 1. male

_____ 2. female

Occupational Title and Socioeconomic Prestige Scores

Below are occupational titles and socioeconomic prestige scores for use in coding question 25, SEI, on the above questionnaire. To find a respondent's prestige score, look through the occupational titles until you find one that matches or is similar to the respondent's occupation. Write the number that appears to the right of the occupation in the space provided for it in the right margin of question 25 on the questionnaire.

The occupational prestige scores were developed by Hodge, Siegel, and Rossi at the University of Chicago. You can learn more about how the prestige scores were obtained by reading Appendices F and G in *General Social Surveys, 1972-1990: Cumulative Codebook* (Davis & Smith, 1990).

Occupational Classification	Prestige Scores
PROFESSIONAL, TECHNICAL, AND KINDRED WORKERS	
Accountants	57
Architects	71
Computer specialists	
Computer programmers	51
Computer systems analysts	51
Computer specialists, n.e.c.	51
Engineers	
Aeronautical/astronautical engineers	71
Chemical engineers	67
Civil engineers	68
Electrical and electronic engineers	69
Industrial engineers	54
Mechanical engineers	62
Metallurgical and materials engineers	56
Mining engineers	62
Petroleum engineers	67
Sales engineers	51
Engineers, n.e.c.	67
Farm management advisers	54
Foresters and conservationists	54
Home management advisers	54
Lawyers and judges	
Judges	76
Lawyers	76
Librarians, archivists, and curators	
Librarians	55
Archivists and curators	66
Mathematical specialists	
Actuaries	55
Mathematicians	65
Statisticians	55
Life and physical scientists	

Occupational Classification	Prestige Scores
Agricultural scientists	56
Atmospheric and space scientists	68
Biological scientists	68
Chemists	69
Geologists	67
Marine scientists	68
Physicists and astronomers	74
Life and physical scientists, n.e.c.	68
Operations and systems researchers and analysts	51
Personnel and labor relation workers	56
Physicians, dentists, and related practitioners	
Chiropractors	60
Dentists	74
Optometrists	62
Pharmacists	61
Physicians, including osteopaths	82
Podiatrists	37
Veterinarians	60
Health practitioners, n.e.c.	51
Nurses, dietitians, and therapists	
Dietitians	52
Registered nurses	62
Therapists	37
Health technologists and technicians	
Clinical laboratory technologists and technicians	61
Dental hygienists	61
Health record technologists and technicians	61
Radiologic technologists and technicians	61
Therapy assistants	37
Health technologists and technicians, n.e.c.	47
Religious workers	
Clergymen	69
Religious workers, n.e.c.	56

Occupational Classification	Prestige Scores
Social scientists	
Economists	57
Political scientists	66
Psychologists	71
Sociologists	66
Urban and regional planners	66
Social scientists, n.e.c.	66
Social and recreation workers	
Social workers	52
Recreation workers	49
Teachers, college and university	
Agriculture teachers	78
Atmospheric, earth, marine, and space teachers	78
Biology teachers	78
Chemistry teachers	78
Physics teachers	78
Engineering teachers	78
Mathematics teachers	78
Health specialists teachers	78
Psychology teachers	78
Business and commerce teachers	78
Economics teachers	78
History teachers	78
Sociology teachers	78
Social science teachers, n.e.c.	78
Art, drama, and music teachers	78
Coaches and physical education teachers	78
Education teachers	78
English teachers	78
Foreign language teachers	78
Home economics teachers	78
Law teachers	78
Theology teachers	78
Trade, industrial, and technical teachers	78
Miscellaneous teachers, college and university	78
Teachers, college and university, subject not specified	78
Teachers, except college and university	
Adult education teachers	43
Elementary school teachers	60
Prekindergarten and kindergarten teachers	60
Secondary school teachers	63
Teachers, except college and university, n.e.c.	43
Engineering and science technicians	
Agriculture and biological technicians, except health	47
Chemical technicians	47

Occupational Classification	Prestige Scores
Draftsmen	56
Electrical and electronic engineering technicians	47
Industrial engineering technicians	47
Mechanical engineering technicians	47
Mathematical technicians	47
Surveyors	53
Engineering and science technicians, n.e.c.	47
Technicians, except health, engineering, and science	
Airplane pilots	70
Air traffic controllers	43
Embalmers	52
Flight engineers	47
Radio operators	43
Tool programmers, numerical control	47
Technicians, n.e.c.	47
Vocational and educational counselors	51
Writers, artists, and entertainers	
Actors	55
Athletes and kindred workers	51
Authors	60
Dancers	38
Designers	58
Editors and reporters	51
Musicians and composers	46
Painters and sculptors	56
Photographers	41
Public relations men and publicity writers	57
Radio and television announcers	51
Writers, artists, and entertainers, n.e.c.	51
Researcher workers, not specified	51
Professional, technical, and kindred workers—allocated	51
MANAGERS AND ADMINISTRATORS, EXCEPT FARM	
Assessors, controllers, and treasurers, local public administration	61
Bank offices and financial managers	72
Buyers and shippers, farm products	41
Buyers, wholesale and retail trade	50
Credit men	49
Funeral directors	52
Health administrators	61
Construction inspectors, public administration	41
Inspectors, except construction, public administration	41
Managers and superintendents, building	38
Office managers, n.e.c.	50

Occupational Classification	Prestige Scores
Officers, pilots, and pursers; ship	60
Officials and administrators; public administration, n.e.c.	61
Officials of lodges, societies, and unions	58
Postmasters and mail superintendents	58
Purchasing agents and buyers, n.e.c.	48
Railroad conductors	41
Restaurant, cafeteria, and bar managers	39
Sales managers and department heads, retail trade	50
Sales managers, except retail trade	50
School administrators, college	61
School administrators, elementary and secondary	60
Managers and administrators, n.e.c.	50
Managers and administrators, except farm— allocated	50
SALES WORKERS	
Advertising agents and salesmen	42
Auctioneers	32
Demonstrators	28
Hucksters and peddlers	18
Insurance agents, brokers, and underwriters	47
Newsboys	15
Real estate agents and brokers	44
Stocks and bonds salesmen	51
Salesmen and sales clerks, n.e.c.	34
Sales representatives, manufacturing industries	49
Sales representatives, wholesale trade	40
Sales clerks, retail trade	29
Salesmen, retail trade	29
Salesmen of services and construction	34
Sales workers—allocated	34
CLERICAL AND KINDRED WORKERS	
Bank tellers	50
Billings clerks	45
Bookkeepers	48
Cashiers	31
Clerical assistants, social welfare	36
Clerical supervisors, n.e.c.	36
Collectors, bill and account	26
Counter clerks, except food	36
Dispatchers and starters, vehicle	34
Enumerators and interviewers	36
Estimators and investigators, n.e.c.	36
Expediters and production controllers	36
File clerks	30
Insurance adjusters, examiners, and investigators	48

Occupational Classification	Prestige Scores
Library attendants and assistants	41
Mail carriers, post office	42
Messengers and office boys	19
Meter readers, utilities	36
Office machine operators	
Bookkeeping and billing machine operators	45
Calculating machine operator	45
Computer and peripheral equipment operators	45
Duplicating machine operators	45
Keypunch operators	45
Tabulating machine operators	45
Office machine operators, n.e.c.	45
Payroll and timekeeping clerks	41
Postal clerks	43
Proofreaders	36
Real estate appraisers	43
Receptionists	39
Secretaries	
Secretaries, legal	46
Secretaries, medical	46
Secretaries, n.e.c.	46
Shipping and receiving clerks	29
Statistical clerks	36
Stenographers	43
Stock clerks and storekeepers	23
Teacher aides, except school monitors	36
Telegraph messengers	30
Telegraph operators	44
Telephone operators	40
Ticket, station, and express agents	35
Typists	41
Weighers	36
Miscellaneous clerical workers	36
Not specified clerical workers	36
Clerical and kindred workers—allocated	36
CRAFTSMEN AND KINDRED WORKERS	
Automobile accessories installers	47
Bakers	34
Blacksmiths	36
Boilermakers	31
Bookbinders	31
Brickmasons and stonemasons	36
Brickmasons and stonemasons, apprentices	36
Bulldozer operators	33
Cabinetmakers	39
Carpenters	40
Carpenter apprentices	40
Carpet installers	47
Cement and concrete finishers	32

Occupational Classification	Prestige Scores
Compositors and typesetters	38
Printing trades apprentices, except pressmen	40
Cranemen, derrickmen, and hoistmen	39
Decorators and window dressers	37
Dental laboratory technicians	47
Electricians	49
Electrician apprentices	41
Electric power linemen and cablemen	39
Electrotypers and stereotypers	38
Engravers, except photoengravers	41
Excavating, grading and road machine operators, except bulldozer	33
Floor layers, except tile setters	40
Foremen, n.e.c.	45
Forgemen and hammermen	36
Furniture and wood finishers	29
Furriers	35
Glaziers	26
Heat treaters, annealers, and temperers	36
Inspectors, scalers, and graders: log and lumber	31
Inspectors, n.e.c.	31
Jewelers and watchmakers	37
Job and die setters, metal	48
Locomotive engineers	51
Locomotive firemen	36
Machinists	48
Machinist apprentices	41
Mechanics and repairmen	
Air conditioning, heating, and refrigeration	37
Aircraft	48
Automobile body repairmen	37
Automobile mechanics	37
Automobile mechanic apprentices	37
Data processing machine repairmen	34
Farm implements	33
Heavy equipment mechanics, including diesel	33
Household appliance and accessory installers and mechanics	33
Loom fixers	30
Office machines	34
Radio and television	35
Railroad and car shop	37
Mechanic, except auto, apprentices	41
Miscellaneous mechanics and repairmen	35
Not specified mechanics and repairmen	35
Millers; grain, flour, and feed	25
Millwrights	40
Molders, metal	39
Molder, apprentices	39
Motion picture projectionists	34
Opticians, and lens grinders and polishers	51

Occupational Classification	Prestige Scores
Painters, construction and maintenance	30
Painter apprentices	30
Paperhangers	24
Pattern and model makers, except paper	39
Photoengravers and lithographers	40
Piano and organ tuners and repairmen	32
Plasterers	33
Plasterer apprentices	33
Plumbers and pipe fitters	41
Plumber and pipe fitter apprentices	41
Power station operators	39
Pressmen and plate printers, printing	40
Pressmen apprentices	40
Rollers and finishers, metal	36
Roofers and slaters	31
Sheetmetal workers and tinsmiths	37
Sheetmetal apprentices	37
Shipfitters	36
Shoe repairmen	33
Sign painters and letterers	30
Stationary engineers	35
Stone cutters and stone carvers	33
Structural metal craftsmen	36
Tailors	41
Telephone installers and repairmen	39
Telephone linemen and splicers	39
Tile setters	36
Tool and die makers	42
Tool and die maker apprentices	41
Upholsterers	30
Specified craft apprentices, n.e.c.	41
Not specified apprentices	41
Craftsmen and kindred workers, n.e.c.	47
Former members of the armed forces	47
Craftsmen and kindred workers—allocated	47
Current members of the armed forces	47
OPERATIVES, EXCEPT TRANSPORT	
Asbestos and insulation workers	28
Assemblers	27
Blasters and powdermen	32
Bottling and canning operatives	23
Chainmen, rodmen, and axmen; surveying	39
Checkers, examiners, and inspectors; manufacturing	36
Clothing ironers and pressers	18
Cutting operatives, n.e.c.	26
Dressmakers and seamstresses, except factory	32
Drillers, earth	27
Dry wall installers and lathers	27
Dyers	25
Filers, polishers, sanders, and buffers	19
Furnacemen, smeltermen, and pourers	33

Occupational Classification	Prestige Scores
Garage workers and gas station attendants	22
Grades and sorters, manufacturing	33
Produce graders and packers, except factory and farm	19
Heaters, metal	33
Laundry and dry cleaning operatives, n.e.c.	18
Meat cutters and butchers, except manufacturing	32
Meat cutters and butchers, manufacturing	28
Meat wrappers, retail trade	19
Metal platers	29
Milliners	33
Mine operatives, n.e.c.	26
Mixing operatives	29
Oilers and greasers, except auto	24
Packers and wrappers, n.e.c.	19
Painters, manufactured articles	29
Photographic process workers	36
Precision machine operatives	
Drill press operatives	29
Grinding machine operatives	29
Lathe and milling machine operatives	29
Precision machine operatives, n.e.c.	29
Punch and stamping press operatives	29
Riveters and fasteners	29
Sailors and deckhands	34
Sawyers	28
Sewers and stitchers	25
Shoemaking machine operatives	32
Solderers	29
Stationary firemen	33
Textile operatives	
Carding, lapping, and combing operatives	29
Knitters, loopers, and toppers	29
Spinners, twisters, and winders	25
Weavers	25
Textile operative, n.e.c.	29
Welders and flame-cutters	40
Winding operatives, n.e.c.	29
Machine operatives, miscellaneous specified	32
Machine operatives, not specified	32
Miscellaneous operatives	32
Not specified operatives	32
Operatives, except transport—allocated	32
TRANSPORT EQUIPMENT OPERATIVES	
Boatmen and canalmen	37
Bus drivers	32
Conductors and motormen, urban rail transit	28
Deliverymen and routemen	28
Forklift and tow motor operatives	29
Motormen; mine, factory, logging camp, etc.	27
Parking attendants	22

Occupational Classification	Prestige Scores
Railroad brakemen	35
Railroad switchmen	33
Taxicab drivers and chauffeurs	22
Truck drivers	32
Transport equipment operatives—allocated	29
LABORERS, EXCEPT FARM	
Animal caretakers, except farm	29
Carpenters' helpers	23
Construction laborers, except carpenters' helpers	17
Fishermen and oystermen	30
Freight and material handlers	17
Garbage collectors	17
Gardeners and groundskeepers, except farm	23
Longshoremen and stevedores	24
Lumbermen, raftsmen, and woodchoppers	26
Stockhandlers	17
Teamsters	12
Vehicle washers and equipment cleaners	17
Warehousemen, n.e.c.	20
Miscellaneous laborers	17
Not specified laborers	17
Laborers, except farm—allocated	17
FARMERS AND FARM MANAGERS	
Farmers (owners and tenants)	41
Farm managers	44
Farmers and farm managers—allocated	41
FARM LABORERS AND FARM FOREMEN	
Farm foremen	35
Farm laborers, wage workers	18
Farm laborers, unpaid family workers	18
Farm service laborers, self-employed	27
Farm laborers, farm foremen, and kindred workers—allocated	19
SERVICE WORKERS, EXCEPT PRIVATE HOUSEHOLD	
Cleaning service workers	
Chambermaids and maids, except private household	14
Cleaners and charwomen	12
Janitors and sextons	16
Food service workers	
Bartenders	20
Busboys	22
Cooks, except private household	26
Dishwashers	22
Food counters and fountain workers	15
Waiters	20
Food service workers, n.e.c., except private household	22
Health service workers	
Dental assistants	48
Health aides, except nursing	48

Occupational Classification	Prestige Scores	Occupational Classification	Prestige Scores
Health trainees	36	Welfare service aids	14
Midwives	23	Protective service workers	
Nursing aides, orderlies, and attendants	36	Crossing guards and bridge tenders	24
Practical nurses	42	Firemen, fire protection	44
Personal service workers		Guards and watchmen	22
Airline stewardesses	36	Marshals and constables	46
Attendants, recreation and amusement	15	Policemen and detectives	48
Attendants, personal service, n.e.c.	14	Sheriffs and bailiffs	55
Baggage porters and bellhops	14	Service workers, except private	
Barbers	38	households—allocated	25
Boarding and lodging housekeepers	22	PRIVATE HOUSEHOLD WORKERS	
Bootblacks	09	Child care workers, private household	23
Child care workers, except private households	25	Cooks, private household	18
Elevator operators	21	Housekeepers, private household	25
Hairdressers and cosmetologists	33	Laundresses, private household	18
Personal service apprentices	14	Maids and servants, private household	18
Housekeepers, except private households	36	Private household workers—allocated	18
School monitors	22	(Not applicable: Unemployed, No father substitute, Not married, Disabled, Retired,	
Ushers, recreation and amusement	15	No answers, and Don't know)	BK

Appendix B **Using SPSS for Your Data**

Getting data ready for analysis with SPSS is really a two-step process. The first step, often called *data definition,* involves establishing a computer file with names for variables, designated places for their storage, any variable or value labels, and missing values that you may wish to associate with each variable. Normally, that would be done using the Add Variable and Define Variable commands in SPSS for Windows. We have saved you the trouble of defining data you collect using the questionnaire in Appendix A. On the disk enclosed with this book is a file named LOCAL.SAV that contains a data definition. We'll show you how to use it a little later.

The second step is editing and coding your data. People do not always follow instructions when filling out a questionnaire. Verbal or written responses have to be transformed into a number code for processing with SPSS. For ease of entry, questionnaires should be edited for proper completion and coding before you attempt to key them into an SPSS file.

Coding Your Data

To the extent we could, we have designed the questionnaire in Appendix A to be self-coding. By having a number next to each response for the closed-ended questions, the interviewer assigns a code as the respondent answers the question. Some questions we have had to leave open-ended, either because there would be too many responses to print on the questionnaire or because we couldn't anticipate all of the possible responses.

Before the data for a single person can be entered into a file, the questionnaire needs to be edited. Each questionnaire should have a unique number in the ID field. We do this not because we want to identify individuals, but because frequently in the coding process, errors are committed that show up later. For instance, we have coded SEX as 1 for male and 2 for female, but in our analysis, we find a respondent with SEX coded 7. What we will need to do is find the record with the erroneous code 7, look up the ID number, go back to the original questionnaire, find out what code SEX should have been, and fix it.

Next in the editing process, we have to code the open-ended questions. All the people coding questions should be following the same written instructions for coding. For instance, at the end of Appendix A, we have included a list of occupations and their socioeconomic statuses for coding SEI, the socioeconomic index. Other coding schemes might not be as elaborate. For instance, in a medical study, patients might be asked about the illnesses that brought them to the hospital. Coding might be as simple as classifying the illnesses as acute or chronic.

Finally, the codes need to be written so that they are easy to read. We have designed our questionnaire to be edge coded. If you look in the right margin, we have put a space for each variable's code. We have included these numbers because some statistics require that variables be placed in specific "columns" across each "record." Happily, that is not a requirement of SPSS for Windows. We'll just use the numbered blanks as a convenient place to write our codes.

To edit your questionnaires, you will need a copy of the codes used to define the LOCAL.SAV file. It's easy to get. Bring up SPSS for Windows and place the disk that shipped with this book in a drive. Then click on the Data window to make it the active window. Once the Data window is in the foreground, click the following sequence:

File → Open → Data

On the File Type window, click on SPSS(*.SAV), then click on Drive and select either the A: or B: drive, depending on which you used for your disk. Now you should see both GSS.SAV and LOCAL.SAV in the window under "File Name." Click on LOCAL.SAV and then on "OK." The file type window should be replaced by a window of empty data cells. This is the empty, but defined, data file for your local data.

To have the codes printed out for your use in coding your data, click Utilities followed by File Info. The codes will print quickly on the screen. You should see the information for SEX in the output window. To have the codes printed, click on File and then Print. If there is a printer connected to your computer, you should have a hard copy of the codes printed in about a minute.

Here is the coding information for the variable RACSEG, responses to question number 12 on the questionnaire, "Do you agree that white people have a right to keep (Blacks/African-Americans) out of their neighborhoods if they want to, and (Blacks/African-Americans) should respect that right?"

```
RACSEG    WHITES HAVE RIGHT TO SEG. NEIGHBORHOOD    17
          Print Format: F1
          Write Format: F1
          Missing Values: 0, 8
          Value       Label
             0 M      NAP
             1         AGREE STRONGLY
             2         AGREE SLIGHTLY
             3         DISAGREE SLIGHTLY
             4         DISAGREE STRONGLY
```

For people who agree strongly that whites have a right to exclude blacks, code 1 is used. For people who slightly agree, code 2 is used, and so on. Notice that code 0, not applicable, has an "M" next to it. That means that code 0 has been designated a missing code. All missing codes are thrown out of the analysis. If respondents fail to answer a question, they should be assigned the missing value code for that variable.

Once you have edited and coded your questionnaires, you can move to the next step, entering data.

Entering Your Data

First, repeat the File → Open → Data sequence again. Click on LO-CAL.SAV again to retrieve the empty data file. Click on the Data window to move it to the front, if it isn't already there. What you should be looking at is an empty data matrix with the names of the variable names across the top and record numbers down the left side. You will notice that the order of the variables across the record is the same as the order of the variables on the questionnaire. We placed them in that order to make data entry easier and less error prone.[1]

You can easily move from cell to cell in the data matrix. Pressing just the Tab key moves the active cell to the right, and pressing the Shift and Tab keys moves the active cell to the left. You can tell the active cell by its thick black border. Pressing the Enter key moves the active cell down to the next record. The directional arrows will also move the active cell, one cell at a time. The mouse can be used to make a cell active just by pointing and clicking. Long-distance moves can be made by pressing Ctrl and Home to move to the left-most cell on the first case and Ctrl and End to move to the right-most cell on the last case.

When you key in data, the data first appear on a line under the name of the file. When you move the active cell, the data jump to the cell. Data may be changed at any time just by moving to the cell and keying in new values.

If a particular case turns into a disaster, you can get rid of the entire case by clicking on the record number at the extreme left of a record and pressing the Delete key.

After you are done entering data, or if you want to stop entering data and continue at a later time, click on File and Save Data. Your data will be saved under the name that was used at the beginning of the session. If you wish to save it under another name, click on File and Save As. Be careful of which disk drive you save to. If the computer is in a public place, you will want to save your work on a removable disk (A: or B:) so that you can take it with you.

If you save your data file at the end of a session, you can pick up where you left off by retrieving it in subsequent sessions. To retrieve a file and start adding data again, just click the File → Open → Data sequence.

Summary

Although there is a fair amount of work involved in doing your own survey and entering your own data, there can also be a special reward or excitement about coming to understand the opinions and behaviors of a group of people with whom you are directly familiar.

Note

1. More detailed instructions for defining a file and entering data may be found in the *SPSS for Windows Release 7.5, Base System User's Guide* or in the *SPSS for Windows, Release 7.5, Student Version.*

Appendix C The Research Report

This book has considered the variety of activities that compose the analysis of social research. In this appendix, we turn to an often neglected subject: reporting your analyses of data to others. Unless the research is properly communicated, all the efforts devoted to the previously discussed procedures will go for naught.

Before proceeding further on this topic, we should suggest one absolutely basic guideline. Good social scientific reporting requires good English (unless you are writing in a foreign language). Whenever we ask the "figures to speak for themselves," they tend to remain mute. Whenever we use unduly complex terminology or construction, communication is reduced. Every researcher should read and reread (at approximately three-month intervals) an excellent small book by William Strunk, Jr., and E. B. White, *The Elements of Style*.[1] If you do this faithfully, and if even 10 percent of the contents rub off, you stand a rather good chance of making yourself understood and your findings perhaps appreciated.

Scientific reporting has several functions, and it is a good idea to keep these in mind. First, the report communicates to an audience a body of specific data and ideas. The report should provide those specifics clearly and with sufficient detail to permit an informed evaluation. Second, the scientific report should be viewed as a contribution to the general body of professional knowledge. While remaining appropriately humble, you should always regard your research report as an addition to what we know about social research. Finally, the report should serve the function of stimulating and directing further inquiry.

Some Basic Considerations

Despite these general guidelines, different reports serve different purposes. A report appropriate for one purpose might be wholly inappropriate for another. This section of this appendix deals with some of the basic considerations in this regard.

From *Research Methods for Social Work,* 2nd edition, by Allen Rubin and Earl Babbie. Copyright © 1993 by Wadsworth, Inc. Reprinted by permission of Brooks/Cole Publishing Company, Pacific Grove, CA 93950.

Audience

Before drafting your report, you must ask yourself who you hope will read it. Normally, you should make a distinction between professional colleagues and general readers. If your report is written for the former, you may make certain assumptions about their existing knowledge and may perhaps summarize certain points rather than explaining them in detail. Similarly, you may use more technical language than would be appropriate for a general audience.

At the same time, you should remain always aware that any science or profession is composed of factions or cults. Terms and assumptions acceptable to your immediate colleagues may only confuse other professionals. That applies with regard to substance as well as techniques. The family sociologist who is writing for a general audience, for example, should explain previous findings in more detail than would be necessary if he or she were addressing an audience of sociologists specializing in the family area.

Form and Length of the Report

We should begin this subsection by saying that our comments apply to both written and oral reports. These two forms, however, will affect the nature of the report.

It is useful to think about the variety of reports that might result from a research project. To begin, you may wish to prepare a short *research note* for publication in an academic or technical journal. Such reports should be approximately one to five pages in length (typed, double-spaced) and should be concise and direct. In such a small amount of space, you will not be able to present the state of the field in any detail, and your methodological notes must be somewhat abbreviated as well. Basically, you should tell the reader why you feel a brief note is justified by your findings, then tell what those findings are.

Often, researchers must prepare reports for the sponsors of their research. These may vary greatly in length, of course. In preparing such a report, however, you should bear in mind the audience for the report—scientific or lay—and their reasons for sponsoring the project in the first place. It is both bad politics and bad manners to bore the sponsors with research findings that have no interest or value to them. At the same time, it may be useful to summarize the ways in which the research has advanced basic scientific knowledge (if it has).

Working papers or monographs are another form of research reporting. Especially in a large and complex project, it will be useful to obtain comments on your analysis and the interpretation of your data. A working paper constitutes a tentative presentation with an implicit request for comments. Working papers can also vary in length, and they may present all of the research findings of the project or only a portion of them. Because your professional reputation is not at stake in a working paper, you should feel free to present tentative interpretations that you cannot altogether justify—identifying them as such and asking for evaluations.

Many research projects result in papers delivered at professional meetings. Often, these serve the same purpose as working papers. You are able to present findings and ideas of possible interest to your colleagues and ask for their comments. Although the length of professional papers may vary depending on the organization of the meetings, we would encourage you to say too little rather than too much. Although a working paper may ramble somewhat through a variety of tentative conclusions, conference participants should not be forced to sit through an oral unveiling of the same. Interested listeners can always ask for more details later, and uninterested ones can gratefully escape.

Probably the most popular research report is the article published in an academic journal. Again, lengths vary, and you should examine the lengths of articles previously published by the journal in question. As a rough guide, however, 20 typed pages is as good as any. A subsequent section on the organization of the report is primarily based on the structure of a journal article, so we shall say no more at this point, except to indicate that student term papers should be written on this model. As a general rule, a term paper that would make a good journal article will also make a good term paper.

A book, of course, represents the most prestigious form of research report. It has all the advantages of the working paper—length, detail—but it should be a more polished document. Because the publication of research findings as a book gives those findings an appearance of greater substance and worth, you have a special obligation to your audience. Although you will still hope to receive comments from colleagues, possibly leading you to revise your ideas, you must realize that other readers may be led to accept your findings uncritically.

Aim of the Report

Some reports may focus primarily on the *exploration* of a topic of interest. Inherent in this aim is the tentativeness and incompleteness of the conclusions. You should clearly indicate to your audience the exploratory aim of the study and point to the shortcomings of the particular project. An important aspect of an exploratory report is to point the way to more refined research on the topic.

Many studies have a *descriptive* purpose, and the research reports from such studies will have a descriptive element. You should carefully distinguish for the reader those descriptions that apply only to the sample and those that are inferred to the population. Whenever inferential descriptions are to be made, you should give your audience some indication of the probable range of error in those descriptions.

Many reports have an *explanatory* aim; the writer wishes to point to causal relationships among variables. Depending on the probable audience for your report, you should carefully delineate the rules of explanation that lie behind your computations and conclusions, and, as in the case of description, you must give your readers some guide to the relative certainty of your conclusions.

Finally, some research reports may have the aim of *proposing action*. For example, the researcher of prejudice may wish to suggest ways in which prejudice may be reduced, on the basis of the research findings. This aim often presents knotty problems, however, because your own values and orientations may interfere with your proposals. Although it is perfectly legitimate for your proposals to be motivated by personal values, you must ensure that the specific actions you propose are warranted by your data. Thus you should be especially careful to spell out the logic by which you move from empirical data to proposed action.

Organization of the Report

Although the organization of reports differs somewhat on the basis of form and purpose, it is possible to suggest a general format for presenting research data. The following comments apply most directly to a journal article, but with some modification they apply to most forms of research reports.

Purpose and Overview

It is always helpful to the reader if you begin with a brief statement of the purpose of the study and the main findings of the analysis. In a journal article, this overview may sometimes be given in the form of an *abstract* or *synopsis*.

Some researchers find this difficult to do. For example, your analysis may have involved considerable detective work, with important findings revealing themselves only as a result of imaginative deduction and data manipulation. You may wish, therefore, to lead the reader through the same exciting process with a degree of suspense and surprise. To the extent that this form of reporting gives an accurate picture of the research process, we feel it has considerable instructional value. Nevertheless, many readers may not be interested in following your entire research account, and not knowing the purpose and general conclusions in advance may make it difficult for them to understand the significance of the study.

An old forensic dictum says: "Tell them what you're going to tell them; tell them; and tell them what you told them." You would do well to follow this dictum in the preparation of research reports.

Review of the Literature

Because every research report should be placed in the context of the general body of scientific knowledge, it is important to indicate where your report fits in that picture. Having presented the general purpose of your study, you should then bring the reader up to date on the previous research in the area, pointing to general agreements and disagreements among the previous researchers.

In some cases, you may wish to challenge previously accepted ideas. You should carefully review the studies that led to the acceptance of those ideas, then indicate the factors that have not previously been considered or the logical fallacies present in the previous research.

When you are concerned with resolving a disagreement among previous researchers, you should organize your review of the literature around the opposing points of view. You should summarize the research supporting one view, then summarize the research supporting the other, and finally suggest the reasons for the disagreement.

To an extent, your review of the literature serves a bibliographic function for readers, indexing the previous research on a given topic. This can be overdone, however, and you should avoid an opening paragraph that runs three pages, mentioning every previous study in the field. The comprehensive bibliographic function can best be served by a bibliography at the end of the report, and the review of the literature should focus only on those studies that have direct relevance to the present study.

Avoiding Plagiarism

Whenever you are reporting on the work of others, it is important that you be clear about who said what. It is essential that you avoid *plagiarism,* the theft of another's words and/or ideas—whether intentional or accidental—and the presentation of those words and ideas as your own. Because this is a common and sometimes unclear problem for college students, let's take a minute to examine it in some detail. Here are the main ground rules regarding plagiarism:

- You cannot use another writer's exact words without using quotation marks (or setting the quote off as an extract) and giving a complete citation, which indicates the source of the quotation such that your reader could locate that quotation in its original context. As a rule of thumb, taking a passage of eight or more words without citation is a violation of federal copyright laws.

- It is also not acceptable to edit or paraphrase another's words and present the revised version as your own work.

- Finally, it is not acceptable even to present another's *ideas* as your own—even if you use totally different words to express those ideas.

The following examples should clarify what is and is not acceptable in the use of another's work.

The Original Work

Laws of Growth

Systems are like babies: once you get one, you have it. They don't go away. On the contrary, they display the most remarkable persistence. They not only persist; they grow. And as they grow, they encroach. The growth potential of systems was explored in a tentative, preliminary way by Parkinson, who concluded that administrative systems maintain average growth of 5 to 6 percent per annum regardless of the work to be done. Parkinson was right so far as he goes, and we must give him full honors for initiating the serious study of this important topic. But what Parkinson failed to perceive, we now enunciate—the general systems analogue of Parkinson's Law.

The System Itself Tends to Grow At 5 to 6 Percent Per Annum

Again, this Law is but the preliminary to the most general possible formulation, the Big-Bang Theorem of Systems Cosmology.

Systems Tend to Expand to Fill the Known Universe[2]

Now let's look at some of the *acceptable* ways you might make use of Gall's work in a term paper.

Acceptable: John Gall, in his work titled *Systemantics,* draws a humorous parallel between systems and infants: "Systems are like babies: once you get one, you have it. They don't go away. On the contrary, they display the most remarkable persistence. They not only persist; they grow."[3]

Acceptable: John Gall warns that systems are like babies. Create a system and it sticks around. Worse yet, Gall notes, systems keep growing larger and larger.[4]

Acceptable: It has also been suggested that systems have a natural tendency to persist, even grow and encroach (Gall 1975, p. 12). [Note: This format requires that you give a complete citation in your bibliography or reference section.]

Here now are some *unacceptable* uses of the same material, reflecting some common errors.

Unacceptable: In this paper, I want to look at some of the characteristics of the social systems we create in our organizations. First, systems are like babies: once you get one, you have it. They don't go away. On the contrary, they display the most remarkable persistence. They not only persist; they grow. [It is unacceptable to quote someone else's material directly without using quotation marks and giving a full citation.]

Unacceptable: In this paper, I want to look at some of the characteristics of the social systems we create in our organizations. First, systems are a lot like children: once you get one, it's yours. They don't go away; they persist. They not only persist, in fact: They grow. [It is unacceptable to edit another's work and present it as your own.]

Unacceptable: In this paper, I want to look at some of the characteristics of the social systems we create in our organizations. One thing I've noticed is that once you create a system, it never seems to go away. Just the opposite, in fact: They have tendency to grow. You might say systems are a lot like children in that respect. [It is unacceptable to paraphrase someone else's ideas and present them as your own.]

All of the preceding unacceptable examples show instances of plagiarism, and they represent a serious offense. Admittedly, there are some "gray areas." Some ideas are more or less in the public domain, not "belonging" to any one person. Or you may reach an idea on your own that someone else has already put in writing. If you have a question about a specific situation, discuss it with your instructor in advance.

We have discussed this topic in some detail because it is important that you place your research in the context of what others have done and said, and yet the improper use of others' material is a serious offense. Mastering this matter, however, is a part of your "coming of age" as a scholar.

Study Design and Execution

A research report containing interesting findings and conclusions can be very frustrating when the reader is unable to determine the methodological design and execution of the study. The worth of all scientific findings depends heavily on the manner in which the data were collected and analyzed.

In reporting the design and execution of a survey, for example, you should always include the following: the population, the sampling frame, the sampling method, the sample size, the data collection method, the completion rate, and the methods of data processing and analysis. Comparable details should be given if other methods are used. The experienced researcher is able to report these details in a rather short space, without omitting anything required for the reader's evaluation of the study.

Analysis and Interpretation

Having set the study in the perspective of previous research, and having described the design and execution of it, you should then present your data. The following major section will provide further guidelines in this regard. For now, a few general comments are in order.

The presentation of data, the manipulations of those data, and your interpretations should be integrated into a logical whole. It is frustrating to the reader to discover a collection of seemingly unrelated analyses and findings with a promise that all the loose ends will be tied together later in the report. Every step in the analysis should make sense—at the time it is taken. You should present your rationale for a particular analysis, present the data relevant to it, interpret the results, and then indicate where that result leads next.

Summary and Conclusions

Following the forensic dictum mentioned earlier, we believe it is essential to summarize the research report. You should avoid reviewing every specific finding, but you should review all of the significant ones, pointing once more to their general significance.

The report should conclude with a statement of what you have discovered about your subject matter and where future research might be directed. A quick review of recent journal articles will probably indicate a very high frequency of the concluding statement, "It is clear that much more research is needed." This is probably always a true conclusion, but it is of little value unless you can offer pertinent suggestions about the nature of that future research. You should review the particular shortcomings of your own study and suggest ways in which those shortcomings might be avoided by future researchers. You also should draw implications for social welfare policy and program development, social work practice, and, if appropriate, social work education. Make sure that the implications that you develop are supported by your findings; do not use this section of the report as a license to make unsupported editorial pronouncements.

Guidelines for Reporting Analyses

The presentation of data analyses should provide a maximum of detail without being cluttered. You can accomplish that best by continually examining your report to see whether it achieves the following aims.

Quantitative data should be presented in such a way as to permit recomputations by the reader. In the case of percentage tables, for example, the reader should be able to collapse categories and recompute the percentages. Readers should be given sufficient information to permit them to compute percentages in the table in the opposite direction from your own presentation.

All aspects of the analysis should be described in sufficient detail to permit a secondary analyst to replicate the analysis from the same body of data. This means that he or she should be able to create the same indexes and scales, produce the same tables, arrive at the same regression equations, obtain the same factors and factor loadings, and so forth. That will seldom be done, of course, but if the report is presented in such a manner as to make it possible, the reader will be far better equipped to evaluate the report.

A final guide to the reporting of methodological details is that the reader should be in a position to replicate the entire study independently. Recall from our earlier discussions in this book that replicability is an essential norm of science generally. A single study does not prove a point; only a series of studies can begin to do so. Unless studies can be replicated, there can be no meaningful series of studies.

We have previously mentioned the importance of integrating data, analysis, and interpretations in the report. A more specific guideline can be offered in this regard. Tables, charts, and figures, if any, should be integrated into the text of the report—appearing near that portion of the text discussing them. Sometimes students describe their analyses in the body of the report and place all the tables in an appendix at the end. This procedure greatly impedes the reader. As a general rule, it is best to (a) describe the purpose for presenting the table, (b) present it, and (c) review and interpret it.

Be explicit in drawing conclusions. Although research is typically conducted for the purpose of drawing general conclusions, you should carefully note the specific basis for such conclusions. Otherwise you may lead your reader into accepting unwarranted conclusions.

Point to any qualifications or conditions warranted in the evaluation of conclusions. Typically, you are in the best position to know the shortcomings and tentativeness of your conclusions, and you should give the reader the advantage of that knowledge. Failure to do so can misdirect future research and result in a waste of research funds.

We will conclude with a point made at the outset of this appendix, as it is extremely important. Research reports should be written in the best possible literary style. Writing lucidly is easier for some people than for others, and it is always harder than writing poorly. You are again referred to Strunk and White's *Elements of Style*. Every researcher would do well to follow this procedure: Write. Read Strunk and White. Revise. Reread Strunk and White. Revise again. That will be a difficult and time-consuming endeavor, but so is science.

A perfectly designed, carefully executed, and brilliantly analyzed study will be altogether worthless unless you are able to communicate your findings to others. This appendix has attempted to provide some general and specific guidelines toward that end. The best guides are logic, clarity, and honesty. Ultimately, there is no substitute for practice.

Notes

1. William Strunk, Jr., and E. B. White, *The Elements of Style,* 3rd ed. (New York: Macmillan, 1979). Another useful reference about writing is H. W. Fowler, *A Dictionary of Modern English Usage* (New York: Oxford University Press, 1965).

2. John Gall, *Systemantics: How Systems Work and Especially How They Fail* (New York: Quadrangle, 1975), 12-14. Note that in the original work Gall previously gave a full citation for Parkinson.

3. John Gall, *Systemantics: How Systems Work and Especially How They Fail* (New York: Quadrangle, 1975), 12.

4. John Gall, *Systemantics: How Systems Work and Especially How They Fail* (New York: Quadrangle, 1975), 12.

Appendix D Answers to Exercises

Chapter 6 Univariate Exercise: Religiosity

Describing Education

The mean education of the respondents is 13.48 years, and two-thirds of them have between 10.56 and 16.40 years of education.

Recoding Age

AGECAT Recoded Age Categories

		Frequency	Percent	Valid Percent	Cumulative Percent
Valid	1 Under 21	42	2.8	2.8	2.8
	2 21-39	625	41.7	41.7	44.5
	3 40-64	613	40.9	40.9	85.3
	4 65 and older	220	14.7	14.7	100.0
	Total	1500	100.0	100.0	
Total		1500	100.0		

Recoding Education

Transform → Recode → Into Different Variables

(Input Variable EDUC, Output Variable: EDCAT

Old and New Values:
    Lowest through 11 → 1
    12 → 2
    13 through 15 → 3
    16 → 4
    17 through 20 → 5

Value Labels:
    1 less than HS
    2 HS grad
    3 some college
    4 college grad
    5 grad studies

EDCAT recoded education

		Frequency	Percent	Valid Percent	Cumulative Percent
Valid	1 less than HS	240	16.0	16.1	16.1
	2 HS grad	419	27.9	28.0	44.1
	3 some college	418	27.9	28.0	72.1
	4 college grad	214	14.3	14.3	86.4
	5 grad studies	203	13.5	13.6	100.0
	Total	1494	99.6	100.0	
Missing	System Missing	6	.4		
	Total	6	.4		
Total		1500	100.0		

Chapter 11 Bivariate Exercise: Religiosity

Correlating Social Class and Religiosity

CHATT Recoded Church Attendance * CLASS SUBJECTIVE CLASS IDENTIFICATION
Crosstabulation

% within CLASS SUBJECTIVE CLASS IDENTIFICATION

| | | CLASS SUBJECTIVE CLASS IDENTIFICATION | | | | |
		1 LOWER CLASS	2 WORKING CLASS	3 MIDDLE CLASS	4 UPPER CLASS	Total
CHATT Recoded Church Attendance	1 About weekly	27.8%	26.1%	35.0%	30.6%	30.7%
	2 About monthly	17.7%	15.5%	14.7%	19.4%	15.4%
	3 Seldom	29.1%	42.8%	36.9%	35.5%	38.9%
	4 Never	25.3%	15.6%	13.3%	14.5%	15.0%
Total		100.0%	100.0%	100.0%	100.0%	100.0%

POSTLIFE BELIEF IN LIFE AFTER DEATH * CLASS SUBJECTIVE CLASS IDENTIFICATION
Crosstabulation

% within CLASS SUBJECTIVE CLASS IDENTIFICATION

| | | CLASS SUBJECTIVE CLASS IDENTIFICATION | | | | |
		1 LOWER CLASS	2 WORKING CLASS	3 MIDDLE CLASS	4 UPPER CLASS	Total
POSTLIFE BELIEF IN LIFE AFTER DEATH	1 YES	86.4%	80.4%	82.2%	66.7%	81.0%
	2 NO	13.6%	19.6%	17.8%	33.3%	19.0%
Total		100.0%	100.0%	100.0%	100.0%	100.0%

PRAY HOW OFTEN DOES R PRAY * CLASS SUBJECTIVE CLASS IDENTIFICATION
Crosstabulation

% within CLASS SUBJECTIVE CLASS IDENTIFICATION

| | | CLASS SUBJECTIVE CLASS IDENTIFICATION | | | | |
		1 LOWER CLASS	2 WORKING CLASS	3 MIDDLE CLASS	4 UPPER CLASS	Total
PRAY HOW OFTEN DOES R PRAY	1 SEVERAL TIMES A DAY	26.7%	32.5%	23.0%	22.2%	26.8%
	2 ONCE A DAY	36.7%	25.8%	34.1%	11.1%	30.2%
	3 SEVERAL TIMES A WEEK	16.7%	12.4%	13.4%	22.2%	13.5%
	4 ONCE A WEEK	6.7%	9.3%	6.9%	11.1%	8.0%
	5 LT ONCE A WEEK	10.0%	18.0%	18.0%	27.8%	17.9%
	6 NEVER	3.3%	2.1%	4.6%	5.6%	3.6%
Total		100.0%	100.0%	100.0%	100.0%	100.0%

These data clearly do *not* confirm the deprivation thesis, nor do they replicate the findings of the original research by Glock et al. In the case of church attendance, in fact, the correlation appears to be in the opposite direction from what was expected: Increasing social class seems to produce more religiosity. On the other two religious indicators, there appears to be no relationship at all.

It bears noting that the original study was limited to Episcopal church members, and the authors warned that the relationship between class and religiosity might not hold up among the general public, where many of those lowest in social class are unchurched.

Chapter 12 Bivariate Exercise: Politics

Age and Politics

What's the relationship between AGE and PARTYID? As you'll see, it's not as clear as that between AGE and POLVIEWS.

PARTY party identification * AGECAT Recoded Age Categories Crosstabulation

% within AGECAT Recoded Age Categories

		AGECAT Recoded Age Categories				
		1 Under 21	2 21-39	3 40-64	4 65 and older	Total
PARTY party identification	1 democrat	19.0%	33.6%	37.7%	45.0%	36.6%
	2 independent	64.3%	39.4%	34.5%	28.2%	36.4%
	3 republican	16.7%	25.6%	26.5%	24.1%	25.5%
	4 other		1.4%	1.3%	2.7%	1.5%
Total		100.0%	100.0%	100.0%	100.0%	100.0%

The first row of percentages goes directly contrary to our expectations: Older people are substantially more likely to call themselves Democrats than are young people. When we examine the Republicans, however, we discover virtually the same thing, although it is not as clear. How can this be?

The explanation is to be found among those identifying themselves as Independents: This is much more common among the young and less common among the old. The clearest relationship in this table is that the likelihood of identifying with *some* political party increases dramatically with age in the table, but there is no clear tendency for that identification to favor one party over another.

Realize that the observed pattern is amenable to more than one explanation. It could be that people become more likely to identify with the major parties as they grow older. On the other hand, the relationship might reflect a *trend* phenomenon: a disenchantment with the major parties in recent years, primarily among young people. To test these competing explanations, you would need to analyze longitudinal data, those representing the state of affairs at different points in time. (The General Social Survey, by the way, has such data.)

Gender and Politics

As you will have discovered for yourself, there is no relationship between gender and political philosophy, although women are slightly more likely to identify with the Democratic party (39%) than are men (31%). This latter relationship may reflect the fact that the Democratic party has been more explicit in its support for women's issues in recent years than has the Republican party. Still, the relationship is not a particularly strong one.

PARTY party identification * SEX RESPONDENTS SEX Crosstabulation

% within SEX RESPONDENTS SEX

		SEX RESPONDENTS SEX		Total
		1 MALE	2 FEMALE	
PARTY party identification	1 democrat	29.7%	42.2%	36.6%
	2 independent	39.8%	33.7%	36.4%
	3 republican	29.3%	22.3%	25.5%
	4 other	1.2%	1.8%	1.5%
Total		100.0%	100.0%	100.0%

Race and Politics

Notice that African-Americans are somewhat more liberal (and less conservative) than whites. Perhaps the difference is less than you expected.

POLREC Recoded POLVIEWS * RACE RACE OF RESPONDENT Crosstabulation

% within RACE RACE OF RESPONDENT

		RACE RACE OF RESPONDENT			Total
		1 WHITE	2 BLACK	3 OTHER	
POLREC Recoded POLVIEWS	1 liberal	25.2%	32.5%	31.1%	26.6%
	2 moderate	37.7%	39.6%	44.6%	38.3%
	3 conservative	37.1%	27.8%	24.3%	35.1%
Total		100.0%	100.0%	100.0%	100.0%

The relationship between race and political party identification, however, is very strong, reflecting the Democratic party's orientation toward minority groups.

PARTY party identification * RACE RACE OF RESPONDENT Crosstabulation

% within RACE RACE OF RESPONDENT

		1 WHITE	2 BLACK	3 OTHER	Total
		RACE RACE OF RESPONDENT			
PARTY party identification	1 democrat	29.5%	69.0%	48.1%	36.6%
	2 independent	38.2%	26.6%	38.3%	36.4%
	3 republican	30.6%	3.1%	13.6%	25.5%
	4 other	1.7%	1.3%		1.5%
Total		100.0%	100.0%	100.0%	100.0%

Class and Politics

If you run the tables relating subjective social class and politics, you are going to discover some surprising results. First, there's no consistent relationship between subjective social class and political philosophy.

POLREC Recoded POLVIEWS * CLASS SUBJECTIVE CLASS IDENTIFICATION Crosstabulation

% within CLASS SUBJECTIVE CLASS IDENTIFICATION

		CLASS SUBJECTIVE CLASS IDENTIFICATION				
		1 LOWER CLASS	2 WORKING CLASS	3 MIDDLE CLASS	4 UPPER CLASS	Total
POLREC Recoded POLVIEWS	1 liberal	28.4%	26.6%	27.0%	22.6%	26.7%
	2 moderate	43.2%	43.7%	34.0%	27.4%	38.1%
	3 conservative	28.4%	29.6%	39.0%	50.0%	35.2%
Total		100.0%	100.0%	100.0%	100.0%	100.0%

The relationship between social class and political party identification, moreover, is not as clear as you might have expected. In part, this reflects Republican party inroads into the working class during the Reagan years.

PARTY party identification * CLASS SUBJECTIVE CLASS IDENTIFICATION Crosstabulation

% within CLASS SUBJECTIVE CLASS IDENTIFICATION

		CLASS SUBJECTIVE CLASS IDENTIFICATION				
		1 LOWER CLASS	2 WORKING CLASS	3 MIDDLE CLASS	4 UPPER CLASS	Total
PARTY party identification	1 democrat	43.2%	37.0%	36.9%	25.4%	36.8%
	2 independent	44.4%	42.1%	30.7%	36.5%	36.4%
	3 republican	11.1%	19.0%	31.0%	38.1%	25.3%
	4 other	1.2%	2.0%	1.4%		1.5%
Total		100.0%	100.0%	100.0%	100.0%	100.0%

Chapter 13   Bivariate Exercise: Abortion

Religion and Abortion

ABORT * RELIG RS RELIGIOUS PREFERENCE Crosstabulation

% within RELIG RS RELIGIOUS PREFERENCE

		RELIG RS RELIGIOUS PREFERENCE					
		1 PROTESTANT	2 CATHOLIC	3 JEWISH	4 NONE	5 OTHER	Total
ABORT	0	19.9%	21.2%	4.2%	9.6%	15.0%	18.3%
	1	36.5%	40.7%	8.3%	25.4%	20.0%	34.8%
	2	43.6%	38.2%	87.5%	64.9%	65.0%	46.9%
Total		100.0%	100.0%	100.0%	100.0%	100.0%	100.0%

ABORT * CHATT Recoded Church Attendance Crosstabulation

% within CHATT Recoded Church Attendance

		CHATT Recoded Church Attendance				
		1 About weekly	2 About monthly	3 Seldom	4 Never	Total
ABORT	0	38.1%	17.7%	7.7%	8.8%	18.3%
	1	34.0%	37.7%	35.4%	29.4%	34.4%
	2	27.9%	44.6%	56.9%	61.8%	47.3%
Total		100.0%	100.0%	100.0%	100.0%	100.0%

Politics and Abortion

Here's how we would describe the relationship between political philosophy and abortion attitudes: Liberals are strongly and consistently more supportive of a woman's right to an abortion than are conservatives, with the moderates falling in between.

Political party identification has little or no impact on abortion attitudes among the general public, despite the differing official positions of the two major parties. You can see this in the tables below.

Percentage Approving of Abortion Under the Following Conditions		*Democrat*	*Independent*	*Republican*	*Other*
ABHLTH	woman's health endangered	93	93	87	69
ABDEFECT	serious defect likely	84	84	74	53
ABRAPE	resulted from rape	87	87	81	56
ABPOOR	too poor for more children	54	49	39	44
ABSINGLE	woman is unmarried	53	46	42	38
ABNOMORE	family wants no more	55	47	41	47
ABANY	for any reason	54	47	42	38

ABORT * PARTY party identification Crosstabulation

% within PARTY party identification

		PARTY party identification				
		1 democrat	2 independent	3 republican	4 other	Total
ABORT	0	14.6%	15.8%	25.8%	46.7%	18.3%
	1	34.0%	38.1%	32.0%	13.3%	34.7%
	2	51.3%	46.1%	42.2%	40.0%	47.0%
Total		100.0%	100.0%	100.0%	100.0%	100.0%

Education and Abortion

ABORT * EDCAT recoded education Crosstabulation

% within EDCAT recoded education

		EDCAT recoded education					
		1 less than HS	2 HS grad	3 some college	4 college grad	5 grad studies	Total
ABORT	0	18.8%	15.2%	20.3%	23.0%	15.9%	18.4%
	1	46.3%	39.8%	32.5%	23.7%	26.5%	34.7%
	2	34.9%	44.9%	47.3%	53.3%	57.6%	47.0%
Total		100.0%	100.0%	100.0%	100.0%	100.0%	100.0%

Race and Abortion

ABORT * RACE RACE OF RESPONDENT Crosstabulation

% within RACE RACE OF RESPONDENT

		RACE RACE OF RESPONDENT			
		1 WHITE	2 BLACK	3 OTHER	Total
ABORT	0	18.0%	19.5%	19.6%	18.3%
	1	34.5%	38.3%	28.3%	34.7%
	2	47.5%	42.1%	52.2%	47.0%
Total		100.0%	100.0%	100.0%	100.0%

Family Matters and Abortion

As you may have guessed, those favoring small families are much more likely to support abortion than are those favoring large families.

ABORT * CHLDIDEL Ideal Number of Children
Crosstabulation

% within CHLDIDEX Ideal Number of Children

		CHLDIDEX Ideal Number of Children			
		1 0-2 children	2 3-4 children	3 5 or more	Total
ABORT	0	11.7%	21.9%	29.2%	17.2%
	1	31.9%	39.4%	23.1%	32.9%
	2	56.4%	38.7%	47.7%	49.9%
Total		100.0%	100.0%	100.0%	100.0%

Notice that separated respondents are more likely to score 2 on the index, indicating unconditional support for abortion.

ABORT * MARITAL MARITAL STATUS Crosstabulation

% within MARITAL MARITAL STATUS

		MARITAL MARITAL STATUS					
		1 MARRIED	2 WIDOWED	3 DIVORCED	4 SEPARATED	5 NEVER MARRIED	Total
ABORT	0	21.8%	20.5%	11.8%	16.7%	15.6%	18.3%
	1	32.9%	35.6%	40.8%	27.8%	35.1%	34.8%
	2	45.3%	43.8%	47.4%	55.6%	49.3%	46.9%
Total		100.0%	100.0%	100.0%	100.0%	100.0%	100.0%

However, there is little difference when we compare those who have ever been divorced with those who have not.

ABORT * DIVORCE EVER BEEN DIVORCED OR SEPARATED
Crosstabulation

% within DIVORCE EVER BEEN DIVORCED OR SEPARATED

		DIVORCE EVER BEEN DIVORCED OR SEPARATED			
		1 YES	2 NO	9	Total
ABORT	0	17.5%	21.9%	100.0%	21.4%
	1	37.7%	32.6%		33.5%
	2	44.7%	45.6%		45.1%
Total		100.0%	100.0%	100.0%	100.0%

Sexual Attitudes and Abortion

As you probably expected, abortion attitudes are related to attitudes toward homosexuality and to attendance at an X-rated movie.

ABORT * HOMOSEX HOMOSEXUAL SEX RELATIONS Crosstabulation

% within HOMOSEX HOMOSEXUAL SEX RELATIONS

| | | \multicolumn{4}{c}{HOMOSEX HOMOSEXUAL SEX RELATIONS} | |
		1 ALWAYS WRONG	2 ALMST ALWAYS WRG	3 SOMETIMES WRONG	4 NOT WRONG AT ALL	Total
ABORT	0	27.2%	3.9%	14.8%	6.9%	18.8%
	1	41.1%	37.3%	29.5%	21.2%	34.1%
	2	31.7%	58.8%	55.7%	71.8%	47.1%
Total		100.0%	100.0%	100.0%	100.0%	100.0%

Chapter 16 Further Bivariate Exercises

Desired Family Size

To recode CHLDIDEL into the two categories mentioned, give these instructions to SPSS:

> Transform → Recode → Into Same Variables
> > 0 through 2 → 1
> > 3 through highest → 2
>
> Value Labels:
> > 1 0 - 2
> > 2 3 or more

Chapter 17 Multivariate Exercise: Religiosity

RINCOME and EDUC are other indicators of social class. Why don't you see how they relate to church attendance.

Chapter 19   Multivariate Exercise:
Attitudes Toward Abortion

Recoding PREMARSX and HOMOSEX

You can create dichotomies for these three sexual attitude variables with a single command, plus another to create new value labels. The logic may be seen in the SPSS syntax below.

Transform → Recode → Into Same Variables

PREMARSX HOMOSEX
  1 through 2 → 1
  3 through 4 → 2

Labels:
  1 WRONG
  2 OKAY

Expanding the Index

To expand the index, try adding these two items, filling in the blanks, of course. Here's the general logic in old-style SPSS commands:

```
IF (PREMARSX ___ ) IND = IND + 1.
IF (HOMOSEX ___ ) IND = IND + 1.
COUNT MISS = IND PREMARSX HOMOSEX (MISSING).
IF (MISS GT 0) IND = -1.
```

Appendix E **Readings**

A Theory of Involvement

Charles Y. Glock

Benjamin B. Ringer

Earl R. Babbie

The preceding analysis has aimed at the elaboration and evaluation of previous speculations and empirical research on the subject of religious involvement. These have been tested in the light of the present data on Episcopal parishioners' religious behavior. In this endeavor, we have sought to ferret out the persistent correlates of religious involvement. While some of the prior findings and expectations have been generally confirmed, some have found little support, and others have been contradicted.

Such an eclectic approach has generated two problems which require some resolution if the analysis is to progress further. One problem is methodological. Since sex, age, family, and socioeconomic status each have an independent effect on involvement, these effects should be controlled as the analysis continues. However, controlling for all of them simultaneously would have the consequence, given the size of the sample, of reducing the number of cases in each cell of future tables to statistically unstable sizes. Some way must be found, therefore, to introduce the necessary controls in a more simplified, but still effective form, enabling the analysis to proceed meaningfully but with a minimum of confusion.

The second problem is of theoretical import: Some recognition of the significant relationships between several independent variables and church involvement has been achieved. The question now arises as to whether these may be ordered within some more general proposition concerning the nature of involvement. Why should being female, older, familyless, and lower class more readily predispose parishioners to church involvement than the opposites of these characteristics?

Reprinted from "A Theory of Involvement," Chapter 5 in *To Comfort and to Challenge: A Dilemma of the Contemporary Church,* Charles Y. Glock, Benjamin B. Ringer, and Earl R. Babbie, 1967, by permission of the University of California Press, Berkeley, California.

An Index of Predisposition to Involvement

In the interest of resolving both problems, a composite index was constructed which simultaneously reflected all four of the characteristics found to have independent effects on involvement. The procedure followed was a relatively simple one. Each parishioner was assigned a score commensurate with his possession of those attributes which were associated with involvement. On the basis of sex, women received a score of 2 and men a score of 0. To this was added a score based on age: 2 for parishioners over fifty years of age, 1 for those between thirty and fifty, and 0 for those under thirty. This combined score was further modified by a score for family status: parishioners who were both childless and spouseless received an additional 2; 1 was given to those with either a spouse or child, and 0 to those having both a spouse and a child. Finally, a score based on socioeconomic status was added: a score of 2 was given to all parishioners low (0 or 1) on the index of social class, 1 for those scored 2 or 3 on class, and 0 for those designated as highest (4) on class. (A more detailed discussion of the predisposition index is presented in Appendix B. [not included in this reading].)

Scores on the composite predisposition index ranged from 0 to 8. In terms of the scoring procedure, parishioners scored 0 on the index would be *young, upper-status men* with *complete families*. Those scored 8 would be *lower status, elderly women* with *neither spouse nor children*. The higher the score, the more the number of attributes possessed by the parishioner which are predisposing to high involvement. As it turns out, no one in the sample was scored at the lowest end (0), but some parishioners were scored at each of the other levels of predisposition to involvement.

The scoring of individual parishioners, it is to be recognized, did not take into account their actual involvement in the church. For example, all women were scored 2 on the basis of sex regardless of whether or not they were deeply involved in the church. All men received 0, even deeply involved men. In each instance, scoring was based on the overall relationship between a given attribute (such as sex) and involvement.

Observations from earlier chapters suggest that the combination of these attributes has a cumulative effect on involvement. For example, sex and social class were seen to affect church involvement jointly. Similarly, missing both family components was reflected in a greater involvement than missing only one. The construction of the composite predisposition index is based on the assumption that a combination of all the attributes should produce an even stronger effect on parishioners' involvement. Parishioners scored 8 on the predisposition index should be the most involved, those scored 1 should be the least involved. Furthermore, involvement should increase steadily with the number of predisposing attributes which parishioners possess. Table 35 tests this basic assumption and strongly supports it.

Parishioners scored lowest on the predisposition index show a mean involvement score of .23. With each successive rise in predisposition score,

TABLE 35
Church Involvement Increases with Increasing Predisposition Scores

| | Index of Predisposition to Involvement | | | | | | | |
| | Low | | | | | | | High |
	1^a	2	3	4	5	6	7	8
Mean involvement scores on C.I.I.	.23	.31	.36	.45	.51	.60	.62	.72
	(23)	(155)	(205)	(312)	(246)	(136)	(91)	(33)

[a] Recall that no parishioner was scored 0 on the index.

there is a corresponding increase in mean involvement. Where it was discovered earlier that one might speak of a person being predisposed to church involvement by virtue of sex, social class, age, or family status, it is now evident parishioners may be classified as more or less predisposed in terms of the number of predisposing attributes they possess. The effects of the several factors are clearly additive.

With few exceptions, the same pattern emerges when the sub-indices of involvement are considered. Minor fluctuations will be noted in regard to ritual involvement, but the overall relationship is still clear. And predisposition scores provide a powerful predictor of parishioners' organizational and intellectual involvement in their church (see Table 36).

The findings of Tables 35 and 36 provide assurance that the predisposition index will satisfy the need for simultaneously controlling for the several attributes as the analysis proceeds. The problem now is to understand why the several attributes, individually and in concert, have the observed effect on parishioners' church involvement.

The Situational Bases of Involvement

At this point, it is important to remember the earlier distinction between factors facilitating and motivating involvement. Facilitating factors, it will be recalled, refer to the degree to which the parishioner's objective situation allows his involvement; motivating factors bear on his desire to be involved.

It is quite conceivable that the relationships discovered thus far are merely examples of the former—differences in opportunities for involvement generated by parishioners' social circumstances. Involvement, at least as it has been measured here, requires an investment of the parishioner's time—time to attend worship services, to participate in organizational meetings, and to read religious literature and periodicals. Such free time, quite possibly, is more readily available to women, to older persons, and to people without family ties, contrasted with men, the young, and those who are bound up in the responsibilities of family life.

A man's occupation generally commands the better part of his day and perhaps invades his leisure as well. While the woman's daily commitments

TABLE 36
Ritual, Organizational, and Intellectual Involvement
All Increase with Increasing Predisposition Scores

| | Index of Predisposition to Involvement | | | | | | | |
| | Low | | | | | | | High |
	1[a]	2	3	4	5	6	7	8
	Mean scores on:							
Ritual involve-ment	.43 (30)	.60 (185)	.60 (258)	.64 (380)	.67 (300)	.71 (185)	.79 (107)	.77 (48)
Organizational involvement	.24 (23)	.32 (160)	.34 (219)	.50 (333)	.54 (262)	.66 (153)	.66 (95)	.71 (36)
Intellectual involvement	.13 (31)	.17 (178)	.24 (242)	.27 (363)	.38 (284)	.41 (177)	.49 (100)	.60 (46)

may be no less demanding, they are, at any rate, normally more flexible. In understanding the effect of family status, the responsibilities of caring for children may often preclude participation in church activities. Regarding age differences, young people are more likely to be preoccupied with the multifarious activities vaguely included in the process of "shaping a future"; older people, on the other hand, have arrived at their "futures," many have retired, and they are generally afforded a greater leisure.

If the concept of leisure is modified to consider those requirements imposed by cultural mores regarding life-styles, social status differentials may also be understood as exemplifying a set of facilitating factors. While the upper-status parishioners may be freed from the mundane drudgeries of life, they are expected to participate in a broader spectrum of secular activities—service, civic, and social. Those with lower social status, on the other hand, may actually be barred from some of these activities, and certainly such participation is not expected of them. Leisure time, so modified, would appear to represent a scarcer commodity for the upper class than for those whose class status places no such demands for secular participation.

The effect of facilitating factors, of course, is cumulative—that is, demands on free time increase with the number of "time-consuming" attributes a person possesses. Hence, while women may have more free time than men, childless women have more than mothers. Taking this into account strengthens the contention that existential differences in opportunities for church involvement contribute to explaining the results reported in Tables 35 and 36. However, this is clearly not the whole explanation.

The nature of the involvement indices themselves precludes this possibility. The indices measure not only how active people are in the church; they also reflect the proportion of a parishioner's total energies which is devoted to it. In particular, the measures of organizational and intellectual involvement, it will be recalled, are indicators of involvement as well as activity. Moreover, intellectual involvement is not a function of available time as much as it reflects the saliency of religion for the individual. If the amount of available time stood alone in differentiating involvement, the relationship between scores on the predisposition index and intellectual involvement should not have appeared.

The explanation in terms of facilitating factors, while making common sense, is not sufficient to incorporate all the various relationships which exist. Hence, while the facilitating effects of these attributes may determine much of one's church involvement, it seems likely that there may be some other dynamic operating with regard to the relationships. But what is that dynamic? What theoretical reconciliation is possible among such diverse attributes?

Societal Values and Involvement

The beginning of an answer has already appeared. Chapter 4 closed with the observation of a similarity in the effects of family status and social class on church involvement. In both instances, the church appeared to serve as an alternative source of gratification for parishioners who were missing something in their secular lives. The church was characterized as a family surrogate for the familyless and as a source of status for those denied it in the secular community. Church involvement was seen as a response to deprivations experienced by parishioners.

In a sense, each of the attributes associated with church involvement represents a departure from the implicit and explicit ideals of American society. First, with regard to sex, there appears little doubt that our society remains, even to this day, a male-dominated one. Despite the extensive inroads into the social, political, and occupational structures gained by women since the passage of the Nineteenth Amendment in 1920, equality of the sexes can scarcely be called a reality even today. Women still fight for equal employment opportunities, are denied serious consideration for many professions, and are still shackled by traditional images concerning the role of the "decent" woman in society. Especially with regard to those functions which are most highly valued by the society, judged by the responsibility and respect involved, it is the service of males which is called for in nearly all instances. Child-rearing is perhaps the single exception to this generalization, insomuch as it is considered a crucial function for the survival and growth of the society. Few if any males, however, exhibit any desire to have child-rearing made their responsibility. On the other hand, many women aspire to positions and occupations now dominated by men.

With respect to age, the flood of adolescent entertainers and the few, conspicuous elder statesmen appear to be exceptions to a general value placed on responsible youth in America. And while even adolescents are expected to grow into mature young adults, the elderly are especially devalued by the norms of contemporary American society. Witness the increasing concern with geriatrics as an effort to prevent old people from becoming a burden on society. While the call for employment of senior citizens may frequently stress the economic value of this important resource, it seldom fails to mention the importance of restoring a sense of meaning to the lives of the elderly. The list of such examples might be continued at length without altering the conclusion that the young, rather than the old, are closer to the mainstream of American values.

The stature of the family as a sacred institution in American society has already been discussed in Chapter 2. Deviations from the normative family pattern evoke feelings of sympathy or rebuke. While the deviant may be pitied for his deprivation in this regard, there is also the implicit feeling that an important norm has been violated, and the deviant is regarded as something of a threat to society. A partial break with the formative pattern seems less critical than a total break. Even if one has no children, it is somehow better to be married than to be single. The most highly valued situation, however, is to have both a spouse and children.

Finally, Americans value, in deeds if not always in words, material wealth and high social status. The theme of upward mobility underlies the American dream. It is central to much of our educational system. Certainly, while few are able to achieve high status and wealth, such are the goals to which most Americans aspire.

It would appear then that those characteristics which are most closely associated with more intense church involvement are, at the same time, least valued by the general society. The data, of course, describe only Episcopalian parishioners. Nonetheless, it seems likely that the same variables would influence church involvement in other denominations as well, although perhaps to different degrees.

It does not necessarily follow that these variables would have the same cumulative effect on influencing church membership per se. As seen in the preceding chapter, the lower and working classes are less likely to provide church members than are the middle and upper classes. Similarly, we suspect that persons deprived of complete families are less likely to be church members than those who are not deprived in this way. The fact that the church and the family are so closely connected is probably a bar to membership on the part of those without families. The church, of course, is only one institution which can help alleviate social deprivation. Lower status and famililess people may turn to other institutions for relief more readily than they turn to the church. The important point is that among people who are attracted to membership, the church wins a greater commitment from those whose attributes are less highly esteemed by the general society.

As far as the data examined thus far in the analysis apply, there should be little doubt that those characteristics which are devalued by the secular society and by the church, are positively related to high church involvement—this is a matter of fact. More interesting is the question of why this should be true. Is there some reason to expect that other devalued characteristics would have the same effect, or is the devalued nature of these particular attributes simply a matter of chance? It has already been suggested that the answer to this puzzle may lie in the gratifications derived from participation in the larger society.

Talcott Parsons laid the groundwork for such an explanation when he chose to approach the broad problem of stratification in terms of moral evaluation.

> Stratification *in its valuational aspect* then is the ranking of units in a social system in accordance with the standards of the common value system.[1]
>
> Specific judgments of evaluation are not applied to the system unit as such—except in a limiting case—but to particular properties of that unit—always by comparison with others in the system. These properties may be classificatory, in the sense of characterizing the unit independently of its relations to other objects in a system as in the case of sex, age or specific abilities, or they may be relational, characterizing the way in which it is related to other entities as in the case of membership in a kinship unit.[2]

The attributes which a society values most it is also more likely to reward. Such rewards appear in different forms: money, power, status, attention, a sense of belonging, and so forth. People who lack the valued attributes are, to some extent, deprived of the concomitant rewards. The church, then, becomes an alternative source of rewards for those who cannot fully enjoy the fruits of secular society. Parishioners who feel outside the mainstream of society by virtue of being familyless find a surrogate family in the church. Elderly parishioners who may feel cast out of the youth-oriented secular society find acceptance within the church. Lower class parishioners are taught that secular status is ultimately irrelevant. Women who are denied serious consideration for the responsible positions in secular society find they can be very important to the life of the church. In sum, the church offers a refuge for those who are denied access to valued achievements and rewards in everyday American life.

This *Comfort Hypothesis* would help explain the observed effects of sex, age, family status, and social class on church involvement. Parishioners whose life situations most deprive them of satisfaction and fulfillment in the secular society turn to the church for comfort and substitute rewards. This is most clearly seen in the case of the two extreme types on the predisposition index. On the one hand, the upper class young father is the darling of our society. His life situation represents much that is considered ideal. He is afforded access to valued achievements and, in turn, is granted greater rewards. As Tables 35 and 36 show, he is hardly involved in the church at all. At the other extreme, the older lower class spinster enjoys little that would be considered ideal in terms of predominant secular values.

Her inability to participate fully and meaningfully in the secular society results in a far greater involvement in church life.

However correct this interpretation may be, it does not encompass the behavior of all parishioners. There remains a minority of members whose social attributes would presumably predispose them away from the church but who are nevertheless highly involved in it. At the other extreme, there are those who have all the characteristics associated with deep involvement, but who are relative apostates. And at every point between these extremes are instances in which the various attributes do not have the expected effects.

These seeming disconfirmations might be accommodated within the general theory in a number of ways. It is possible that the effects of some of these attributes are conditioned by other aspects of the parishioner's total life situation. For example, among women who report holding office in secular organizations, social class does not affect church involvement. While the lack of education and income would normally be felt as a deprivation, the feeling of devaluation is evidently alleviated through the acquisition of status by other means. The church is one but not the only source of comfort for the socially deprived.

Furthermore, no claim is made that the attributes examined in this study are the only factors determining a person's subjective status within the society. Many people are deprived of secular rewards by virtue of their race. National origins prevent others from fully participating in American social life. Similarly, certain bizarre physical deformities deprive people of participation to a greater extent than would be warranted by their physical limitations. There are theoretical grounds for expecting that these forms of deprivation would affect the extent of church involvement, although the present data do not permit an empirical test of the expectation.

If it were possible to exhaust the indicators of social deprivation, it is still unlikely that a complete understanding of church involvement would be forthcoming. The phenomenon is clearly more complex than that. Nevertheless, it should be evident that the *Comfort Hypothesis* provides one important avenue toward the explanation of religious differences.

Summary and Conclusions

This short chapter has represented an attempt to synthesize what had been observed earlier and to establish a more general theoretical framework for understanding religious involvement. The result has been the discovery of a very strong cumulative relationship between the possession of four attributes and extensive participation in church life. Parishioners whose life situations most deprive them of prestige and gratification in the secular society are the most involved in the church. The church, then, was characterized as an alternative source of rewards for the socially deprived.

This interpretation would seem to be in harmony with the observations of contemporary critics of the church. However, before considering that issue, as well as the more general question of this study's implications for the church's role in society, it seems wise to examine the church's effectiveness in challenging its parishioners. If the church is found to perform both a comforting and challenging role, the implications will be different than if we learn that it serves a comforting function only. Whether parishioners are challenged by their commitment to adopt values promulgated by the church is the subject of Part Two of the book.

Notes

1. Talcott Parsons, "A Revised Analytical Approach to the Theory of Social Stratification," in *Essays in Sociological Theory* (Glencoe, Ill.: The Free Press, 1954), p. 388. (Emphasis in the original.) An earlier statement of this position may be found in Parsons' 1940 essay: "An Analytical Approach to the Theory of Social Stratification," reprinted in the same volume.

2. *Ibid.,* p. 389.

The Social Bases of Abortion Attitudes

Elizabeth Addell Cook

Ted G. Jelen

Clyde Wilcox

Most of this book will offer explanations for differences in abortion attitudes in the mass public. In this chapter, we describe social group differences in abortion attitudes. How do members of various social groups differ in their attitudes toward abortion? Do young people have different attitudes than their parents and grandparents? Do men think differently than do women? Do blacks and whites have different attitudes? Do the rich and poor think differently, or southerners and those who live in the northeast? What are the group bases of abortion attitudes?

Social characteristics are often useful predictors of attitudes. Might members of various social groups hold different political attitudes? First, members of social groups have different objective interests. Impoverished Americans are more likely to favor spending on social programs, at least in part because they are more likely to benefit from them. Wealthy Americans are more likely to favor cuts in the capital gains tax rate because such an action would decrease their tax bill, but it would have little direct effect on the tax payments of the working poor. Parents of small children favor more spending for schools because their children will benefit, whereas retired Americans are less supportive of spending on education because they will not benefit directly.

Of course, self-interest is not the only explanation for social group differences. Various social groups have different life experiences and may be socialized into different roles in society. Affluent blacks may be more supportive of government spending on social programs than affluent whites because they encounter friends and relatives who benefit from these programs. Men may be less willing than women to support programs for

Reprinted from "The Social Bases of Abortion Attitudes," Chapter 2 in *Between Two Absolutes: Public Opinion and the Politics of Abortion,* Elizabeth Addell Cook, Ted G. Jelen, and Clyde Wilcox, 1992, by permission of Westview Press, Boulder, Colorado.

the disadvantaged because they are less likely to be encouraged to show sympathy toward others. Those with a college education have experienced an entirely different type of socialization than those who did not finish high school. This socialization can lead those with college degrees to be more tolerant of those with whom they disagree and to be more supportive of gender and racial equality.

Of course, many social group (or demographic) differences in attitudes are attributable to other factors. For example, southerners are more likely to hold orthodox religious beliefs, and older citizens are more likely to approve of distinct and unequal sex roles. When we find that southerners are less supportive of legal abortion than northerners, therefore, this may be due to greater religiosity among southerners. In the next two chapters we will focus on the attitudinal and religious basis of these group differences. Similarly, when we find that the oldest citizens are less supportive of legal abortion than those who grew up during or after the 1960s, this may be due to the traditional views of the oldest Americans on the role of women in families. In this chapter, we will first present an overview of abortion attitudes in America, then discuss social group differences in support for and opposition to legal abortion.

Attitudes toward Legal Abortion: Methods of Analysis

In almost every year since 1972, the National Opinion Research Center (NORC) at the University of Chicago has conducted a national survey of social and political attitudes. This General Social Survey (GSS)[1] has included a battery of six questions measuring support for legal abortion. These items ask respondents whether they believe that it should be possible for a pregnant woman to obtain a legal abortion:

- if there is a strong chance of serious defect in the baby
- if she is married and does not want more children
- if the woman's own health is seriously endangered by the pregnancy
- if the family has a very low income and cannot afford any more children
- if she became pregnant as a result of rape
- if she is not married and does not want to marry the man

These six items can be used to measure attitudes toward legal abortion. By counting the number of circumstances under which each respondent supports legal abortion, we have created a scale that runs from 0 (when the respondent approves of abortion under no circumstances) to 6 (when he or she approves of abortion in all six circumstances).

Because these questions have been asked for eighteen years, we were able to examine changes in attitudes toward abortion. Throughout this book, we generally concentrate our analysis on recent attitudes (the GSS surveys from 1987 through 1991). When attitudes or relationships have changed over time, however, we report and try to explain those changes. These GSS data constitute the core of our analysis, but we use other survey data when they are needed to more fully describe abortion attitudes.

Statistical analysis reveals that the public sees these six questions as measuring two related but distinct attitudes: support for abortion in circumstances of physical trauma (where the mother's health is in danger, where the fetus is seriously defective, or when the pregnancy results from rape) and support for abortion in social, more "elective" circumstances (poverty, when an unmarried woman does not want to marry the father, or when a married couple wants no more children). In this book we refer to these sets of circumstances as *traumatic abortion* and *elective abortion.*[2]

Because each set of circumstances contains three separate questions, the scales we have created to measure these attitudes range from 0 (when the respondent supports abortion in none of the circumstances) to 3 (when the respondent favors abortion in all three circumstances). For most purposes, we simply report relationships involving the combined abortion scale. We use the traumatic/elective distinction when the pattern of relationships differs for the two components of abortion attitudes.

The distinction between traumatic and elective circumstances is an important one to public attitudes, but most abortions in the United States are done for elective reasons. A very recent survey of abortion patients revealed that only seven percent listed one of the three traumatic reasons as their primary reason for getting an abortion. Most abortion patients indicated financial problems, the desire to avoid raising a child outside of marriage, or their belief that they were not yet mature enough to raise a child as their primary reason for obtaining an abortion.[3]

In this book, we divide Americans into three groups: pro-life respondents who oppose abortion in all six circumstances, pro-choice citizens who favor legal abortion in each circumstance, and situationalists who think abortion should be legal in some but not all circumstances. We make more precise distinctions among the situationalists in Chapter 5.

Abortion Attitudes: An Overview

There is a general societal consensus that abortion should be legal in each of the traumatic circumstances. Seventy-six percent of those surveyed from 1987 through 1991 supported abortion under all three circumstances in our trauma scale—mother's health, fetal defect, and rape, with only 7 percent opposing abortion in all three circumstances. In contrast, the public is deeply divided on abortion in elective circumstances. Nearly half (47 percent) of all respondents between 1987 and 1991 opposed abortion in all three social circumstances (poverty, unmarried woman, or a couple who wants no more children), while more than a third (37 percent) support legal abortion under all three conditions.

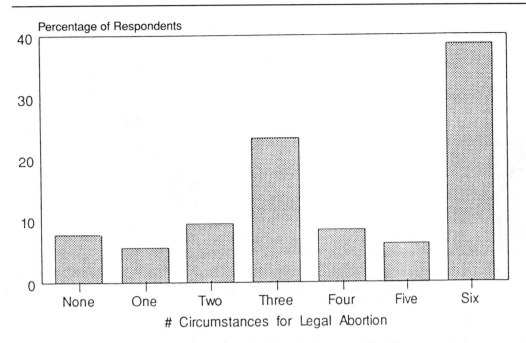

Figure 2.1. Respondents Favoring Abortion in Zero to Six Circumstances
SOURCE: Compiled from the General Social Survey, 1987-1991.

In all of the surveys between 1972 and 1991, more Americans have favored unlimited access to abortion than have favored banning abortions under all circumstances. In the period 1987 to 1991, only 8 percent of respondents opposed abortion in all six circumstances, but 39 percent favored abortion in all six instances. Figure 2.1 shows the distribution of attitudes on support for legal abortion, and Figure 2.2 shows attitudes on traumatic and elective abortion. Although Figure 2.1 shows that few Americans favor an outright ban on abortion, Figure 2.2 shows that Americans are deeply divided on allowing abortion for social reasons.

Activists on both sides of the abortion debate frequently assert that the majority of Americans support their position. Pro-choice activists point out (correctly) that the public does not want a ban on abortion. Pro-life activists note (also correctly) that the public disapproves of abortion on demand. In fact, the majority of Americans hold positions that do not fall neatly in either camp—they support legal abortions in some but not all circumstances.

The narrow majority of Americans in every survey favored limited legal access to abortion. Between 1987 and 1991, 53 percent favored some limitations on access to abortion without an outright ban. A majority of those who favored limited access to abortion favored allowing it in all three of the traumatic circumstances, but in none of the three elective circumstances. Thus, neither the pro-life nor pro-choice movement has the support of an absolute majority of Americans.[4]

Figure 2.3 shows public attitudes toward legal abortion since 1972. The lines are remarkably flat, suggesting that abortion attitudes are generally stable in the aggregate.[5] For eighteen years, the "average" position on

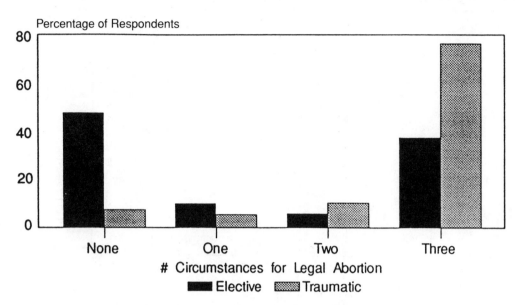

Figure 2.2. Respondents Favoring Abortion in Elective and Traumatic Circumstances
SOURCE: Compiled from the General Social Survey, 1987-1991.

abortion has hovered near allowing abortion in four of the six possible circumstances, allowing abortions in between two and three traumatic circumstances, approving of abortion in between one and two elective circumstances.

Figure 2.4 shows support for legal abortion since 1972 plotted on a narrower range that emphasizes the small changes in attitudes over time. A closer look reveals that support increased in 1973 after the *Roe v. Wade* decision and remained relatively high until the early 1980s, when support declined. This decline was greatest in support for elective abortion. After 1989, support for legal abortion increased again to levels that nearly matched those of the 1970s.

It may be that the decline in support for legal abortion in the early 1980s was influenced by the strong pro-life position of President Ronald Reagan. During this period, the percentage of those taking a pro-life position did not increase nor did the percentage of pro-choice citizens markedly decrease; instead those Americans who supported abortion in some but not all circumstances reduced the number of circumstances under which they favored legal abortion.

An explanation for the recent increase in support is less obvious. Data from *CBS News/New York Times* public opinion polls from 1985 through 1989 reveal that support began to gradually build in mid-1987 but jumped sharply between July 1988 and January 1989. This change occurred *before* the *Webster* decision, so that decision could not have led to attitude change.

Some analysts have argued that public support for legal abortion increased in *anticipation* of a Supreme Court ruling of greater limits on legal abortion.[6] We think this unlikely. It is true that with each new conser-

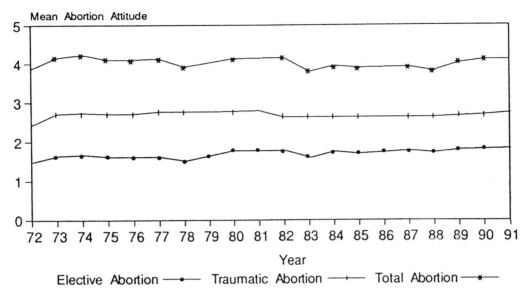

Figure 2.3. *Mean Level of Support for Legal Abortion under Various Conditions*
SOURCE: Compiled from the General Social Survey, 1972-1991.

vative Court nomination (especially Judge Robert Bork), the uncertain future of *Roe* was prominently discussed in the media. Yet the public did not pay close attention to the policy implications of Supreme Court confirmation debates.

If the increased support for legal abortion in 1989 was due to the anticipation that *Webster* would return the abortion issue to state legislatures, attitude change should be larger among those who would be most likely to have heard of the pending case. In fact, attitude change was slightly lower among the best educated respondents and among those who regularly read a newspaper. Moreover, data from a national opinion poll by *CBS News/New York Times* in autumn 1989 revealed that more than 70 percent of the public were not aware of the *Webster* decision soon after the opinion was handed down. We interpret these data to suggest that the public did not increase in support for legal abortion in anticipation of future Court decisions that would restrict *Roe,* but there is insufficient survey data to test this hypothesis fully. It is possible, however, that the increasing support for legal abortion since 1989 is in part a response to continued media attention to the changing membership of the U.S. Supreme Court and to the likely overruling of *Roe,* and to visible organized activity by pro-choice groups. If *Roe* is overturned soon, this would suggest further increases in the numbers of pro-choice citizens.

We have seen that the public is generally supportive of legal abortion for circumstances that involve physical trauma, but deeply divided over circumstances that are more social in origin. In 1990, ABC News surveyed the general public to determine their willingness to personally undergo an abortion under a series of different circumstances. The questionnaire listed

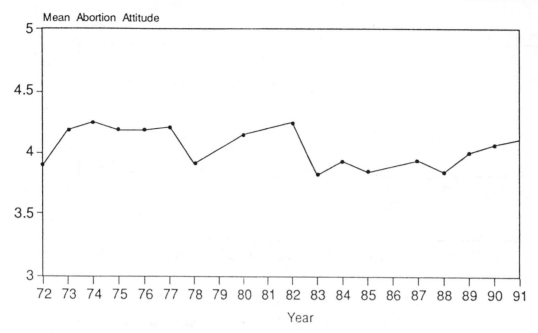

Figure 2.4. Mean Support for Legal Abortion: A Closer Look
SOURCE: Compiled from the General Social Survey, 1972-1991.

seven distinct circumstances, ranging from a painful disease that would cause the child's death by age 4 (63 percent said they would abort) to abortion for sex selection (3 percent indicated that they would abort). In all, 70 percent of the public indicated their willingness to abort under at least one circumstance, and 30 percent indicated willingness to abort in three or more different situations.

Of course, these questions were hypothetical. Faced with a concrete decision, probably many of those who indicated a willingness to abort would hesitate, and many who indicated that they would not abort would seriously consider the alternative. What these data do show is that most Americans not only want to keep abortion legal under situations of physical trauma, but also would consider personally aborting under difficult circumstances.

State Differences in Abortion Attitudes

If the Supreme Court overturns *Roe,* abortion regulation will return to state governments. By mid-1991, two states and one territory (Louisiana, Utah, and Guam) had passed stringent restrictions on abortion, and other states had passed legislation calling for parental notification or consent and/or waiting periods. Some states did not limit access to abortion. Although Governor Robert Martinez of Florida called a special session of the legislature to limit abortion, the legislature refused to comply. Moreover, the state of Maryland (which is heavily Roman Catholic) recently legislated a guarantee of abortion rights, and in late 1991 the Republican governor of Massachusetts, William Weld, introduced a similar legislative package.

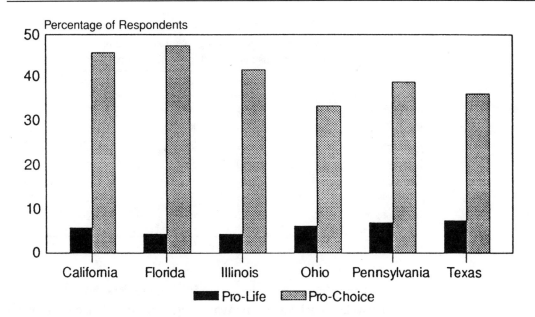

Figure 2.5. Pro-life and Pro-choice Respondents in Selected States
SOURCE: Compiled from the 1989 *CBS News/New York Times* Surveys.

If abortion is to be decided at the state level, interstate differences in abortion attitudes become important. The 1989 *CBS News/New York Times* national survey discussed above was administered along with separate surveys in Florida, California, Illinois, Pennsylvania, Texas, and Ohio. Figure 2.5 shows the percentage of respondents in each state who took consistently pro-choice or pro-life positions. There are important state differences, with more than 45 percent of residents of California and Florida consistently supporting legal abortion but only 35 percent of those in Ohio.

In Table 2.1 we show the percentage of respondents in each state who favor legal abortion under each circumstance. It is interesting that in all six states (and in the national survey), the public generally orders these seven items in the same way. Support is highest for abortions when the mother's health is in danger and lowest for a professional woman who does not want to interrupt her career. There are few state differences in support for abortion when the mother's health is in danger, and there is wide support for legal abortion for all three traumatic circumstances. State differences are far larger on abortion for social reasons. In California, Florida, and Illinois, there are narrow majorities favoring legal abortion in all circumstances except for professional women who would abort to maintain their careers. In Texas, in contrast, majorities oppose legal abortion for all four social reasons, including poverty and unmarried women.

The *CBS News/New York Times* survey did not include any states that passed stringent abortion restrictions in 1989 or 1990.[7] A University of New Orleans survey in 1990 revealed that pro-life and pro-choice forces constituted an identical 21 percent of the Louisiana sample, with 53 percent favoring some restrictions. There had been a slight increase in support for

TABLE 2.1
Respondents Supporting Legal Abortion in
Various Circumstances, 1989, by State (in percent)

	CA	FL	IL	OH	PA	TX
Mother's health	94	94	94	92	92	92
Rape	86	88	86	86	85	84
Fetal defect	79	79	75	73	75	72
Poverty	60	60	57	49	52	47
High school student	56	56	52	46	50	46
Interrupt career	46	47	42	37	37	35

SOURCE: *CBS News/New York Times* survey, 1989.

legal abortion since a similar poll in 1988, but these data show that citizens of Louisiana are much less supportive of legal abortion than citizens in the United States in general or in the six states in the *CBS News/New York Times* survey.

Group Differences in Abortion Attitudes

In the rest of this chapter, we examine demographic, or social group, differences in attitudes toward legal abortion. Where we observe differences between social groups, we attempt to explain them. Often this explanation consists of a discussion of the ways that other demographic characteristics or attitudes influence the attitudes of the social groups in question. When we say that, for example, blacks are less supportive of legal abortion than whites because they have lower levels of education, are more likely to hold orthodox religious beliefs, and are more likely to have large families, we suggest that there is nothing inherent in race that influences support for abortion—rather, African-Americans are less supportive because of their other social characteristics and attitudes. This means that if we compare (for example) African-American and white evangelical Christians with high school degrees and five children, we will find no significant differences in abortion attitudes.

In the next two chapters, we more fully examine two other sources of abortion attitudes. In Chapter 3, we examine the effects of attitudes on related issues such as feminism, euthanasia, and ideal family size, while Chapter 4 deals with the effects of religion. Many of the demographic differences in this chapter are ultimately explainable by differences in these related attitudes and behaviors.

Gender and Racial Differences

Spokespersons for both pro-life and pro-choice groups often claim that women should be especially supportive of their cause. Some pro-life groups claim that the special role of women in procreation makes them less likely than men to support legal abortion and that this gender difference should be largest among those with young children. Some pro-choice spokespersons argue that because women bear a disproportionate share of the costs of unwanted pregnancies, they should be more supportive of legal abortion.

In fact, there is practically no relationship between gender and attitudes toward legal abortion. Women are slightly less supportive of legal abortion than men, but the differences are very small. The gender gap is somewhat larger among older Americans, but only among those citizens over 65 are these differences large enough to be confident that women are significantly less supportive of legal abortion. Men are significantly more supportive of legal abortion than homemakers, but among men and women who work outside the home there is no difference in degree of support for legal abortion. Interestingly, among those respondents with small children, the gender gap entirely disappears.

Racial differences do exist, however. For all but one of the surveys between 1972 and 1991, whites were more supportive of legal abortion than African-Americans. Why do these racial differences occur? Differences between whites and blacks have been the subject of a good deal of academic study.[8] African-American women are twice as likely to have abortions as are white women, although this is primarily because they are more likely to become pregnant.[9] A similar percentage of white and black pregnancies end in abortion. Nonetheless, abortions are more common among African-Americans, yet blacks are less supportive of legal abortion. Between 1987 and 1991, 40 percent of whites supported abortion under all circumstances, compared with only 30 percent of blacks. Racial differences are largest among the oldest Americans, and during much of the 1980s these differences were larger among those who lived in the South.[10]

Why are blacks more likely than whites to oppose abortion? Several factors come into play. First, African-Americans are more likely than whites to have been raised in rural areas or in the South, and to have lower levels of education. These factors all influence abortion attitudes, as we will see below. Second, African-Americans are much more likely to oppose euthanasia (mercy killing), which is shown in Chapter 3 to be a strong predictor of abortion attitudes. Finally, blacks are more likely to hold orthodox religious beliefs, to attend doctrinally conservative churches, to attend church regularly, and to pray frequently. In Chapter 4, we will see that religious attitudes and behaviors are the strongest predictors of abortion attitudes.

Once we have held constant demographic factors, attitudes toward sexual morality, and religious affiliations and behaviors, racial differences in abortion attitudes disappear. This means that blacks are less supportive of legal abortion than whites because of their social characteristics, attitudes toward sexual morality, and religion. Indeed, after we control for attitudes and religion, African-Americans are significantly *more* supportive of legal abortion than whites.

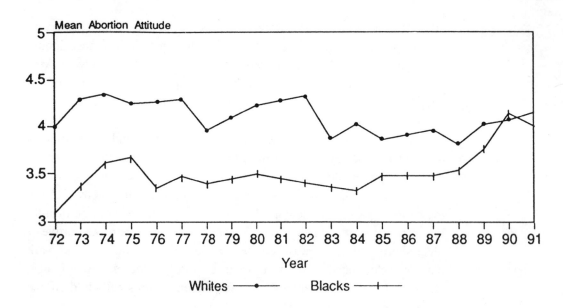

Figure 2.6. Mean on Legal Abortion Scale for Blacks and Whites, 1972-1991
SOURCE: Compiled from the General Social Survey, 1972-1991.

Over the past several years, racial differences in abortion attitudes have declined. Figures 2.6 and 2.7 show that between 1985 and 1991, the racial gap in abortion attitudes narrowed, and in the 1990 survey, blacks were actually *more* supportive of legal abortion than whites.[11] Indeed, the increase in support for legal abortion observed above in 1989 and 1990 was largely confined to the African-American community. The African-American respondents to the GSS surveys in 1989, 1990, and 1991 were more supportive of legal abortion than were black respondents in any previous years.

Several factors combined to change black attitudes on legal abortion during this period. First, as the oldest generation of African-Americans has died off, it has been replaced by a younger generation that is far more supportive of legal abortion. This oldest generation of blacks was strongly opposed to legal abortion, but from 1989 to 1991 there were fewer of this generation in the population. In addition, the average education level of blacks has climbed steadily during this period, and education is strongly associated with support for legal abortion. Finally, there has been a decline in the religiosity and religious orthodoxy of blacks (especially outside of the South) during this period, and a subsequent change in certain social issue attitudes.

Education and Social Class Differences

Of all the social characteristics that help us understand abortion attitudes, education is the strongest predictor. Opposition to legal abortion is highest among those who have dropped out of high school and lowest among college graduates. The effects of education are generally strong and exist across the entire range of educational attainment, with each increasing year

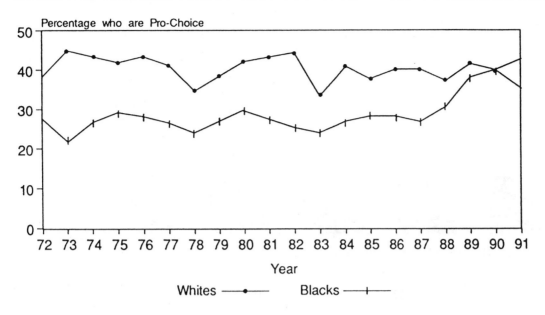

Figure 2.7. Pro-choice Respondents by Race, 1972-1991
SOURCE: Compiled from the General Social Survey, 1972-1991.

of education leading to more liberal beliefs about abortion. Between 1987 and 1991, only 21 percent of those who dropped out of school before completing high school supported abortion in all circumstances, but nearly two-thirds of those who had attended graduate school supported unlimited access to abortion. The strength of this relationship is shown graphically in Figure 2.8.

Why is education associated with liberal attitudes on abortion? In part, education is associated with other attitudes and characteristics that predict abortion attitudes. College-educated citizens are more tolerant of sexual behavior outside of marriage and are more likely to support gender equality. They are more likely to favor small families and to value their control over the size and timing of their families. They are also less likely to attend church regularly, or to hold orthodox religious beliefs. Once controls for these religious characteristics and social attitudes are introduced, the effects of education are reduced. Yet even after controls for all types of social characteristics, attitudes, and religious beliefs, education remains a strong predictor of liberal attitudes on abortion.

One reason for the relationship between education and abortion attitudes may lie in the other values and attitudes that education fosters: Education is a strong predictor of tolerance of unpopular opinions, support for civil rights for racial and behavioral minorities, and the rights guaranteed (and implied) in the Bill of Rights. Increases in formal schooling appear to lead to exposure to alternative beliefs and values and to inculcate a general value of respect for such opposing viewpoints. Education may therefore lead citizens to view issues in terms of individual liberties, which is the framework that pro-choice activists use for their arguments.

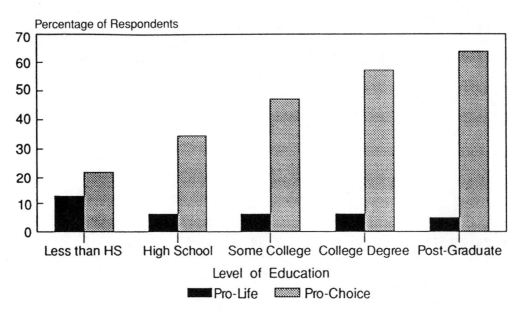

Figure 2.8. Pro-life and Pro-choice Attitudes by Level of Education
SOURCE: Compiled from the General Social Survey, 1987-1991.

We also know, however, that those who do go on to college already hold somewhat different attitudes even before their exposure to higher education. M. Kent Jennings and Richard G. Niemi interviewed a set of high school students in 1965, then reinterviewed them in 1973.[12] They found that those who would later go on to college showed higher levels of civic tolerance while they were high school seniors than those who terminated their education with high school and that this gap widened by 1973, presumably as a result of the continued education of the college students. In other words, some of the relationship between college education and support for legal abortion is possibly due to self-selection—pro-choice high school students may be more likely to continue their education in college than their pro-life counterparts. However, an important part of the relationship between high levels of education and liberal attitudes toward legal abortion is clearly due to the socializing experiences of education.

Other characteristics of socioeconomic status also predict support for legal abortion. Those citizens in high-prestige jobs and who have high family incomes are also more supportive of legal abortion.

These patterns are partly but not entirely attributable to the relationship between education and social class. High family income often characterizes two-career couples, who generally want to control their fertility, and this accounts for part of the relationship between income and abortion attitudes. For high-income, two-career families, the opportunity costs of an unexpected pregnancy may be very high. Even after controls for education and two-income couples, however, occupation and income are weak but significant predictors of support for legal abortion.

TABLE 2.2
Demographic Variables and Abortion Attitudes, 1987-1991 (in percent)

	Pro-life	Situationalist	Pro-choice	Mean Value
Men	41	53	6	4.08
Women	37	54	9	3.84
Housewives	29	60	11	3.52
Whites	40	52	8	3.99
Blacks	33	58	9	3.71
High school dropout	21	66	13	3.19
High school grad.	34	60	6	3.85
Some college	45	49	6	4.20
College degree	56	38	6	4.45
Post-graduate	63	32	5	4.71
Raised—Live				
South—South	28	63	9	3.54
South—North	36	52	12	3.66
North—South	47	45	8	4.22
North—North	43	50	7	4.10
Raised				
On farm or in country	28	61	11	3.47
Small or medium city	39	54	7	3.95
Suburbs or big city	51	44	5	4.45

Final column is the mean value (on six-point legal abortion scale) for each group.
SOURCE: General Social Survey.

Geographic Differences

Where people live influences their attitudes toward legal abortion. More importantly, where they were raised plays an even greater role. Those Americans raised in the South are less supportive of legal abortion than those raised elsewhere, regardless of where they currently live. Those raised in rural areas are more likely to oppose legal abortion than those raised in a city, regardless of where they currently live. The data in Table 2.2 show the differences in attitudes.

In part, the explanation for these geographic patterns lies with other demographic variables. Southerners and those who live in rural regions have lower levels of education than other Americans, and blacks disproportionately live in the rural South. Even more important are the religious characteristics and social attitudes that are fostered in rural regions and in the South. Rural residents and those in the South are more likely to hold orthodox religious views and be highly involved in their religion, and it appears that those raised in these areas maintain at least some of their religious characteristics when they move. Moreover, southerners and rural residents are less likely to support gender equality and are more likely to be conservative on questions of sexual morality and other issues.

Generational Differences

Abortion is a topic that affects the young somewhat differently than the old. Young men and women are more likely to confront unwanted pregnancies; for people over 50, abortion is unlikely to affect their lives directly. It seems likely, then, that abortion attitudes will differ across age groups. Two different processes could produce differences on abortion attitudes among different age groups. First, attitudes can change over the life cycle. Second, different generations of citizens may hold different sets of beliefs. It is possible that abortion attitudes could change during the life cycle. Life-cycle changes may occur as people age and their lifestyle changes.

At different ages, people have different circumstances and different needs, and these may lead to different attitudes as well. This life-cycle pattern could be linear—as people get older, they may become more conservative on abortion, or life-cycle differences could follow a more complex pattern.

Let us consider one hypothetical example of a life-cycle pattern to abortion attitudes. It could be that young, predominantly single people would generally favor legal abortion, but that those in their late twenties and early thirties, many of whom have young children, might be less supportive. Parents of teenaged children (especially daughters) may be more supportive, since they fear the consequences to their children of unwanted pregnancies, while grandparents of young children might be less supportive. In this hypothetical life-cycle pattern, those who face the highest costs of unplanned pregnancies (either for themselves or their offspring) are the most supportive of a legal abortion option, and those with young children or grandchildren are less supportive.

A second process can produce age-related differences in abortion attitudes: Generational differences may persist throughout the life cycle. Karl Mannheim argues that those who came of age during the same time (called cohorts) and who also shared unique political and social experiences could form a political generation.[13] This generation would remain distinctive in its attitudes and orientations as it passed through the life cycle. Generational effects would occur when a particular cohort retains the historical imprint of the social and historical context in which its members grew up and came of age.

A variety of studies has shown that the political circumstances existing when people reach adulthood may continue to influence them throughout their lives. These generational differences have been found in a number of areas. Those people who reached adulthood during the Great Depression have been generally more financially cautious than those who grew up during the booming 1950s. Some scholars have argued that those who grew up during World War II generally view military force as essential to deter aggression, but those who came of age during the Vietnam War are more skeptical of the use of force.[14]

We can test whether a life-cycle or a generational account of abortion attitudes provides a better explanation by comparing the attitudes of various generations over time. Although our data do not allow us to see if specific people change their attitudes, if each successive generation becomes more conservative when it reaches the age at which most women begin their families or becomes more liberal when its children are in their teens, we will have evidence of one type of life-cycle effect. If each generation remains relatively constant in its attitudes, but is notably different in ways that reflect the circumstances that existed when its members became adults, we will have evidence of generational effects.

In order to examine possible generational differences, we must identify cohorts (people who turned age eighteen during a specified time period) who have had distinctly different experiences. We have posited six possible generations that might differ on abortion attitudes. Five of our generations are adapted from the work of Virginia Sapiro.[15] Sapiro defined seven coming-of-age cohorts by historical events affecting women. We define the cohorts according to when respondents reached age eighteen, and these parallel many of Sapiro's cohorts, including those who came of age during or before the Great Depression (prior to or during 1933), those who came of age before or during World War II (1934-1944), a *Feminine Mystique* cohort from the 1950s (who reached eighteen between 1945 and 1960), a sixties cohort (1961-1969), and a women's liberation cohort that came of age during the early years of the women's movement in the 1970s (1970-1979). Finally, we add a Reagan cohort (not included in Sapiro's earlier work) that reached age eighteen after 1979.

Kristin Luker characterizes the period prior to 1960 as the "century of silence," during which there was little organized challenge to the status of abortion as regulated primarily by medical doctors. In the 1960s, however, abortion-reform forces began to push for easier access to abortion. The claim that women had a "right to control their bodies" was made during this period, when advocates of legal abortion had the rhetorical field to themselves. The 1960s was also the decade in which the birth control pill became widely available, ensuring women greater control of their fertility. After the *Roe v. Wade* decision in 1973, however, pro-life forces organized and began to publicize their position widely. Thus, those who came of age during the 1970s experienced both the rise of the women's movement and that of the pro-life movement. Sapiro's women's liberation cohort is also the cohort that was first exposed to the arguments and organizing of pro-life activists.

The 1980s saw the increasing politicization of the abortion issue, with the national Republican party officially adopting a pro-life position and most national Democrats publicly endorsing legal abortion. Those who came of age in the 1980s saw a popular conservative president espouse a pro-life position. Thus the 1960s, the women's liberation, and Reagan cohorts were socialized in eras with differing laws regulating abortion and

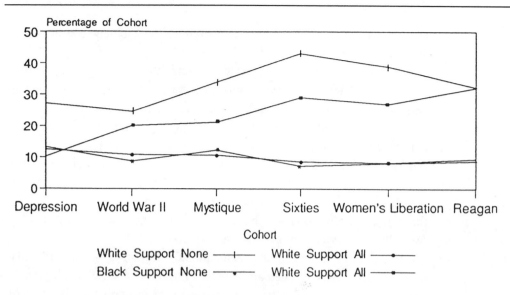

Figure 2.9. Support for Legal Abortion under Six Circumstances by Cohort
SOURCE: Compiled from the General Social Survey, 1985-1988.

different levels of elite debate on abortion. We expect smaller differences between those cohorts that came of age prior to 1960, for there were no notable changes in legal abortion during this period. Nonetheless, because part of the abortion debate concerns gender roles and these cohorts experienced differences in roles available to women, we do expect some slight cohort differences among these older respondents. In addition, we are unable to predict the direction of the responses of those who came of age during the 1970s. This cohort was exposed to the efforts of the women's movement to build feminist consciousness and also to those of the pro-life forces to regulate abortion access.

Figure 2.9 shows the percentage of whites and blacks in each generation who consistently oppose or support legal abortion. The figure shows that among blacks, support is highest among the youngest citizens, but for whites, support is highest for men and women who came of age during the 1960s and 1970s. This lowered support for legal abortion among the youngest white respondents is not accompanied by an increase in the number who take positions consistently opposing legal abortion. Indeed, the Reagan generation whites are the most supportive of legal abortion under the three traumatic circumstances. Younger whites are not joining the pro-life cause, but they approve abortion in fewer circumstances than those who came of age during the 1960s.

Instead, younger whites are less likely to approve of elective abortion than those who came of age during the 1960s. The data in Table 2.3 show that whites who came of age during the Reagan era are less likely than their somewhat older counterparts to approve of legal abortion when the mother is unmarried or when a married couple wants no more children. In contrast, young blacks are *more* likely than other blacks to approve of abortion in these circumstances.

TABLE 2.3
Support for Legal Abortion by Cohort, 1987-1991 (in percent)

	Depression	WWII	Mystique	1960s	Women's Lib	Reagan
WHITES ONLY:						
Trauma						
None	12	10	9	7	5	4
All	74	77	75	79	79	81
Elective						
None	56	51	49	44	42	44
All	29	30	37	43	46	37
N	389	637	880	814	1045	688
Health of mother	83	88	88	91	93	94
Rape	80	83	81	83	85	89
Fetal defect	78	81	80	83	83	85
Poverty	40	42	44	50	53	49
Single mother	35	40	42	49	50	43
No more children	34	38	42	49	50	44
BLACKS ONLY:						
Trauma						
None	20	16	12	9	5	3
All	41	56	65	75	76	76
Elective						
None	65	57	56	51	42	43
All	18	24	24	39	34	34
N	47	96	164	138	248	158
Health of mother	82	82	86	90	93	90
Rape	55	65	75	83	83	86
Fetal defect	54	63	69	78	82	80
Poverty	33	35	38	45	47	51
Single mother	22	30	30	42	40	39
No more children	22	34	34	44	49	46

SOURCE: General Social Survey.

These generational changes appear to persist through the life cycle. The data in Table 2.4 show that the relative ordering of the different generations has remained nearly constant since 1972. This constancy implies that abortion attitudes are generational, and although adults do change their attitudes, this change is not related to stages of the life cycle.[16]

TABLE 2.4
Cohort Differences in Abortion Attitudes: Longitudinal Trends, 1972-1991

	1972-76	*1977-80*	*1981-85*	*1986-91**
WHITES ONLY:				
Depression	3.99	3.94	3.72	3.57
WWII	4.17	4.18	3.78	3.74
Mystique	4.12	3.97	3.93	3.85
1960s	4.45	4.28	4.19	4.12
Women's liberation	4.30	4.25	4.19	4.24
Reagan			3.79	4.07
BLACKS ONLY:				
Depression	2.53	2.33	2.24	2.73
WWII	2.85	2.86	3.00	3.13
Mystique	3.93	3.73	3.22	3.40
1960s	3.88	4.08	3.99	3.95
Women's liberation	3.78	3.61	3.65	3.99
Reagan			3.61	4.00

Mean values for each cohort on six-point legal-abortion scale. Higher scores indicate greater support for legal abortion.
*Data in this column for blacks are for 1987 to 1990.
SOURCE: General Social Survey.

As a further test of the life-cycle theory, we compared young women with children and those who have no children. One version of this theory would predict that those young women with children would be less supportive of legal abortion because at that stage of their lives they are less likely to experience unwanted pregnancies and possibly make them more likely to believe that the fetus represents human life.[17] Luker has argued that some housewives were fearful that their status as mothers was devalued by the feminist movement and felt they had a vested interest in preserving the sanctity of motherhood. Restrictive attitudes about abortion were seen as an important component of a "pro-family" ideology.

Predictably, young women with children were less supportive of legal abortion. However, this difference was entirely accounted for by differences in education, occupational status, attitudes, and religion. Young mothers are less supportive of legal abortion than other young women not because their babies make them more likely to believe that an embryo is a human life, but because their education, occupational status, and religion make them both more likely to have children at a young age and less likely to support legal abortion. In contrast, those women who choose to have their children later in life are more likely to value control over their childbearing decisions.

These data suggest that abortion attitudes vary across generations but do not change as individuals move through their life cycle. Why, then, are younger whites less supportive of legal abortion than those who came of age during the 1960s? Several possible explanations exist. First, it is possible that the pro-life movement, which began organizing after the *Roe v. Wade* decision in the early 1970s, has influenced the attitudes of younger whites. The evidence does not support this explanation. First, the youngest whites are actually slightly *less* likely than older whites to take a consistently pro-life position and more likely to support legal abortion under all three traumatic situations. Second, in data from the American National Election Study (ANES) in 1988, the youngest whites were somewhat less favorable toward pro-life activists than older whites.[18] Although this evidence is not conclusive, it seems to us that the explanation of this generational pattern must lie elsewhere.

A second possible explanation is that Ronald Reagan influenced young people (especially young Republicans) by his strong opposition to legal abortion. This explanation fits the racial differences in generational patterns, where the youngest blacks are the most supportive of legal abortion. Young blacks were quite negative toward Reagan, so his persuasive powers are more likely to be effective on young whites than on blacks.[19]

Yet once again the data do not support the hypothesis. Although young whites liked Reagan more than their older counterparts, feelings toward Reagan are not at all related to abortion attitudes among this group. Young whites who were most positive toward Reagan in 1984 were no more likely to favor restrictions on abortion than those who did not like Reagan. Thus, we can reject the opinion leadership of a popular, conservative president as a possible explanation for generational differences in abortion attitudes.

A third potential explanation for the decline of support for legal abortion among younger whites is that they are more conservative in general than those who came of age during the 1960s. Again the data do not support this explanation. Younger whites are slightly less supportive of gender equality than the 1960s and 1970s cohorts, but these differences are small. They are the most permissive generation on issues of sexual morality and the most likely to call themselves liberals. Of course, this generation is also more Republican than the older generations and more likely to have supported Reagan. At most, however, the Reagan generation shows evidence of a confused ideology, not a consistently conservative pattern.

We believe that the Reagan generation came of age during a period in which the media presented a consistent message that abortion was ultimately a woman's choice but one that should not be taken lightly. We are persuaded by Condit's evidence (discussed in Chapter 1) that the media consensus during the 1980s was critical of abortions that were chosen without a compelling justification. Condit's claim fits well with these data, for the Reagan cohort of whites is primarily different from its older counterparts on two abortion items—when a married couple wants no more children and when a pregnant, unmarried woman does not want to marry.

In both cases, the Reagan cohort may feel that the need for abortion under these circumstances is not compelling. Younger respondents may be less likely to feel that there will be a substantial societal stigma for an unmarried mother. Unmarried motherhood has become more widespread since the 1960s, and the popular media (especially television) have treated unmarried mothers in a much more positive light in recent years than previously. During the 1991-1992 television season, popular television character Murphy Brown deliberately had a baby out of wedlock, as the fictional character desired a child, but did not wish to be married. Vice President Dan Quayle attacked the script as an example of the decline of traditional values.

The Reagan generation may also be more likely to believe that a married couple should have just "been more careful" and not gotten pregnant in the first place. Younger Americans may underestimate the chances of contraceptive failure, for they have had less chance to experience it. We noted in Chapter 1 that a married couple who correctly used the most successful contraception available still bore a sizable risk of an unwanted pregnancy. Young people have had less time to experience this type of contraceptive failure themselves and are less likely to know someone else who has. A woman of twenty-one who has been consistently contracepting for three years using a method 99 percent successful in each year bears only a 3 percent chance of becoming pregnant during this period. A similar woman from the sixties generation who is now 40 would have experienced a 20 percent chance of pregnancy using this same method, as would her friends of the same age. A woman of the sixties generation is therefore more likely to be aware of the probabilistic nature of contraceptive failure than a young woman of the Reagan generation. If the Reagan generation underestimates the chance of contraceptive failure, young whites may believe that such pregnancies should simply have been avoided. Thus the Reagan cohort may disapprove of abortions in these two circumstances because they do not find these situations compelling justifications for abortion.

Demographic Differences in Abortion Attitudes: Multivariate Analyses

How do these demographic variables combine to explain abortion attitudes? In order to determine how useful each demographic variable is in explaining abortion attitudes, we use a statistical procedure called multiple regression. This technique enables us to determine how much effect a variable (say, education) has on abortion attitudes when other variables have been held constant.

The nine demographic variables combined to explain approximately 9 percent of the variation in abortion attitudes. This relatively low figure suggests the need for additional explanations of abortion attitudes. In the next two chapters, we consider the effects of other, related attitudes and of religion on abortion attitudes.

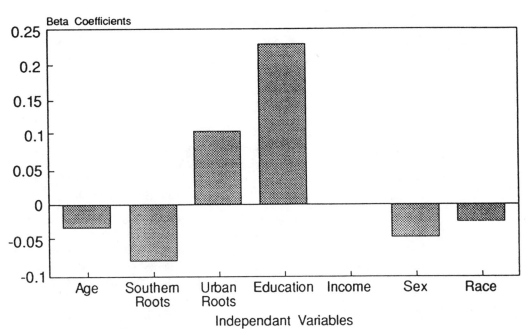

Figure 2.10. Demographic Predictors of Abortion Attitudes
SOURCE: Compiled from the General Social Survey, 1987-1991.

Figure 2.10 presents the results of the analysis. The height of the bar is proportional to the strength of the relationship between the variable and overall abortion attitudes. Those bars that lie below the line suggest that the relationship is negative. For example, the bar representing those raised in the South lies below the line, indicating that those who grew up in the South are less supportive of legal abortion. In contrast, the bar for education is above the line, indicating that those with higher levels of education are more supportive of abortion than those who completed less formal education. A detailed presentation of the results can be found in the Appendix [not included with this reading].

Among the social variables that we have considered here, education is by far the most important predictor. Geographic variables are also important, with those who were raised in the South or in rural areas markedly less supportive of legal abortion. Women were significantly less supportive of abortion, and further analysis shows that this relationship is entirely due to less support among housewives. Income and race are not significant predictors of abortion once other variables are controlled. In other words, we cannot dismiss the possibility that the observed relationships are not attributable to sampling error.

Conclusions

Memberships in social groups do help us account for differences in attitudes toward legal abortion to some extent. Differences in education, region, and family structure all help explain some of the variation in abortion attitudes. However, the explanatory power of such demographic variables is rather weak, and much remains to be explained after the effects of these variables have been taken into account. What is needed is a more detailed analysis of the reasons people have for their abortion attitudes, and it is to this task that we now turn.

Notes

1. These data and others in this book are made available by the Inter-University Consortium for Political and Social Research. We are responsible for all interpretations. James Davis and Tom Smith, *General Social Surveys, 1972-1991* [machine readable data file]. Chicago: National Opinion Research Center (1991).

2. The dimensionality of the abortion items has been widely documented, and we have confirmed this with factor analysis. Moreover, we find that this same factor structure holds for the somewhat different items included in the 1989 *CBS News/New York Times* survey in several different states. In using this terminology, we are mindful that all abortions are traumatic for the women involved, and that all abortions are in some sense elective. Moreover, extreme poverty is a traumatic circumstance. Some other researchers have used the terms "hard" and "soft" reasons for abortion, but we believe that elective and traumatic convey more of the core of the distinction. Note that the distinction between these two sets of items is not our own categorization, rather it emerged from the pattern of public response to these questions.

3. Aida Torres and Jacqueline Forrest, "Why Do Women Have Abortions?" *Family Planning Perspectives* 20 (1988), pp. 169-176.

4. We refer to only those citizens who oppose abortion in all circumstances as pro-life supporters. Because some pro-life organizations allow for exemptions when the mother's life is in danger, this may seem an arbitrary decision. We make this choice for two reasons. First, political actors call themselves pro-life or pro-choice for political reasons. Although President Bush calls himself pro-life, he has at various points endorsed exemptions for the life and health of the mother, for rape and incest, and for severe fetal defect. This position would be at 3, near the mid-point of our scale. Similarly, some of those who call themselves pro-choice favor restrictions. It is therefore cleaner to limit our pro-life and pro-choice categories to those positions held by most activists on both sides. Second, note that the GSS question refers to the *health,* not life of the mother. Pro-life activists are quite wary of this exception. Prior to the *Roe* decision when states were allowed to regulate abortion, several states with exemptions for the mother's health allowed that clause to become quite elastic—for example, allowing doctors to certify that a live birth would upset the mother and therefore interfere with her *mental* health.

5. Abortion attitudes appear to be remarkably stable at the individual level as well. See Philip E. Converse and Gregory B. Markus, "Plus ca Change . . . The New CPS Election Study Panel," *American Political Science Review* 73 (1979), pp. 32-49.

6. Malcolm L. Goggin and Christopher Wlezien, "Interest Groups and the Socialization of Conflict: The Dynamics of Abortion Politics" (paper presented at the annual meeting of the Midwest Political Science Association in Chicago, 1991). Goggin and Wlezien argue that interest group activity in anticipation of *Webster* may have influenced public attitudes.

7. Pennsylvania passed a package of restrictions including parental consent; spousal notification; a twenty-four hour waiting period; requirements that doctors

inform patients of the development of their fetuses; health risks from abortion and alternatives to abortion; and a requirement that abortion providers supply the state health department with information about each procedure, including the basis for determining the gestational age of the fetus.

8. For a discussion of racial differences in abortion attitudes, see M. Combs and S. Welch, "Blacks, Whites, and Attitudes Toward Abortion," *Public Opinion Quarterly* 46 (1982), pp. 510-520; E. Hall and M. Ferree, "Race Differences in Abortion Attitudes," *Public Opinion Quarterly* 50 (1986), pp. 193-207; P. Secret, "The Impact of Region on Racial Differences in Attitudes Toward Legal Abortion," *Journal of Black Studies* 17 (1987), pp. 347-369; C. Wilcox, "Race Differences in Abortion Attitudes: Some Additional Evidence," *Public Opinion Quarterly* 54 (1990), pp. 248-255; C. Wilcox, "Race, Religion, Region, and Abortion Attitudes," *Sociological Analysis* (1992), forthcoming.

9. S. Henshaw and J. Silverman, "The Characteristics and Prior Contraceptive Use of U.S. Abortion Patients," *Family Planning Perspectives* 20 (1988), pp. 158-168.

10. P. Secret, "The Impact of Religion on Racial Differences in Attitudes Toward Legal Abortion," *Journal of Black Studies* 17 (1989), pp. 347-369. But see also C. Wilcox, "Race, Religion, Region, and Abortion Attitudes," *Sociological Analysis,* forthcoming.

11. In the late 1980s, the GSS began asking many of its questions of two-thirds of all respondents. This allowed NORC to include more questions, but it reduced the already small number of black respondents to the abortion items. Beginning in 1988, therefore, we have averaged the respondents in each year with those in the previous year for Figure 2.6. This allows us to smooth trends in black attitudes by reducing sampling error.

12. M. Kent Jennings and Richard G. Niemi, *Generations and Politics* (Princeton: Princeton University Press, 1981).

13. Karl Mannheim, "The Problem of Generations," in Philip Altbach and Robert Laufer, eds., *The New Pilgrims* (New York: David McKay, 1972).

14. See Graham Allison, "Cool It: The Foreign Policy Beliefs of Young America," *Foreign Policy* 1 (1971), pp. 150-154; Ole Holsti and James Rosenau, "Does Where You Stand Depend on When You Were Born? The Impact of Generation on Post-Vietnam Foreign Policy Beliefs," *Public Opinion Quarterly* 44 (1980), pp. 1-22; and Michael Roskin, "From Pearl Harbor to Vietnam: Shifting Generational Paradigms," *Political Science Quarterly* 89 (1974), pp. 563-588. Yet other studies show an opposite pattern, with those who came of age during World War II the least supportive of military action in the Persian Gulf; those who grew up during the Vietnam war were the most supportive. See Clyde Wilcox, Joseph Ferrara, and Dee Allsop, "Before the Rally: Public Attitudes on the Iraq Crisis" (paper presented at the annual meeting of the American Political Science Association, Washington, D.C., September 1991).

15. Virginia Sapiro, "News from the Front: Intersex and Intergenerational Conflict over the Status of Women," *Western Political Quarterly* 33 (1980), pp. 260-277.

16. These data show evidence of period effects, with all generations becoming more conservative during the mid-1980s and more liberal at the end of that decade.

17. Alternatively, pro-choice activists would hypothesize that women who have experienced childbirth would be less likely to want other women to go through the experience unless they chose to.

18. For details of this and other tests of explanations for generational differences, see Elizabeth Cook, Ted G. Jelen, and Clyde Wilcox, "Generations and Abortion," *American Politics Quarterly,* forthcoming.

19. A more likely influence on the attitudes of young blacks would be Rev. Jesse Jackson, who took a pro-choice position in his 1984 and 1988 presidential campaigns, despite his earlier pro-life position.

Ideal Family Size as an Intervening Variable between Religion and Attitudes towards Abortion

Mario Renzi

Previous research has shown a fairly consistent relationship between religion and/or religiosity and attitudes toward abortion. Data from a 1972 national sample is presented showing the importance of ideal family size as an intervening variable in this relationship and argues for its inclusion in subsequent research in this area.

The research on the relationship between religious affiliation and attitudes towards abortion has consistently taken a position of a direct causal relationship between religion and these attitudes. Finner and Gamache (1969) in their study demonstrate that multidimensional measures of religious commitment are directly related to attitudes towards induced abortion. This relationship is supported by the introduction of the following control variables: sex, age, marital status, education, income, religious self identification, political self identification, and religious affiliation, none of which significantly affected the relationship of religious commitment and abortion attitudes. Subsequent research has further contributed to these findings by investigating different populations, using other control variables or modification of the measurement of the religious variable. Research by Richardson and Fox (1972) was conducted on a sample of state legislators using voting record on abortion legislation as the dependent variable. Religious affiliation was found to have a direct relationship to their dependent variable after the introduction of the control variables of age, party affiliation, and constituency.

Reprinted by permission from Mario Renzi, "Ideal Family Size as an Intervening Variable between Religion and Attitudes towards Abortion," *Journal for the Scientific Study of Religion,* 1975, vol. 14, pp. 23-27.

AUTHOR'S NOTE: The author would like to thank Paul Gustafson for his comments and direction in regard to an earlier draft.

A comparative perspective was added to this research by Balakrishnan et al. (1972). Using a sample of married women in Toronto, they found that religious affiliation, particularly Catholic vs. non-Catholic, as well as frequency of church attendance were the most powerful predictors of attitudes towards abortion. The control variables of age, income, education, and size of birthplace were not as important as religion in explaining the variation in abortion attitudes.

Two of the most recent studies were conducted on a college student population (Clayton and Tolone 1973) and on a sample of professional social workers and nurses (Hertel et al. 1974). Clayton and Tolone (1973: 28) used the following control variables: sex, class rank (freshman and other), birth order, size of community, parental income, religious identification, and frequency of church attendance while Hertel et al. (1974: 27-28) used sex, race, age, profession, and occupational prestige. As with the earlier research, these control variables did not significantly modify the relationship of religion and/or religiosity with attitudes towards abortion. Given the various populations researched, as well as the numerous control variables introduced, the religion and/or religiosity relationship to abortion attitudes appears well established.

However there is another body of research findings dealing with religion which leads one to a possible variable which is consistently absent from the above research. As early as 1960, it was found that Catholic married women wanted and expected to have a larger number of children than non-Catholic married women (Whelpton et al. 1966: 90). Subsequent research (Westoff et al. 1963; Ryder and Westoff 1968) further supported these findings. The most recent study by Brackbill and Howell (1974), while based on junior high, high school, and college students, does show the continued importance of a religious differential in family size preference.

Religion appears then to be systematically related to desired family size. If one conceptualizes abortion as simply one more device to control family size, it would seem important to introduce family size as a control variable in any analysis of the relationship of religion and attitudes towards abortion. This is what we intend to do in this research note, as an attempt to see if religion continues to have a direct influence on attitudes towards abortion when preferred family size is held constant.

Methods

The data for this research note were taken from the National Data Program for the Social Sciences. The data collection was under the supervision of the National Opinion Research Center. The survey was conducted in March of 1972 on a cross-sectional national sample of non-institutionalized adults 18 years of age or older. The N was 1,613.[1]

Three variables are of concern in this research note: religion, preferred family size, and attitudes towards abortion. In regard to religion respondents

TABLE 1
Percent Agreeing to a Legal Abortion by Religion and Ideal Family Size

| | Situation of Pregnancy | | | | | |
	Woman's Health Endangered by Pregnancy	Became Pregnant as a Result of Rape	Strong Chance of Birth Defect in Baby	Family Has Low Income and Can't Afford More Children	Woman Not Married and Does Not Want to Marry the Man	Woman Married and Does Not Want Any More Children
			Small Families			
Protestants (N)	91 (442)	87 (441)	89 (438)	60 (436)	57 (430)	52 (441)
Catholics (N)	93 (138)	85 (133)	83 (134)	49 (136)	44 (134)	40 (133)
			Large Families			
Protestants (N)	78 (539)	71 (526)	70 (527)	37 (522)	30 (523)	26 (532)
Catholics (N)	78 (254)	68 (253)	65 (250)	31 (251)	27 (253)	24 (260)
	$\chi^2 = 35.4$	$\chi^2 = 52.7$	$\chi^2 = 84.2$	$\chi^2 = 70.8$	$\chi^2 = 90.8$	$\chi^2 = 88.1$
	df = 3	df = 3	df = 3	df = 3	df = 3	df = 3
	$p < .001$	$p < .001$	$p < .001$	$p < .001$	$p < .001$	$p < .001$

were categorized into Catholics and Protestants,[2] and respondents with other religious affiliations were excluded because of the small size of this population represented in any national sample. Preferred family size was operationalized by responses to a question about the ideal number of children for a family.[3] Those respondents who indicated 2 or less children as ideal were categorized as preferring small families, while those who indicated 3 or more were designated as preferring large families.

Attitudes toward abortion were tapped by six questions, with each indicating a condition of pregnancy, and the respondents were asked whether or not it should be possible for a pregnant woman in each of these conditions to obtain a legal abortion.[4] Only responses of yes or no are included in our analysis. Chi square was used to measure the statistical significance of any observed differences.

Results

Table 1 presents the data on the relationship of religious affiliation and attitudes towards abortion when preferred family size is held constant. In general the data support our position that preferred family size is an important intervening variable in the relation between religion and abortion attitudes. First, comparing members of the same religious groups who differ on family size preference, the data indicate that preferred family size appears to have an independent relationship to abortion attitudes. This is supported by noting that under each of the pregnancy situations Catholics and Protestants who prefer small families are consistently more liberal than corresponding religious group members who prefer large families. The range of difference on abortion attitudes for the two Catholic groups is 15 to 18 percent, while the differences for the two Protestant groups is 8 to 27 percent.

However, it also appears that preferred family size has a slight interactive effect with religion upon abortion attitudes. Comparing the differences between Protestants and Catholics with the same family size preference, the data in general indicate that under the specification of small family size the difference between the religious groups is more substantial than between the religious groups who prefer large families. In four of the six situations of pregnancy the differences between Catholics and Protestants who prefer small families is greater than 5 percent, while only in one situation of pregnancy is the difference between Catholics and Protestants who prefer large families greater than 5 percent.

In summary, the data in Table 1 indicate that preferred family size has a relationship to abortion attitudes relatively independent of religious affiliation. However, it also appears that this variable has an important specifying effect on the relationship of religion and abortion attitudes, in that the greatest differences between religious groups with respect to attitudes towards abortion in general occur only with the specification of small family size.

Discussion

Much of the previous research (noted above) on the relationship between religion and/or religiosity as it influences attitudes towards abortion attempts to argue for a direct causal relationship between a "religious factor" and attitudes towards abortion. This specific theoretical orientation is consistent with the one called by White (1968) the theory of "psychological consonance." According to White, this theoretical approach is based on two postulates. The first of these postulates is that the theology of the religion with which one is affiliated is the primary source of religious influence,[5] and, second, that persons who believe their theology seek a consonance between that theology and their attitudes and behaviors in other spheres of social life.

White then continues to critique this approach of direct theological influence. He argues that a more appropriate approach is to conceptualize religious groups as spheres of interaction and that this interaction generates group specific norms. These group specific norms may or may not be logically linked to theology but they are to White the primary source of the "religious factor." White therefore seems to be calling for greater care as to possible intervening factors in the religion, attitude, and behavior process.

The data in this research note lends support to the appropriateness of White's caution to the specific area of research dealing with the relationship of religion and attitudes towards abortion. Our findings suggest that the influence of religion is more indirect, and that preferred family size is an important specifying variable to be considered in further research in the area. Such subsequent research on abortion attitudes should be concerned then with two questions: 1) the influence of religion on family size preference, and 2) other normative factors of religious groups as they influence this preference, e.g., ethnicity.

The above conclusions are offered in a preliminary way given the somewhat small but consistent differences found in this data. We recognize that other factors such as denominational differences among Protestants and the extent of religious involvement are not included in this research. Furthermore, alternative explanations exist for these findings. It is possible that preferred family size is an indirect measure of religious commitment, religious orthodoxy or some other dimension of the religious factor. Questions such as these, however, await research designed specifically to address the relationship of religion and/or religiosity to abortion attitudes rather than secondary analysis as is reported here. Nonetheless we do feel that this research raises questions with the position that because abortion is a "moral" issue theology must be the most important factor.

Notes

1. Further information on the data as well as the exact wording of all the questions used can be found in Davis (1972).

2. We recognize that this operationalization of the variable of religion is most elementary and much more refined measures exist, but we feel that such operationalizations await a more lengthy and systematic analysis than can be accomplished in a paper such as this.

3. This research is based on secondary analysis, and while a question tapping preferred family size which explicitly refers to the respondent's family would be more useful, such a question was not available to us. For a discussion of the conceptual problems involved with this variable see Ryder and Westoff (1969).

4. For a more detailed analysis of abortion attitudes see Ryder and Westoff (1971: 267-293) as well as Blake (1971).

5. Recent work by Clayton and Gladden (1974), among others, attempting to show the overriding importance of an ideological factor in multidimensional of religiosity is consistent with this postulate.

References

Balakrishnan, T. T., Shan Ross, John D. Allingham, and John F. Kanter. 1972. "Attitudes toward abortion of married women in metropolitan Toronto." *Social Biology* 19:36-42.

Blake, Judith. 1971. "Abortion and public opinion: The 1960-1970 decade." *Science* 171:540-49.

Brackbill, Yvonne, and Embry M. Howell. 1974. "Religious differences in family size preference among American teenagers." *Sociological Analysis* 35:26-39.

Clayton, Richard R. and William L. Tolone. 1973. "Religiosity and attitudes towards induced abortion: An elaboration of the relationship." *Sociological Analysis* 34:26-39.

————, and James W. Gladden. 1974. "The five dimensions of religiosity: toward demythologizing a sacred artifact." *Journal for the Scientific Study of Religion* 13:135-43.

Davis, James A. 1972. *Codebook for the Spring 1972 General Social Survey.* Chicago: National Opinion Research Center/University of Chicago.

Finner, Stephen L. and Jerome D. Gamache. 1969. "The relationship between religious commitment and attitudes towards induced abortion." *Sociological Analysis* 30:1-12.

Hertel, Bradley, Gerry E. Hendershot, and James W. Grimm. 1974. "Religion and attitudes toward abortion: A study of nurses and social workers." *Journal for the Scientific Study of Religion* 13:23-34.

Richardson, James T. and Sandy Wightman Fox. 1972. "Religious affiliation as a predictor of voting behavior in abortion reform legislation." *Journal for the Scientific Study of Religion* 11:347-59.

Ryder, Norman B. and Charles F. Westoff. 1969. "Relationship among intended, expected, desired, and ideal family size: United States 1965." Washington, DC: National Institute of Child Health and Human Development, Center for Population Research.

————, and ————. 1971. *Reproduction in the United States: 1965.* Princeton: Princeton University Press.

Westoff, Charles F., Robert G. Potter, and Philip C. Sagi. 1963. *The Third Child.* Princeton: Princeton University Press.

Whelpton, Pascal K., Arthur A. Campbell, and John E. Patterson. 1966. *Fertility and Family Planning in the United States.* Princeton: Princeton University Press.

White, Richard H. 1968. "Toward a theory of religious influence." *Pacific Sociological Review* 11:23-28.

Religion, Ideal Family Size, and Abortion: Extending Renzi's Hypothesis

William V. D'Antonio

Steven Stack

Recent research has noted a negative relationship between ideal family size (IFS) and proabortion attitudes (AA) which is independent of religious affiliation. The present investigation extends the investigation of this relationship in several ways. First, we find considerable variation in abortion attitudes among the Protestant denominations; this finding warrants a denomination-specific analysis. Second, controlling for religious affiliation within Protestantism, we find numerous examples of the spuriousness of the IFS-AA relationship. Third, the 1973 U.S. Supreme Court decision regarding abortion is found to have limited impact on the number of significant associations between IFS and AA. At the same time, for most denominations, IFS remains a significant predictor of AA. Fourth, we assess the importance of IFS relative to seven other independent variables in a multiple regression analysis and find that IFS is a significant predictor of an index of overall abortion attitudes. While Renzi's hypothesis is therefore successfully extended in each stage of this analysis, numerous exceptions appear, particularly for denominations with strong proabortion sentiments. Finally, we note that IFS may have a limited history as a predictor variable if a national consensus emerges around the two child family.

Research on the relationship between religious affiliation and attitudes towards abortion has shown a consistent pattern, that is, those who express a religious commitment in one form or another, or who attend church regularly, are less likely to support proabortion stands than those with weaker or no church linkages. Renzi (1975) further reported that people's family size preference (PFS) acted as an intervening variable between religion and abortion attitudes.[1] More recently, Arney and Trescher (1976) clarified the relation between religious denomination and attitudes toward abortion by controlling for religious participation. They found littler differ-

---

Reprinted by permission from William V. D'Antonio and Steven Stack, "Religion, Ideal Family Size, and Abortion: Extending Renzi's Hypothesis," *Journal for the Scientific Study of Religion,* 1980, vol. 19, pp. 397-408.

ence in the distributions of responses of Catholics and Protestants who attended church less than once a month. Among Catholics and Protestants who attended church more than once a month (called the more committed), Catholics were more likely than Protestants to oppose abortion. In addition, Arney and Trescher (1976) note, since the Supreme Court decision of 1973 in favor of abortion, a "substantial increase in approval of abortion among both committed Protestants and Catholics, although the increase among Protestants is for soft reasons (see explanation below) while among Catholics this increase is for hard reasons only" (p. 120).

Renzi reported that when "comparing members of the same religious group who differ on family size preference, preferred family size appeared to have an independent relationship to abortion attitudes." Catholics and Protestants who preferred small families were consistently more supportive of abortion than their counterparts preferring large families. Renzi concluded that family size preference was indeed an intervening variable between religion and attitudes toward abortion. At the same time he reported that PFS also appeared to act as an independent variable regardless of religion.

In this paper, we take another look at the question and expand the analysis to include the following issues: (a) within Protestantism is there a variation in attitudes towards abortion that is obscured when all Protestants are combined into one category? (b) within Protestant denominations, is the variable of ideal family size significantly related to abortion attitudes (AA)? (c) did the U.S. Supreme Court decision on abortion have any impact on the relationship between IFS and abortion attitudes? (d) what is the importance of IFS compared with other factors in explaining the variance in abortion attitudes? Research (deBoer, 1977-78) has shown that the main variables influencing abortion attitudes are: sex (women more than men oppose abortion); creed and church attendance (Catholics and those who attend church regularly are more likely than others to oppose abortion); age (those older than 45 are more likely than those under 45 to oppose abortion); and education (the less formally educated are more likely than the more formally educated to oppose abortion). These variables will be included with IFS in a multiple regression analysis.

Methodology

The data source in this investigation is the same as in Renzi's, the NORC General Social Survey. We utilize two NORC surveys, one from 1972 and another from 1975, to assess the impact of the U.S. Supreme Court decision on abortion attitudes. These surveys are based on a cross sectional national sample of 1,613 persons in 1972 and 1,490 persons in 1975. All respondents interviewed were over 18 years of age. All were living in noninstitutionalized arrangements within the United States. Block quota sampling was used in 1972, and a combination of block quota and probability sampling was

TABLE 1

Members of Each Religious Denomination Favoring Abortion by Abortion
Possible Situations for 1972 and 1975 (in percentages)

Abortion Situation	Non-bel.	Jew	Episc.	Presb.	Meth.	Luth.	Oth Prot.	Bapt.	All[a] Prot.	Cath.
					1972					
Health	95	96	100	92	92	91	85	79	87	84
Rape	91	98	100	91	86	81	72	69	79	75
Defect	91	93	97	90	88	82	76	69	80	72
Low income	79	80	76	65	56	45*	45	35*	48	38*
Not marry	73	84	75	54	52	43*	36	29*	42	33*
Not want	75	72	69	55	47	31*	35	26*	38	30*
Total N	83	54	33	80	232	139	185	324	1,031	413
					1975					
Health	98	96	98	93	91	96	93	87	91	86
Rape	93	100	93	93	85	92	81	76	84	79
Defect	95	95	89	89	87	88	80	77	84	77
Low income	77	91	77	69	51	62*	45	43*	53	45*
Not marry	76	82	71	63	47	59*	38	35*	46	43*
Not want	74	86	71	58	42	55*	36	36*	44	39*
Total N	113	23	44	76	175	139	182	309	975	363

NOTE: To determine whether or not the changes from 1972 to 1975 were significant, we used a test for differences between proportions. For a discussion of this technique, see Loether and McTavish (1974: 189-192). The test is tailored for two unequal N's and independent samples. We found through use of Cramer's V that the variations in abortion attitudes that existed between the six Protestant denominations were all significant at the .05 level, in both time periods. Most of the variation significance was caused by the fact that the Baptists (the largest Protestant denomination) had the most restrictive attitudes on abortion in all situations. Lumping Protestant denominations into one broad category obscures the differences. Cramer's V was adopted instead of Tschuprow's T since the T statistic can attain unity only when the number of rows and columns are not equal. For this reason V is judged to be preferable to T (Blalock, 1979: 305). Another alternative, the Contingency Coefficient, was not utilized since its upper limit is .707, making it more difficult to interpret than the other measures.

[a]Includes Protestants without a specific denominational identity.

*Change from 1972 to 1975 is significant, $p < .05$, one-tailed test.

used in 1975. (For a further description of the sampling techniques used see Davis 1978:171-75.)

Attitudes towards abortion are measured in terms of the respondent's approval or disapproval of six abortion situations. These six situations are divided into two sets: in one the reason for getting an abortion is said to be "hard," and in the other it is considered "soft." The three "hard" situations are those in which the woman's pregnancy is: (1) beyond her control because of rape, (2) involves a major health hazard to her, or (3) involves a risk of a severe birth defect in the baby. The soft reasons for abortion involve situations in which: (4) the woman does not want the baby because the family has a very low income and cannot afford more children, (5) the woman is not married and does not want to marry the father, or (6) she is married and simply does not want to have more children. (For the section of the paper dealing with the regression analysis, an index of abortion attitudes was constructed by summing the respondents' scores on the six abortion questions. Scores were "one" if opposed and "two" if supportive of abortion on the particular question. The index had a coefficient of reproduceability of .940 and a coefficient of scalability of .807.)

Religious affiliation includes nine categories: Catholic, Baptist, Methodist, Lutheran, Presbyterian, Episcopalian, Other Protestant, Jew, and Nonbeliever. One limitation of this classification scheme is that it does not subdivide the category "other Protestant," which includes approximately ten percent of the sample. However, these finer categories would be so small as to preclude analysis.

Renzi used ideal family size as his measure of preferred family size, which leads to some terminological confusion (see Ryder & Westoff, 1969). In this paper we will use the term ideal family size (IFS), since it seems to reflect more accurately the question used in the NORC studies: "What do you think is the ideal number of children for a family to have?"

Furthermore, Renzi dichotomized respondents' answers into "small" (two or fewer children) and "large" (three or more), thereby masking possible variation. To avoid this problem, we coded the responses from a low of zero to a high of five or more. Hence, we use a six part ordinal scale in place of Renzi's dichotomous ordinal scale.

Analysis

To determine whether variations existed on attitudes toward abortion among Protestants in 1972 and 1975 and whether variation between denominations declined over time, we carried out a number of statistical comparisons.

Table 1 presents the data on the percentage of each religious group who favor abortion in each of the six abortion situations. For both 1972 and 1975 considerable differences in AA exist among the Protestant religions. For example, for the year 1972, on the issue of abortion for health reasons, the percentage of Protestants favoring abortion ranged from a low of 79 percent for Baptists to a high 100 percent for Episcopalians. The variation tends to be greater for the soft reasons than for the hard reasons. For example, the range in the percentage favoring abortion is 21 points on the hard reason of health whereas it is 55 points on the soft reason of not wanting to marry the father of the child. In this latter case, in fact, three Protestant denominations each gave less than majority support to this abortion possible situation (Table 1, 1972 data).

Comparing the variation among Protestants to differences between Catholics and all Protestants, we see that the diversity of opinion on abortion among Protestant denominations is indeed masked if one sticks to Renzi's dichotomous measure. For example, the difference in Catholic-Protestant percentages is less than four points for the health reason and ten points for the "low income" reason. A further analysis of denominational differences in the IFS-AA is warranted by these data. We will save the discussion of the 1975 data for the section on the effects of the Supreme Court ruling on AA.

Table 1 makes clear that certain Protestant denominations are more liberal on abortion than others. Baptists stand out as being the most conservative on the abortion issue, followed by the category Other Protestants. (In fact, the category is made up of small, conservative groups.) Presbyterians and Episcopalians are the most liberal on the issue. A majority of the members of these two latter groups favor abortion for all six reasons, soft and hard alike. Methodists and Lutherans take a more "middle of the road" position, with almost twice as much support for the hard as compared with the soft reasons. Nevertheless, their support generally is considerably higher than that of the Baptists.

Comparing Protestants with non-Protestants, Baptists more closely resemble Catholics than do any of the other Protestant groups; less than a six point difference obtains in the ratings of Catholics and Baptists for each of the six abortion situations. Jews and nonbelievers are even more liberal on abortion than either Presbyterians or Episcopalians. While these two sets of liberal religious positions are similar when it comes to the hard abortion situations, greater levels of liberalism are found among the non-Protestant categories for soft reasons. Finally, while most religions were more liberal on most abortion situations in 1975, the relative positions of the different religions stayed approximately the same.

Further evidence on the significant variation in AA was provided by restricting the analysis to the six Protestant denominations. Cramer's V statistic of association between Protestant religious affiliation and AA was significant at the .05 level for all six abortion situations (see note to Table 1). However, the level of consensus on some abortion situations, mainly the hard reasons, for some of these denominations is so high (sometimes 100 percent) that in these situations we would expect the IFS variable, as well as other possible independent variables, to have little bearing on AA; little or no variation exists to explain. While Renzi found a significant relationship between religion (measured in dichotomous terms) and AA, we can specify that this is true only for those denominations not having a high level of consensus on AA. In addition, we anticipate that the IFS-AA relationship will be greater in soft situations rather than hard, inasmuch as more consensus on AA exists for hard situations.

Table 2 presents the Kendall's tau measures of association between IFS and AA for each of nine religious denominations and each of the six abortion situations. Restricting our analysis for the moment to the 1972 data, we see that IFS is not always significantly related to AA when we control for religion. In 14 cases the tau value is not significant. However, thirty-seven of the Kendall's taus are significant. On the whole, IFS is still a significant predictor of AA, but there are numerous exceptions. The exceptions to the general rule follow a pattern involving the degree of consensus on proabor-

TABLE 2

Measures of Association (Kendall's tau) Between Ideal Family Size and
Proabortion Attitudes, by Religious Affiliation, 1972, 1975

Religious Affiliations	Health	Rape	Defect	Low Income	Not Marry	Not Want
1972						
Catholic (398)	.16*	.19*	.18	.16*	.15*	.13*
Jewish (53)	.28*	.17	.24*	.40*	.40*	.34*
Nonbelievers (76)	−.01	.02	.11	.21*	.26*	.26*
Baptist (312)	.18*	.23*	.26*	.19*	.15*	.18*
Methodist (223)	.02	.16*	.10	.21*	.30*	.21*
Lutheran (133)	.14*	.29*	.29*	.32*	.22*	.36*
Presbyterian (79)	.01	−.02	−.06	.16	.17	.20*
Episcopalian (33)	—a	—a	.16	.41*	.46*	.42*
Other Protestant (176)	.18*	.14*	.25*	.15*	.24*	.26*
1975						
Catholic (348)	.23*	.18*	.25*	.27*	.21*	.22*
Jewish (21)	−.16	—a	.28	.50*	.85*	.34
Nonbelievers (107)	.04	.19*	.13	.11	.10	.03
Baptists (304)	.07	.13*	.08	.21*	.22*	.24*
Methodists (170)	.22*	.15*	.20*	.25*	.21*	.21*
Lutheran (139)	.19*	.09	.27*	.24*	.26*	.26*
Presbyterian (74)	.06	.22*	.14	.31*	.35*	.32*
Episcopalian (44)	.22	.11	.06	.02	.02	.05
Other Protestant (173)	.08	.03	.18*	.20*	.24*	.25*

a All persons approved of abortion.
*Statistically significant at the .05 level.

tion attitudes by hard and soft reasons. Given the high level of consensus on hard reasons, we find that only 14 out of 27 Kendall's taus are significant where it comes to the hard reasons. In contrast, where there are lower levels of agreement (the soft reasons for abortion), nearly all of the measures of association are significant (25 out of 27 cases). Hence, on the hard reasons such as rape and birth defects, we often find that persons support abortion regardless of their reported IFS. (A similar pattern shows up in the 1975 figures.)

On the soft reasons for abortion, there is considerable disagreement between denominations, and lack of majority support among four of the denominations. In these situations IFS appears to play a significant role in shaping abortion sentiments. Those preferring small families are significantly more likely to be proabortion, regardless of religious affiliation.

A second prediction to be tested was that the IFS-AA relationship would tend to be significant among denominations with low levels of proabortion consensus. This is largely borne out by comparing the data in Table 1 with those in Table 2. For example, the IFS-AA relationship is significant on all three hard abortion situations for Catholics, Baptists, and other Protestants. These are precisely the groups that have the lowest support for abortion (between 69 and 84 percent approve of abortion for hard reasons), and hence the lowest level of consensus. Within these groups, when there is somewhat greater disagreement on AA, IFS can help explain the variation.

A third concern of our analysis was to determine if abortion attitudes and the IFS-AA relationship for the various denominations had changed following the U.S. Supreme Court decision on abortion. A trend toward greater support would be expected. Table 1 shows that the percentage of persons in each religious denomination who supported abortion increased in 40 of the 54 cells between 1972 and 1975. While this is the direction of change that was anticipated, a related issue concerns how many of these increases between 1972 and 1975 were significant. Using a significance test for differences in proportions (Loether & McTavish 1974:189-92), we determined that only six of the 1972-1975 changes were significant at the .05 level. The six significant increases were for Catholics and Baptists on each of the three soft abortion situations. Hence, the Supreme Court's ruling on abortion is associated with a significant liberalization of attitudes on abortion for only two denominations. The finding takes on added importance, perhaps, given that these are the two largest denominations. At the same time, since these denominations were least supportive of abortion for soft reasons in 1972, there was more possibility of change for Baptists and Catholics than for the other religious groups.

Given the general drift towards greater acceptance of abortion that followed the Supreme Court decision, we would anticipate less variance in AA and somewhat fewer significant IFS-AA relationships once we control for religious affiliation. Thus, we expected that the associations between Protestant denominations and AA might be significantly smaller for 1975 than for 1972.

The data (Table 1) do not support our prediction. To assess whether or not significant decreases in the measure of association were present among Protestant denominations Kendall's (1962:62-63) test for differences in correlations was applied. The results were negative; none of the 1972-1975 differences in Cramer's V were significant at the .05 level. In all cases the Cramer's V for 1975 was smaller than that for 1972. The direction of the difference was as predicted, but none was significant. However, the difference in the 1972-1975 Cramer's V statistics for the abortion situation for health reasons does meet the standards for significance at the .10 level. Measured in the terms of this test, then, the Supreme Court decision cannot be said to have brought the Protestant denominations closer together.

Table 2 concerns the relationship between Ideal Family Size and Abortion Attitudes. The data support the hypothesis of the declining importance of IFS. In 1972 40 of the associations between IFS and AA were significant. In 1975 only 32 were significant. The decline was disproportionately in the area of soft reasons, the area that is marked by higher levels of proabortion consensus in 1975 than in 1972. In the case of the Methodists we found that all IFS-AA relationships were significant. This was what we would anticipate given the Methodists' relative lack of change of abortion attitudes between 1972 and 1975.

Regression Analysis

While we have extended Renzi's finding that IFS is negatively related to a proabortion attitude for specific denominations, there remain some further questions such as the possible spuriousness of this relationship and the question of the relative importance of IFS in determining the variance in abortion attitudes. For example, from the work of Arney and Trescher (1976) we know that education was the leading determinant of abortion attitudes. While IFS was not included in the analysis of Arney and Trescher, we would anticipate a negative correlation between education and ideal family size; the better educated prefer smaller families. Once we control for education, then, the relationship between IFS and proabortion attitudes might vanish. In addition, we need to weigh the importance of IFS relative to other factors shaping attitudes on this issue: age, frequency of church attendance, sex, race, and the size of the place of residence (Arney & Trescher 1976). That is, is IFS as important a factor as church attendance, sex, etc., in the shaping of attitudes on abortion? The previous research has either dealt with simple bivariate relationships or has introduced only one control variable. The present investigation utilizes the techniques of multiple regression analysis in order to rank the importance of the relevant independent variables.

The results of the first regression analysis are given in Table 3. The dependent variable, the index of proabortion attitudes, was constructed by combining the scores on the answers to the six items regarding abortion. The t-statistic associated with IFS indicates that the relationship with abortion attitudes is significant and in the expected direction. Even if we control for religious affiliation, church attendance, and the other independent variables, greater IFS means less approval of abortion. In like manner, education, church attendance, sex, age, and religion (measured in terms of a dummy variable where 0-Protestant, 1-Catholic)[2] exert a significant impact, in the expected direction, on abortion attitudes.

While IFS is significantly related to attitudes on abortion, and while this relationship is independent of seven control variables, there remains the issue of how strongly it is related to the dependent variable relative to the other factors. To weigh the importance of the variables, we can look at the absolute values of their beta coefficients; the greater a variable's beta coefficient, the greater its importance in explaining the variation in the dependent variable. By this criterion, church attendance is the most important variable associated with abortion attitudes (beta = −.253); years of education is the second most important variable (beta = .242); ideal family

TABLE 3
Effects of Education, Age, Religion, Church Attendance, Sex, Race,
Ideal Family Size, and City Size on the Index of Proabortion Attitudes, 1975
($N = 1,113$)

Variable	Regression Coefficient	Standard Error	Beta	T	P (1 Tail)
Education	.153	.019	.242	2.174	.000
Age	.011	.003	.101	3.436	.001
Religion	−.264	.122	−.061	−2.163	.016
CA	−.193	.022	−.253	−8.970	.000
Sex	.192	.108	.049	1.782	.038
Race	−.152	.184	−.024	−.830	.204
IFS	−.262	.035	−.212	−7.491	.000
City size	.000	.000	.047	1.628	.052

Intercept 8.517
$R = .4287$
$R^2 = .1836$
$F = 31.073, p < .00001$

size is in third place (beta = −.212). The other variables are considerably less important, the next largest beta being age (beta = .101). All the variables taken together explain 18 percent of the variance in abortion attitudes. While IFS is not the strongest predictor of abortion attitudes, it ranks among the top three in the present study.

The regression results in Table 3 regarding religious affiliation should be taken as problematic since all Protestants are lumped together. There remains the question of whether IFS is a significant predictor of AA in specific denominations. One way to answer this question is to run a separate, conditional analysis for each denomination.[3]

Table 4 provides the beta coefficients for each of seven regressions for the seven specific denominations. Two religious groups, Jews and Episcopalians, were dropped from the analysis because of their limited numbers (less than 45 persons). The rank orders of beta coefficients for these denomination-specific regressions follow some of the same patterns found in the regression based on the entire sample. For example, church attendance and education still tend to be the most important variables associated with the variance in AA. The only exception to this pattern is the case of the religious "nones." For those without a religious affiliation, sex is the most important predictor of AA wherein females are more likely to approve of abortion than are males. However, this was only one of two regressions where significant results for the sex status variable were found. In contrast, church attendance was significant six out of seven times; education, five out of seven.

The results in Table 4 show that IFS remains an important variable in the denomination specific regressions. Ideal family size is among the top

TABLE 4

Effects of the Independent Variables on the Index of Proabortion Attitudes
for Specific Denominations (1975)

Independent Variables	Non-bel.	Presb.	Meth.	Luth.	Cath.	Bapt.	All Prot.
EDUCATION	.201*[a]	.147	.296*	.227*	.057	.305*	.299*
CHURCH ATT.	−.041	−.331*	−.194*	−.268*	−.386*	−.192*	−.220*
IFS	—[b]	−.241*	−.200*	−.067	−.243*	−.248*	−.203*
RACE	—[b]	−.026	−.143	−.049	.056	−.044	−.099*
AGE	.128	—[b]*	.133	.171	.030	.134*	.118*
N	90	52	107	98	237	193	624
adj. R^2	.05	.13	.14	.06	.23	.18	.22

[a]Beta coefficient.
[b]F level insufficient for further analysis.
*Statistically significant at the .05 level.

three predictors in five of the seven regressions. The only exceptions are for nonbelievers and Lutherans.[4]

The amount of variance explained ranges from five percent for the religious nones to 23 percent for Catholics. The multiple R's reported here were adjusted for the problem of shrinkage in relatively small samples. All of the multiple R's were significant at the .05 level.

If the number of significant relationships is taken as the test of our seven variable model, the model works best for the category of all Protestants, where all six variables are significant. This regression, however, masks the fact that many relationships do not hold for specific Protestant denominations. For example, age is significant only for Baptists. The model is weakest in explaining the AA of religious nonbelievers. For this group, only two predictors are significant, and only five percent of the variance is explained. Additional research might look at the role of religion of origin of religious nones in order to increase the variance explained.

Discussion/Conclusion

We hypothesized that a reexamination of the data presented by Renzi on the relationship between attitudes toward abortion and religion would be further clarified by subdividing the general category "Protestant" into the various denominations. Specifically, we examined more closely the relationship Renzi had found between ideal family size and abortion: as IFS increased, support for abortion decreased.

Our reanalysis has indeed supported the general finding. At the same time, we have been able to show that, while ideal family size appears to act as an independent variable on attitudes toward abortion, within Protestantism there is a considerable variation in support of abortion whether or not ideal family size is taken into account. As a matter of fact, the attitudes of Baptists more closely approach those of Catholics in all abortion situations than they do those of other Protestants. Thus, to combine Protestants, especially given the large proportion of respondents in the United States who identify themselves as Baptists, only tends to obscure the differences that actually exist between denominations.

The findings also indicate that the U.S. Supreme Court decision on abortion had at best only a modest effect on the liberalization of already fairly strong proabortion sentiments. This supports the position that the court's decision was more consequence than a cause of proabortion attitudes. The modest increase in proabortion attitudes associated with the court's decision did, however, reduce the variation in AA and, hence, decreased the impact of IFS in explaining AA.

The results of the regression analysis for both the sample as a whole and for specific denominations indicate that IFS is a leading determinant of AA. While education level and the measure of religiosity (church attendance) tend to be more powerful predictors of AA, it seems that IFS, a neglected factor, deserves more attention than it has received. We turn now to a brief discussion of the possible reasons for this association.

We may speculate about why IFS seems to interact with religion to be such an important predictor variable in abortion possible situations. Jews have had a long history of accepting the two-child family as normative (Scanzoni & Scanzoni 1976); support for large families comes only from Orthodox Jews, a small minority in the United States. Orthodox Jews also take a strong anti-abortion stand. Thus, we would hypothesize that if we had a large enough sample of Jews so as to be able to control for Orthodox Jews, we would be able to eliminate the relationship of IFS to abortion.

Episcopalians and other mainline Protestant denominations came to terms with birth control and the two-child family over a 25 year period beginning with the Lambeth Conference of 1930. IFS is less a predictor variable for these denominations than it remains for Baptists and the more fundamentalist sects. We would hypothesize that with an adequate sample to control for Northern and Southern Baptists, IFS would be further diminished as a predictor variable.

The Catholic Church has only recently come to accept the idea of family size limitation, and the hierarchy's continued opposition to contraceptive birth control and abortion are too well known to need elaboration here (Potvin & Burch 1968). We would hypothesize that the continued strong relationship between IFS and abortion attitudes within Catholicism reflects the ongoing struggle between a younger, ever more autonomous laity, which sees the two-child family as ideal and uses contraception to achieve the goal, and the older, more traditional Catholic laity.

IFS may not be so much a variable independent of religion as it is a *reflection* of religious ideology, another indicator of people's religious orientations. People may continue to be religious, but in a much less absolutistic way than their forebears. They may even see a large family as ideal, but not at the risk of the health of the mother, nor begotten under conditions of rape or incest. Likewise, the changes between 1972 and 1975 suggest that acceptance of abortion even for soft reasons is reaching broad consensus levels, regardless of orientation to family size.[5] At the same time, there appears to be a broad and emerging consensus among all people, regardless of religious affiliation, toward the two-child family as ideal. Thus, whatever the power of this variable in the 1970s, it may well have a limited history.

Notes

1. The phrase "family size preference" as used by Renzi refers to the responses to the following question: "What do you think is the ideal number of children for a family to have?" We think the phrase "ideal family size" more accurately describes the question, so we will use it rather than "family size preference" in our own analysis.

2. The treatment of religious affiliation as a dummy variable in the first part of the regression analysis is clearly not consistent with the previous section of the analysis which seeks to decompose Protestantism into its respective denominations. These preliminary regression results should be taken with great caution since all Protestants are grouped together, and the considerable variation in denominational AA is masked.

3. Another approach to the inspection of the denomination specific-IFS interaction is to introduce a multiplicative interaction term to the regression analysis. This was done in a separate analysis using the following procedure. The responses to the NORC question on religious affiliation, which provides data on Protestant affiliations, were recorded into a rank order according to the average proportion favoring abortion in the six abortion situations. An interaction term was calculated by multiplying this new ordinal scale by IFS. The correlation between the interaction term and IFS was rather large, indicating a potential problem of severe multicollinearity. The Klein test for severe multicollinearity was positive. This precluded a meaningful regression analysis of the impact of the interaction term on AA.

4. The remaining four predictor variables are less often associated with AA. Sex is significant only for nonbelievers and all Protestants. Size is significant twice (for Baptists and all Protestants). Race emerges as significant only once (all Protestants). For all significant relationships the signs of the betas are in the expected direction. Even the nonsignificant betas have signs in the expected direction except for the case of city size for Catholics.

5. Recent polls show that most Americans now see the two-child family as ideal. And Westoff, after a careful examination of fertility trends over the past 50 years, concludes that there is little or no evidence of a return to the three- or four-child family as normative. Rather, he sees it as more probable that U.S. fertility levels will stabilize at or below the two-child level. See Charles F. Westoff, "Some speculations on the future of marriage and fertility," *Family Planning Perspectives*, Vol. 10, No. 2, March/April, 1978, pp. 79-83.

References

Arney, William R. and William H. Trescher. 1976. "Trends in attitudes toward abortion, 1972-1975." *Family Planning Perspectives* 8:117-24.

Blalock, Hubert. 1979. *Social Statistics.* New York: McGraw-Hill.

Davis, James, Thomas W. Smith, and C. Bruce Stephenson. 1978. *General Social Survey: Cumulative Codebook.* Chicago: National Opinion Research Center.

deBoer, Connie. 1977-1978. "The polls: Abortion." *Public Opinion Quarterly* 41: 553-64.

Kendall, Maurice. 1962. *Rank Order Correlation Methods.* London: Charles Griffin and Co., Ltd.

Loether, Herman J. and Donald G. McTavish. 1974. *Inferential Statistics for Sociologists.* Boston: Allyn and Bacon.

Potvin, Raymond and Thomas K. Burch. 1968. "Ideal family size and religious orientation among U.S. Catholics." *Sociological Analysis* 29:28-34.

Renzi, Mario. 1975. "Ideal family size as an intervening variable between religion and attitudes towards abortion." *Journal for the Scientific Study of Religion* 14: 23-27.

Ryder, Norman and Charles Westoff. 1968. *Relationship Among Intended, Expected, Desired, and Ideal Family Size: United States 1965.* Washington, DC: Center for Population Research.

Scanzoni, Letha and John Scanzoni. 1976. *Men, Women and Change.* New York: McGraw-Hill Co.

References

Alwin, Duane F. 1989. "Changes in Qualities Valued in Children in the United States, 1964 to 1984." *Social Science Research, 18,* 195-236.

Blake, Judith. 1989. *Family Size and Achievement.* Berkeley: University of California Press.

Cook, Elizabeth Addell, Jelen, Ted G., & Wilcox, Clyde. 1992. *Between Two Absolutes: Public Opinion and the Politics of Abortion.* Boulder, CO: Westview.

D'Antonio, William V., & Stack, Steven. 1980. "Religion, Ideal Family Size, and Abortion: Extending Renzi's Hypothesis." *Journal for the Scientific Study of Religion, 19,* 397-408.

Davis, James A., & Smith, Tom W. 1992. *The NORC General Social Survey: A User's guide.* Newbury Park, CA: Sage.

———— 1996. *General Social Surveys, 1972-1996: Cumulative Codebook.* Chicago: National Opinion Research Center.

Glock, Charles Y., Ringer, Benjamin B., & Babbie, Earl R. 1967. *To Comfort and to Challenge.* Berkeley: University of California Press.

Renzi, Mario. 1975. "Ideal Family Size as an Intervening Variable Between Religion and Attitudes Towards Abortion." *Journal for the Scientific Study of Religion, 14:*23-27.

Smith, Tom W., & Arnold, Bradley J. 1996. *Annotated Bibliography of Papers Using the General Social Survey,* 11th ed. Chicago: National Opinion Research Center.

Weber, Max. 1958. *The Protestant Ethic and the Spirit of Capitalism.* Translated by Talcott Parsons. Reprint, New York: Scribners.

Index/Glossary

Richardson, J. T., 295
Ringer, B. B., 8, 101, 104, 106, 182, 183, 185, 250
Roe v. Wade, 274, 275, 276, 285, 289
Roper Center for Public Opinion Research, 222
Rosenau, J., 285, 293
Roskin, M., 285, 293
Ross, S., 296
Ryder, N., 304
Ryder, N. B., 296, 297, 299

S

Sagi, P. C., 296
SAM, 223
Same pairs, 135, 136, 137, 138, 139
sampling error—The extent to which a probability
      sample of a given design is expected to vary from
      perfectly representing the population from which it
      was drawn.
Sampling error, 20, 21, 159, 160, 162, 164, 166, 170
Sapiro, V., 285, 293
SAS, 5, 223
Scanzoni, J., 311
Scanzoni, L., 311
scattergramA graphic plotting of the values of two
      variables, with one variable serving as the *x*-axis
      and the other the *y*-axis of the graph. A regression
      line is the attempt to summarize the distribution of
      points in a scattergram.
Scattergram, 142, 152
secondary analysis—The analysis of data previously
      collected by some other researcher. Your use of the
      GSS data is an example of this.
Secondary analysis, 222, 223
Secret, P., 279, 293
Sexual behavior attitudes, 23, 97-98, 175
      abortion attitudes, 126-127, 208-210
ShowCase, 223
Silverman, J., 279, 293
Slope, 156
Smith, T. W., 19, 220, 221, 222, 271, 292, 303
SNAP, 223
Social class, religiosity and, 106, 183-184
Social inquiry, explanatory, 7
Social-political opinions, 22
Social research, 1, 3
      logic, 1
      theory, 7
SOS, 223
specification—An outcome in multivariate analysis in
      which we specify the conditions under which a r
      elationship holds true. Thus, for example, sexual
      intercourse can cause pregnancy, but only among
      women.
Specification, 192, 193
SPSS, 1, 3, 5-6, 30, 34, 52, 127, 131, 151, 154, 163, 223,
      224
      coding data, 233-235

correlation computation, 145-146
Count, 88-94
Crosstabs, 73-77, 139, 176, 185
data definition, 233
entering data, 235-236
launching, 26, 37
mastering, 65
powerful tool, 25
programmed statistics, 16
saving work, 57-58
SPSS/PC+, 5
SPSSX, 5
Studentware, 5, 20
      useful tool, 25, 94
      Version 7.5, 5, 6
Stack, S., 212
standard deviation—A measure of dispersion
      appropriate to ratio variables.
Standard deviation, 47, 144
Standardized slope, 188
STATA, 223
STAT80, 223
Statgraf, 223
statistical significance—A measure of the likelihood that
      an observed relationship between variables in a
      probability sample represents something that exists
      in the population rather than being due to sampling
      error.
Statistical significance, 149, 159, 176
      versus substantive significance, 164, 172
Statpak, 223
StatPro, 223
STATS PLUS, 223
Statview, 223
Stephenson, C. B., 303
Strunk, William, Jr., 237, 245
Survey Mate, 223
SURVTAB, 223
SYSTAT, 223

T

TECPACS, 223
Tests of significance, 159
      versus measures of association, 164
      See also Analysis of variance (ANOVA);
            Chi-square; *t* tests
theory—An interrelated set of general principles that
      describes the relationships among a number of
      variables.
Theory, 8, 109
Thought experiments, 129, 152
Tolone, W. L., 296, 298, 299
Torres, A., 272, 292
Trescher, W. H., 301, 302, 308
***t* test**—A class of significance tests used to test for
      significant differences between different kinds of
      means. In this book, the independent samples *t* test

is used to test whether the observed difference
between two means could have easily happened by
chance, or if it so unlikely, we believe the difference
we see in our sample also exists in the population
from which the sample was taken. [QU: if it so]
  t tests, 164-169, 172
    shortcomings, 170
    2-tailed probability, 167-168

U

U.S. Census Bureau, 4, 19-20, 222
univariate analysis—The analysis of a single variable
  for the purpose of description. Contrasted with
  bivariate and multivariate analysis.
Univariate analysis, 35, 95-100
  graphic display, 43-45
  See also Abortion; Composite index; Composite
    measures; Political orientations; Religiosity

V

validity—The extent to which an empirical measure
  actually taps the quality intended.
Validity, 11
  problems, 11-12
  versus reliability, 13
variable—Logical set of attributes. For example, gender
  is a variable comprised of the attributes male and
  female.
Variables, 7, 14, 17
  categorical, 45
  continuous, 45, 54-55, 150, 152
  dependent, 153
  discrete, 45
  dummy, 185
  independent, 109, 153
  interval, 15-16
  nominal, 14-15, 16, 134, 157
  ordinal, 15, 16, 41, 134, 157
  ratio, 15, 16, 152, 157
Variables, modifying:
  recode, 47-56
Variance, 144

W

Weber, M., 212
Welch, S., 279, 293
Westoff, C. F., 296, 297, 299, 304, 312
Whelpton, P. K., 296
White, E. B., 237, 245
White, R. H., 198
Wilcox, C., 119, 121, 279, 285, 289, 293, 294
Within-group differences, 170
Wlezien, C., 274, 292

Z

z score—A conversion for interval and ratio variables
  that uses the mean and standard deviation of a
  variable to transform measurement into standardized scores called *z* scores. Useful for comparing
  variables that come from distributions with different
  means and standard deviations.
  z scores, 144